Reforming the Revolution

Reforming the Revolution

China in Transition

Edited by

Robert Benewick and Paul Wingrove

MACMILLAN
EDUCATION

Contents

vi *Contents*

List of Contributors

Robert Benewick   School of English and American Studies, University of Sussex

Marc Blecher   Department of Government, Oberlin College, Ohio, USA

Terry Cannon   School of Humanities, Thames Polytechnic

Richard Conroy   Organisation for Economic Cooperation and Development, Paris

Elisabeth Croll   British Resource Unit for the Sociology and Anthropology of China, School of Oriental and African Studies, University of London

John Gardner   Department of Government, University of Manchester

Sheila Hillier   Joint Department of Sociology Applied to Medicine, The London Hospital Medical College

Keith Lewin   Centre for Graduate Studies in Education, University of Sussex

Martin Lockett   Oxford Institute of Information Management, Templeton College, Oxford

Robin Munro   Department of Chinese, Polytechnic of Central London

Tony Saich   Sinologisch Instituut, University of Leiden, Netherlands

Gerald Segal   Department of Politics, University of Bristol

Anne Wedell-Wedellsborg   Institute of East Asian Studies, University of Aarhus, Denmark

Gordon White   Institute of Development Studies, University of Sussex

Paul Wingrove   Division of Politics, School of Humanities, Thames Polytechnic

Introduction: China in the 1980s

Robert Benewick and Paul Wingrove

This book is an attempt to understand the decade since the death of Mao Zedong, the period we describe as 'reforming the revolution'. For such an understanding it is necessary to examine, albeit selectively, the most important political social, economic and cultural developments, the dramatic shift towards the outside world, and the major transformations at every level from family to state, during the period.

What is novel, we hope, is the attempt to conduct our examination in a way that will be meaningful to the general reader and to the student new to the study of China. Accordingly, leading scholars in the field have been specially commissioned to contribute to this volume. It is not a compendium of conference papers where specialists gather to form a consensus or air their differences. From their different perspectives our contributors have attempted to provide a basis for an initial understanding of the dilemmas in China's difficult task of 'reforming a revolution', although they do demonstrate the variety of conclusions that is bound to emerge from any discussion of the transformation of China. This is hardly surprising, given the uncertainties in China itself, the disagreements and backtrackings in the leadership, and the presentation of policies in the carefully chosen language of the controlled media.

Measuring a decade

The titles of recent books on contemporary China read like a thesaurus entry. They abound with words like 'change',

1

'development', 'flux', 'growth', 'innovation', 'mobilisation', 'revolution', 'transition', 'transformations', 'struggle', and so on, reflecting the dynamic reality of the People's Republic of China (PRC) since its founding in 1949. They document the fact that since that date China has undergone a period of restless change more rapid than any country in the world. Rather than simply catalogue the changes and upheavals of that period, which would be a monumental task, it is sufficient to note the landmarks: the highly successful land-reform movement of the early 1950s, the collectivisation of agriculture from the mid-1950s, the disastrous years of the Great Leap Forward (1958–60), the dislocations of the Great Proletarian Cultural Revolution (1966–76), and the relocations of the post-Mao economic programme, including the decollectivisation of agriculture. Finally, whereas the first thirty years of the PRC were characterised by Maoism, much of the last decade is characterised by its secularisation, its transformation into a shell of continuity and legitimacy.

The chronicle of change has an oscillating, occasionally lurching, almost frenetic quality. Flexibility is manifest in the willingness to experiment and the constant search for solutions, but this combines and conflicts with a rigidity express-ed, for example, in a penchant for models and bureaucratic patterns of behaviour. The latest Chinese model is 'socialism with Chinese characteristics'. To some this is only a meaning-less slogan ('Chinese, but not socialist'), but it nonetheless stands in a diverse tradition of economic models of develop-ment in socialist countries which stretch from Lenin's New Economic Policy by way of Stalin's industrialisation, Mao's communes, the economic reform experiences of Czechoslova-kia and Hungary, to Deng's decade of experimentation and the recent stirrings in Gorbachev's USSR. There is little orthodoxy here, and therefore little heresy.

While the focus may be on change and its rapid, often turbulent and uneven pace, an equally remarkable feature of the PRC has been its persistent or underlying stability.

For any nation the balance between change and stability is delicate, and when change is rapid it is precarious. It is tempting to argue that the PRC has ultimately been able to maintain this balance because of an authoritarian tradition of political rule. Such an approach ignores the magnitude of the problems confronting the political leadership and the fierce debates about the appropriate strategies to adopt. It devalues the intensity of the political rivalries and what is at stake in the succession struggles.

At the same time, it is important to avoid the myopic approach which concentrates purely on power struggles to the exclusion of the longer-term considerations – the maintenance or restoration of the delicate balance between continuity and change is much more complex. This is apparent when the enormous tasks that confront Chinese decision-makers are considered: for example, feeding the world's largest population, let alone improving a desperately low standard of living. However effective its family planning policies may be for controlling a population explosion, the natural population growth alone has staggering implications for food supply. The most optimistic estimates place China's arable land at 15 per cent of the total land mass, but there is little doubt that it is declining and that 12 per cent may be more a realistic estimate. Grain production is the seedbed of Chinese politics, past and present. Disagreements over which strategy to pursue are as sharp as the personal political rivalries among the leadership, and to some extent underpin those struggles.

It follows that revolution is not to be viewed simply as a single event or period of struggle; nor reform as a decision or series of decisions. Nor is it particularly revealing simply to indulge in the practice of labelling and re-labelling the leadership factions. What is involved is a long-term process which balances a revolutionary tradition and reform strategies. Just how fragile these sets of balances are is evident in the history of the PRC. It is suggested by the student demonstrations of 1986 which were followed in early 1987 by the resignation of Hu Yaobang who, as General-Secretary of the Communist Party, was considered the second most powerful person in China.

It is therefore not surprising that many commentators believe that China has reached a watershed. The resignation of Hu Yaobang represents more than a leadership crisis. What is at stake are the balances between stability and change and revolution and reform. We have argued that this is a continuing and complex process and as such cannot be resolved at a single Party Congress.

Up to the end of 1986, however, it seemed as if Deng Xiaoping had achieved some sort of resolution, and also the Communist miracle – sweeping economic reform without the popular political upheavals or irremovable elite resistance that broke the reformers in the USSR and Eastern Europe. Deng had the advantage of being able to gain the limited support of his political opponents with his re-establishment of order and a measure of justice in the wake of the chaos of the Cultural Revolution; he also won popular support through the rising standard of living he provided. But those were advantages negated, ultimately, by Deng's own encouragement in 1986 of the debate on 'political reform' which, leading to the debate on 'political liberalisation' and the student protests, at least temporarily tipped the balance against Deng in the leadership of the Party. The events of 1986 certainly sharpened, for Deng, the dilemma of communist states, attempting to reconcile the requirements of political discipline and economic liberalisation, with one force – the power of the Party – ultimately unable to accommodate some of the political implications of economic reform.

The future is no longer clear, if indeed it ever was. Societies develop to some degree in ignorance of the plans of political leaders, and are not simply the sum of the policies of the latest Five Year Plan or Central Committee circular. Thus although some still ask if China is becoming 'capitalist', that arguably overstates the economic changes on the one hand, while on the other it ignores some of the other elements in the present transformation of Chinese society.

Work in prospect

Most attention in the West has focused on the new economic programme, particularly the rural reforms. But since the decisions affecting programmes and pace are political ones,

ais book begins with an examination of the political before
ursuing the economic, social, cultural and international
imensions.

John Gardner guides the reader through the changes in
olitical leadership of the period, which saw the accession of
Ieng Xiaoping and his colleagues and the consolidation of
ieir position at the Third Plenum of the Central Committee
1 December 1978. For them economic reforms have been the
riority but, as Tony Saich argues, reform of the political
ystem has been on the agenda throughout the 1980s. Despite
ignificant opposition from within the Communist Party
CCP) and the People's Liberation Army (PLA), important
hanges have taken place. The position of the CCP is crucial
ince any fundamental reforms would decrease its power.
Hence China's leaders have been cautious in taking on this
ask. The sensitivity of the Party's role is suggested by the
eactions to the student demonstrations of 1986. Saich
oncludes, however, that further reforms of the political
ystem are necessary for China to meet the demands of an
ncreasingly complex society.

Political participation is generally viewed as an outstand-
ng characteristic of the PRC. Benewick examines the
ttempts to move from the mass mobilisations of the Maoist
eriod to more structured forms of participation. He surveys
he opportunities available, concentrating on the direct
lections to the county-level people's congresses. It is impor-
ant not to exaggerate the possibilities for effective participa-
ion, but at the same time the value being placed on it should
ot be underestimated.

Perhaps the most important events since the Third Plenum
f 1978 were the student demonstrations of 1986 leading to
Hu Yaobang's resignation. Wide-ranging discussions on the
ieed for political reforms to ensure the continued success of
he economic reforms preceded the demonstrations. While the
students' motives were mixed, they did bring to a head the
conflicts within China's leadership over these reforms, and
the implications of these matters are the subject of Munro's
in-depth study.

As previously indicated, the economic reforms have been
the centrepiece of the post-Mao transformations. White

provides an analysis of what he describes as the 'reform paradigm' which has replaced the essentially Soviet-style planning system. The reshaping of the economy has favoured a re-orientation towards light industry, agriculture and consumer goods, international economic ties, the diversification of ownership and the re-instatement of markets. Serious issues nonetheless remain unresolved, not least the fundamental nature of 'socialism'.

The question that follows is how to evaluate the process of reforming the revolution: what has taken place, as well as what has not. Blecher presents both the weaknesses of collectivisation and the success of the reforms in the countryside, but he is neither willing to dismiss the former nor uncritically accept the latter. The reader is thereby presented with a more balanced view of collectivisation during the Maoist period than is evident in much of the recent literature. At the same time Blecher finds much that is disturbing for development and stability, and for the proclaimed socialist principles of the reforms. The implementation of the urban and industrial economic reforms is more problematic, as the Chinese leaders themselves expected. Lockett describes the development of the system of economic planning and outlines the proposed reforms. Since the political opposition in this sphere is more truculent, he foresees a future of policy development in fits and starts.

In addition to overcoming opposition, technological and scientific advance are necessary if China is to achieve its modernisation goals. Conroy describes the technological needs and indicates the difficulties of absorbing the new technology, as well as the economic, cultural and political constraints. The critical role of technology is also the theme of Cannon's chapter on overseas trade. The policies that have been adopted to attract foreign technology and investment are explained, as are the obstacles, especially the problem of payment. While technology may be a priority, it has to compete with other imports including consumer goods. As Cannon concludes, trade policies, let alone technology, cannot be insulated from politics.

Just how far-reaching is the impact of the reforms is illustrated by Croll's study of the family. The household has come to prominence as the most important socio-economic and political unit in rural China, and is becoming increasingly important in the urban areas. Benefits have accrued to the household in the form of higher incomes and diversified consumption patterns, but simultaneously new sources of tension and conflict have been created, and there are increased welfare responsibilities.

The economic reforms have also had a profound effect on health care, a field in which China has made extraordinary progress in the forty years since liberation. There is a new emphasis on quality, both of care and of health facilities. On the other hand, there is a tendency to regard health as an aspect of consumption rather than social provision. Hillier appraises the consequences of the changes in direction, drawing on China's own experiences as well as those of the West.

Lewin considers the development of education policy since 1976 and assesses the reforms within the largest education system in the world. Current policy contains elements that fuelled the Cultural Revolution, but these are overshadowed by a new purposefulness which is pragmatically determined, an unprecedented openness, and an impressive quantitative expansion. Whether this can be matched by quality is the greatest challenge.

The literary flowering is a striking aspect of the era of the secularisation of Maoism. Anne Wedell-Wedellsborg explains its vitality but also draws attention to the constraints on its development. She detects three different schools, but what characterises each is a concern for the individual, which is a marked departure from the past.

Segal argues that China's governing principle is to seek a peaceful international environment for 'reforming the revolution'. It is not surprising, therefore, that China views its relations with the two superpowers as its foreign policy priority. In attempting to achieve a more balanced position between the two, China is described by Segal as a 'talented if cheeky player'. Wingrove reminds us that China's foreign policy also has a decidedly regional dimension. Enduring considerations are the fear of encirclement and historic pride, while the new dimension is the economic, with China's regional diplomacy reflecting the need for co-operation with neighbouring states in order to achieve the economic goals determined by the Party leadership.

1

The Politics of Transition

John Gardner

Mao's death on 9 September 1976 was by no means unexpected. He was then in his eighty-third year, had become increasingly infirm as the 1970s progressed, and the official media had signalled his decline.

Yet little had been done to ensure an orderly transition. The Cultural Revolution which Mao instigated had resulted in the death and disgrace first of Liu Shaoqi and then of Lin Biao, both of whom had been identified in turn as his successor. The passing of Zhou Enlai in January 1976 had removed from the scene China's greatest diplomat. The dismissal of Deng Xiaoping in April 1976 had similarly neutralised the most outspoken leader of those powerful interests in the leadership which sought to curb the radical excesses of the previous decade.

Factionalism was prevalent throughout the elite, and the appointment of Hua Guofeng, a comparatively inexperienced and unknown 'outsider' to the posts of Premier and First Vice-Chairman of the Party's Central Committee, in April 1976, inspired little confidence that this could be more than a stop-gap solution. After ten years of political instability, which at times had produced virtual anarchy, and frequent changes of both leadership and policy, the general populace was demoralised, fearful and cynical.

In fact, Hua Guofeng quickly demonstrated that he had been underestimated. Although only emerging as a leader of

9

national importance in the 1970s, he had acquired considerable political and administrative skills earlier in his political career in Hunan province, and used these to good effect. In the last few months of Mao's life he created a power-base among senior cadres, including those in the People's Liberation Army (PLA), and also acquired a measure of public support by his efficient handling of relief operations after the Tangshan earthquake disaster. His political calculations at the time of Mao's death must have suggested that a move against the most extreme leftists in the leadership would be well received.

Consequently, less than a month after Mao's death Hua arrested Jiang Qing, Mao's widow, and three of her most prominent supporters, Zhang Chunqiao, Yao Wenyuan and Wang Hongwen. In addition to the 'Gang of Four', as this group became branded, a considerable number of lesser leftists were also imprisoned. Hua justified his actions by claiming that the Gang had attempted to usurp Party and state power. To prepare public opinion they had not only used the media to attack their opponents and extol their own virtues (which they undoubtedly did) but had also resorted to forgery. They were also alleged to have plotted some form of armed uprising (Onate, 1978).

Hua's account of the Gang's misdeeds also went to great lengths to distance Mao from them. The propaganda barrage launched from October 1976 onwards emphasised that Mao had long been estranged from his wife and had criticised her and her followers on numerous occasions. It was he who had coined the term 'Gang of Four' when supposedly warning them against underhand and factionalist behaviour. Similarly, the horrors of the Cultural Revolution were attributed to their distortion of Mao's principles and policies.

Whatever liberties may have been undertaken with the truth, the arrest and discrediting of the Gang was extremely popular. Hua was immediately appointed Chairman of the Party Central Committee and of its Military Affairs Commission, and also became custodian of Mao's works, a role of great importance in a society where policy for so long had been justified by reference to ideology (Ting Wang, 1980).

Hua also sought to consolidate his position as Mao's

successor by resorting to a very Maoist technique, the personality cult. Much was made of a note Mao had apparently given to Hua in April 1976 which stated, in part, 'With you in charge, I'm at ease', and this was reinforced by the widespread distribution of a picture giving an artist's impression of the celebrated occasion. It was also asserted that Hua's appointment as *First* Vice-Chairman showed that Mao had 'explicitly designated' him as his successor, as that post had never previously existed. Mao was also said to have instructed that it was necessary 'to do propaganda and give publicity to Comrade Hua Guofeng to make him known to the people of the whole country step-by-step'.

Leaders who had themselves displayed loyalty to Maoist principles were enlisted to endorse Hua. Pre-eminent among these was Chen Yonggui, the semi-literate peasant whose supposed commitment to Mao's ideas of self-reliance had raised him from the humble role of leader of the Dazhai production brigade to Politburo membership. Although the 'achievements' claimed for Dazhai were later revealed to be somewhat fraudulent, in 1976 they were widely regarded as representing the best of Maoism, and Chen's support for Hua was clearly of great value. According to Chen, Mao had 'complete faith' in Hua, had 'selected' him as his successor, and had also 'trained' him (*Peking Review*, 7 January 1977). The clear implication was that Hua's elevation had not been unexpected or arbitrary: he had been 'groomed' for leadership. Chen praised Hua's qualities, which included loyalty, selflessness, modesty and prudence. Hua, he said, was democratic and approachable, a wise leader with a gift for uniting people to work together.

A spate of books and articles testified to Hua's diligence, his devotion to Mao throughout his career, and his ability to retain 'the common touch'. According to one typical account, a poor peasant who had received Hua in his home in the early 1960s reported:

When Chairman Hua lived in my house, he worked day and night for the Party. He never seemed to get tired. He ate what we ate and was never fastidious about his food and clothes. He took part in labour and often had heart-to-heart talks with the poor and lower-middle peasants as well as chatting with the children. He never put on airs and was like a member of the family. (*Peking Review*, 25 February 1977)

Nothing was too unimportant to be used to advantage. One story told how in 1971 Hua had visited a school where one of his children was studying and insisted on being treated like any other parent. A cartoon strip showed a cyclist falling off his bicycle and scattering the vegetables he was carrying. Hua was at hand to pick them up. Apart from somewhat contradictorily publicising his becoming modesty by the device of the personality cult, Hua also consciously assumed his patron's style. Like Mao, he began to provide the press with inscriptions in his own calligraphy. On 1 August 1977 the fifty-sixth anniversary of the PLA was marked by the publication of a photograph of Mao in military uniform and of Hua similarly attired. Hua also modified his appearance, allowing his 'military' cropped hair to grow, and sweeping it back from the temples to give him a distinct resemblance to Mao.

To compensate for his lack of experience in foreign affairs and the fact that he was an unfamiliar figure outside of China, Hua devoted a good deal of his time to receiving foreign visitors, and this was duly reported to establish his image as a world leader. His ideological credentials were also bolstered by the republication of articles he had written in his Hunan days and, more importantly, by his authoring of a study of the fifth volume of Mao's selected works which was published on 15 April 1977. Hua's interpretation was, of course, uncritical. Indeed, at the beginning of the year Hua had produced an instruction which was to become known as the 'two whatevers' when he wrote: 'We must resolutely uphold whatever policy decisions Chairman Mao made and unswervingly carry out whatever Chairman Mao instructed' (*People's Daily* in SWB:FE, July 1981, No. 6683).

Superficially, Hua's protestations of loyalty to Mao, coupled with his role as custodian of Mao's ideological heritage, placed him in a very strong position in that he could justify policy shifts by the publication of judicious selections from Mao's writings and speeches. What he hoped to do was to maintain that the Cultural Revolution had been basically correct in conception but that Mao's aims had been 'distorted' by the Gang of Four. Thus he had produced 'evidence' to distance Mao from his wife and to demonstrate his own role as the determined opponent of the Gang. Fundamentally, however, this was an extremely difficult stand to maintain. On the one hand, his claim to be Mao's faithful follower meant that he could only move away from Maoist positions relatively slowly if he were to maintain credibility. On the other hand, it inevitably raised questions about the return of Deng Xiaoping to high office. Deng's opposition to the Gang was a matter of incontrovertible fact, and his early return was seen by Hua as a threat to the consolidation of his own position as supreme leader, and was an even greater danger to the political position of others who had offered little or no opposition to the Gang of Four in Mao's lifetime.

Deng had massive support. A Party member since 1924, Deng's record of outstanding ability and services to the revolutionary cause had, after 1949, given him a series of top-ranking posts in the Party, government and military which provided him with political credentials second to none, including a 'constituency' among cadres in all spheres and at all levels. Few, if any, could match him for his forthright expression of views, which had led to his fall in the Cultural Revolution and again in 1976. Admiration for his courage extended well beyond official circles.

Consequently, from October 1976 onwards there was a lengthy debate and struggle which concentrated not so much on whether Deng should be rehabilitated but when this should be, and how far his rehabilitation should go. Hua attempted to play for time both in order to bolster his own position and to obtain from him certain assurances of support and co-operation. Those who supported Deng worked assiduously to force Hua's hand.

At a very public level, many wallposters appeared at the time of the first anniversary of Zhou Enlai's death (January 1977) calling for Deng's return. No doubt some were spontaneously produced by ordinary citizens, but it seems probable that many were instigated by senior officials. Deng's supporters also started a 'whispering campaign', dropping heavy hints that he was about to be brought back. Some senior leaders appear to have applied pressure by refusing to attend top-level meetings until the question of Deng was settled.

Deng himself facilitated his return by writing to Hua on two occasions supporting his action in arresting the Gang of Four and requesting that Deng should give him some 'front-line work' to do. In July he was formally restored to all his posts. When Deng addressed the Eleventh Party Congress in August it was to emphasise that what China needed was 'less empty talk and more hard work'. A new Party Constitution gave priority to the 'Four Modernisations' (of agriculture, industry, science and technology, and defence) and demanded strict discipline and an end to factionalism. Early in 1978 the Fifth National People's Congress adopted a new State Constitution which provided a detailed framework for the rebuilding of governmental and legal institutions.

Deng's establishment of power

Once restored to office, Deng lost little time in directing his efforts to the pursuit of modernisation: he initially assumed responsibilities for the development of science, education and intellectual life generally. He rallied the intellectual community to adopt high standards once more and supported calls to 'let a hundred flowers bloom', recognising that intellectual life could not flourish under too great a degree of ideological control. In March and April 1978 Deng addressed major national conferences on science and educational work respectively, emphasising the need for talent and expertise, and proper rewards for the talented.

As part of his encouragement for an intellectual awakening, Deng also called for a more critical approach to Mao. As early as May 1977 he had taken issue with the 'two whatevers' thesis, describing it as 'unacceptable':

We cannot mechanically apply what Comrade Mao Zedong said about a particular question to another question, what he said in a particular place to another place, what he said at a particular time to another time, or what he said under particular circumstances to other circumstances. Comrade Mao Zedong himself said repeatedly that some of his own statements were wrong. He said that no one can avoid making mistakes in his own work unless he does none at all. He also said that Marx, Engels, Lenin and Stalin had all made mistakes – otherwise why did they correct their manuscripts time and time again? (Deng Xiaoping, 1983, p. 51)

On 9 May 1978 an article entitled 'Practice is the sole criterion for testing truth' appeared in an internal publication of the Central Party School, which was headed by Hu Yaobang, a leading supporter of Deng. The following day it was reprinted in the *Guangming Daily*, the national newspaper devoted primarily to intellectual concerns. The title of the article was a phrase of Mao's, and the article reiterated a 'basic principle of the Maoist theory of cognition', namely, that 'only social practice can test whether a theory correctly reflects objective reality and is true.' It emphasised that 'we must dare to touch and to get clear the rights and wrongs' regarding the 'forbidden areas' set up by the Gang of Four (*People's Daily* in SWB:FE, July 1981, No. 6683).

On 2 June 1978 Deng addressed an All-Army Conference on Political Work and criticised those who forgot or opposed Mao's method of 'seeking truth from facts'. Mao, Deng said, had no time for the 'misguided mentality of those who, in discussions with the Communist Party, could not open their minds without citing a book, as if whatever was written in a book was right' (Deng Xiaoping, 1984, p. 129).

Deng's desire to 'shatter spiritual fetters' had important ramifications for the political leadership because it conflicted directly with the stance taken by Hua and his supporters, most prominent of whom was Wang Dongxing. One of the least known of China's top leaders, Wang was a security specialist whose devotion to Mao went back to the 1930s, when he was his personal bodyguard. Although he was one of those who had turned on Mao's widow in October 1976, Wang had been reluctant to censor media discussion of Deng's views.

By the autumn of 1978, however, support for Deng was rising rapidly. It was not so much Deng's popularity among 'the masses' that mattered as the growing influence of cadres in leading positions who shared his views. In a detailed study of central and provincial leaders in the Party and state apparatus, Goodman (1979) has demonstrated that there was a 65 per cent turnover of personnel between September 1976 and April 1978. It would be wrong to assume that all those who lost their jobs were dedicated leftists and that all their replacements were loyal to Deng, but the trend was certainly in that direction. The growing constituency of veteran cadres who had suffered in the Cultural Revolution greatly strengthened Deng's hand. Moreover, the trend was to continue. In October 1977 Hu Yaobang had called for 'liberating large numbers of cadres who for various reasons had not been rehabilitated and assigned work'. Hu, then director of the Central Committee's Organisation Department (which had major responsibilities for personnel matters) was instructed to rehabilitate 'the victims of miscarriages of justice' in the Cultural Revolution and 'this work gathered pace' (*People's Daily*, in SWB:FE, July 1981, No. 6683).

By the end of 1978 Deng and his supporters were able to consolidate their position when a lengthy Central Work Conference was convened in November, followed by the Third Plenum of the Eleventh Central Committee which met in late December. The Third Plenum was later to be described not only officially but accurately as a 'turning point of profound historical significance' in the history of the Party; it 'put an end to the situation in which the Party's work had been stagnating since October 1976 and began to correct the leftist mistakes committed before and during' the Cultural Revolution (*People's Daily*, in SWB:FE, July 1981, No. 6683).

At these meetings there was considerable criticism of Mao, although leaders differed as to how far it was advisable or desirable for the Party to wash its dirty linen in public. Wang Dongxing and Hua Guofeng came under fire for their unwillingness to admit Mao's mistakes, and Hua had to make a self-criticism on this matter.

The communique of the Third Plenum made it clear that 'seeking truth from facts' was the new ideological orthodoxy, noting that it would not be Marxist to demand that a revolutionary leader be free of all shortcomings and errors. It would also not conform to Comrade Mao Zedong's consistent evaluation of himself. The 'shortcomings and mistakes' of the Cultural Revolution were to be 'summed up at the appropriate time'. Four veteran leaders who had suffered in the Cultural Revolution or earlier were formally rehabilitated, including Peng Dehuai, who had been purged in 1959 after he had criticised the Great Leap Forward.

In effect the Plenum produced a brief guide to the reform programme which Deng was to push forward as China entered the 1980s. China was henceforth to focus its attention on 'socialist modernisation'. This required great growth in the productive forces, which in turn necessitated numerous changes in methods of management, action and thinking. The radical style of the Great Leap Forward and later campaigns was unsuitable, and the stress was to be placed on political stability and working 'according to objective economic laws'. The Party was to stop substituting itself for the government and, in industry, the government was to stop making decisions that were best left to enterprise administrations. The responsibilities of managers were to be increased, and an efficient system of rewards and punishments, promotions and demotions, was to be introduced. In agriculture the 'socialist', but politically ambiguous, principle of 'to each according to his work' was to be properly implemented and the importance of an element of free enterprise was acknowledged, although it is unlikely that the leadership had any idea at the time just how far this would actually go (see Chapter 6). It was also promised that democracy and legality would be strengthened.

The Plenum also made leadership changes, electing important reformers to high office. Chen Yun, a distinguished economic specialist who had opposed Maoist excesses, was made a member of the Standing Committee of the Politburo and also a Vice-Chairman of the Central Committee. Hu Yaobang was elected to the Politburo.

The Plenum also marked the beginning of the end for Hua and his supporters, but the way Hua was removed was gradual and cushioned, in marked contrast to the treatment given to fallen leaders under Mao. Thus his resignation from

the Premiership in September 1980 was presented as a natural
response to a major speech on leadership reform made by
Deng the month before, which had criticised the 'lifelong
tenure' system of holding office (Deng Xiaoping) 1983,
pp. 302–25). The following year Hua was required to surren-
der his chairmanship of both the Central Committee and
Military Affairs Commission, and he received some public
criticism. But his achievements were also recognised and he
retained some status first as a Vice-Chairman of the Central
Committee and, after the abolition of such posts in 1982, by
retaining his membership of that body. This was an excellent
illustration of Deng's desire to establish new 'rules of the
game' to institutionalise and humanise the political process.
The official verdict on Mao, that he was a great revolutionary
who made mistakes in his later life, was encompassed in a
'Resolution on Party History' agreed at a Central Committee
plenum in 1981, and it was another example of the desire to
strike a proper balance (Xinhua in SWB:FE, June 1981,
No. 6764).

The rise of the modernisers and the limits of reform

From 1979 to 1986 Deng was clearly recognisable as China's
top leader and presided over the reform drive. The impact of
the policies he and his colleagues inspired are considered
elsewhere in this book, and this section will concentrate on the
transformation of the Chinese elite during these years. Elite
replacement has been one of the dramatic and ultimately far-
reaching aspects of the modernisation programme, with the
rise of a generation of 'new men' and, occasionally, 'new
women' to positions of influence. At the same time questions
of leadership personnel have imposed limitations on the speed
of reform programmes in all areas and on their nature.

Beginning with the highest leadership, it may be noted that
Deng refused to formalise his supremacy by assuming the
chairmanship of the Central Committee. Indeed that post,
along with vice-chairmanships, was abolished in 1982 in
favour of a more collective leadership. As a member of the
Standing Committee of the Politburo and Chairman of the

Military Affairs Commission, from 1981 Deng was a key figure in a constitutional sense but did not automatically outrank other senior leaders. Indeed his assumption of the chairmanship of the Central Advisory Commission was indicative of his belief that the elderly should start to make way for younger leaders. The Commission, created by the Twelfth Party Congress in 1982, consisted of leaders who had been Party members for at least forty years and who were now to serve in a consultative role rather than a decision-making one. By becoming Chairman, Deng attempted to endow the new body with status in an effort to encourage his contemporaries to vacate positions of power to which they had tenaciously clung since 1949 in favour of younger, fitter, better educated and more reform-minded people.

In 1981 the Standing Committee of the Politburo (the most important decision-making body) contained two other veterans of Deng's vintage, Chen Yun and Li Xiannian, who initially shared with him an enthusiasm for reform, although later they were to take issue with various aspects of his policies. Two other members were Deng's protégés. Hu Yaobang, 66, had been appointed to the post of Party General-Secretary in 1980, then replaced Hua as Chairman in 1981; after the abolition of that post he served as General-Secretary until January 1987. Zhao Ziyang, 60, had become Premier in 1980, a post he continued to hold until early 1987, when he also became Acting General-Secretary of the Party being confirmed in the post by the Thirteenth Party Conference in October 1987. In November he resigned his Premiership. At the end of Mao's life Zhao had instituted economic reforms in Sichuan Province which in some respects heralded those which followed the Third Plenum. The remaining members were Hua and Ye Jianying. Ye enjoyed considerable prestige, especially in the PLA, and was the least reform-minded of the senior leaders. He was, however, also the oldest and in poor health. Hence Deng could rely on majority support for a vigorous programme of economic modernisation, particularly in so far as this called for the promotion of younger leaders with relatively high levels of education and professional competence.

An early sign of the rise of a modernising elite came at the

Twelfth Party Congress in 1982, which saw a considerable influx of 'new blood'. Sixty per cent of the members of the Central Committee were elected for the first time. Two-thirds of them were described as 'well-qualified professionals' from various economic departments. Seventeen per cent were 'professional and technological cadres' as opposed to only 2.7 per cent elected to the Eleventh Central Committee in 1977. Similarly, at the next Central Committee elections in 1985, three-quarters of the new intake were people with higher education, and their average age was fifty (*Beijing Review*, 6, 13 and 20 September 1982; 30 September, 7 and 14 October 1985). The average age of the new Central Committee elected by the Thirteenth Party Congress in autumn 1987 was 55, lower by four years than the average age of the previous Central Committee.

The contribution of relative youth, good education and relevant experience, characteristic of Central Party leaders who have risen in the 1980s, may be illustrated by brief reference to four leaders who first attained Central Committee rank in 1982. Qiao Shi, then in his late fifties, had held responsible posts in the steel industry and was also a Party specialist in international relations. After joining the Central Committee he served a spell as head of its Organisation Department and in 1986 was assigned to give fresh stimulus to an anti-corruption drive originally introduced in 1982. He has been described as 'a notable example of China's group of rising technocrats' (Barnett, 1985). In November 1987 the first plenary session of the Thirteenth Party Congress elected him to the five-man Standing Committee of the Politburo.

The three others were all born in 1929. Li Peng was a former Vice-Minister of Water Conservancy and Power, and became a Vice-Premier in 1983. An engineering graduate, he received part of his education in the Soviet Union. As an energy specialist he had experience of a sector of the economy which, like steel, was of crucial importance to any economic development plans. After 1982 Li's major responsibilities involved areas as diverse as nuclear power plants, electronics, the development of rural energy, and environmental protection. In 1985 he was appointed to head the newly established

State Education Commission, created to direct and co-ordinate the over-compartmentalised and inefficient education sector. Li Peng was also elected to the Politburo Standing Committee in November 1987.

Tian Jiyun, like Li a Vice-Premier, had worked with Zhao Ziyang in the 1970s. A graduate and finance economics specialist, he played an active part in the controversial price reform of the mid-1980s.

Hu Qili graduated in engineering from Beijing University and thereafter specialised in Youth League and Party work. By the mid-1980s he was one of the most travelled of China's leaders, having not only visited Third World and Communist countries, but also the United States, France and West Germany. In the 1980s his principal responsibilities were in the fields of educational and economic reform. Hu joined Li Peng and Qiao Shi in the Standing Committee in November 1987.

These four are outstanding representatives of the rising central Party elite, but they are by no means untypical in terms of their comparatively high education, professionalism, knowledge of the outside world and 'youthfulness' in Chinese terms. Moreover, the central state apparatus has also seen the elevation of younger leaders. Of forty-five people holding ministerial rank or its equivalent in September 1985, two were in their forties and twenty-two were between fifty and fifty-nine. Only three were seventy or over.

Deng and his colleagues were not content simply to revamp the central leadership. At lower levels of the system elite replacement also occurred on a massive scale. Goodman's studies of leadership change in the provinces have revealed that despite the convulsions of the Maoist era, the *type* of leader found there scarcely changed between 1949 and 1980. Some 80 per cent were born before 1919, almost all were male, and few had any significant academic education. During the 1980s a combination of old age and leadership change swept away most of this generation. By the summer of 1985 the average age of provincial leaders was fifty-three, and some 20 per cent were under forty. People who had served before the Cultural Revolution had virtually disappeared. Moreover, by 1985 over half the provincial Party secretaries were graduates (Goodman, 1986, pp. 123–30; Goodman, Lockett and Segal, 1986, p. 20).

The rise of the qualified has been even more notable in other spheres. In 1985 a survey of 3000 key industrial enterprises revealed that 89 per cent of factory directors had received higher education, as had 81 per cent of Party secretaries. One-fifth of the 'leading cadres' were under forty.

Such personnel changes were impressive and important but were nevertheless limited in their impact, one simple reason being that the educational system of the 1960s and 1970s had failed to produce enough qualified people to meet present needs. Thus in late 1984 it was reported that only 4 per cent of Party members had received higher education, and over 50 per cent had only been to primary school and were illiterate (Xinhua in SWB:FE, November 1984, No. 7808). Similarly, an official report of February 1985 expressed concern over the education of the twenty-two million cadres then in post. This report noted that although 24 per cent had received higher education, 37 per cent had not gone further than primary or junior school. Of nine million engaged in professional and technical work, only 1.3 million were classified as senior- or medium-level personnel. There was a particular shortage of economic specialists in such fields as planning, finance and trade, monetary affairs, and technical and general management. It was estimated that China would need 8.53 million such specialists by the end of the century, a twelve-fold increase (Beijing Radio in SWB:FE, November 1984, No. 7869). In like manner, a Central Committee circular in the spring of 1985 demonstrated that secondary schools were still failing to produce more than a fraction of the intermediate-level technicians that China needed (Communist Party of China, 1985). Consequently, the reformers' desire to improve the calibre of leadership at lower levels was constrained by the shortage of candidates who were manifestly superior in education, training and ability to those already in post.

Another obstacle was opposition based on personal considerations and came from those groups whose interests were threatened by the policies of the 1980s. These included elderly veterans who refused to accept that university degrees were an adequate substitute for their own decades of practical experience, or that a seat on the Central Advisory Commission was adequate recompense for a life of service to the revolution, and who looked askance at the prospect of losing power, status and the perquisites of office. Ye Jianying was an eminent member of this category, hanging on to office despite desperately poor health until his eighty-ninth year when, in September 1985 at a Special Party Conference, he joined over a hundred Party veterans in a collective letter of resignation. It was at this Conference that a number of the younger, professional leaders entered the Politburo, replacing veteran cadres. Resentment and resistance was also strong in the PLA, which was the major institution to suffer in the reforms. Sections of the military protested against policies designed to curtail PLA influence in both the Party and state structures, which resulted in a major reduction in the percentage of senior positions going to army personnel, most notably at Central Committee level.[1] This in turn had adversely affected the national defence budget, with the civilian leadership deciding to modernise that sector by concentrating on education and training rather than by simply relying on the acquisition of sophisticated and expensive equipment, and by financing the purchase of the latter by reducing military manpower by one million by 1987. Although the professionally skilled and educated benefited from the new approach, it had little to offer the many who were unable to meet the new standards required. Instead of being able to expect promotion on the basis of long service, such people were now likely to find themselves demobilised into a civilian job market with no great interest in absorbing the PLA's 'rejects'.

More generally, throughout society there was opposition from leftists who had advanced up the career ladder during the Cultural Revolution and who had no desire to be dislodged by the rectification drive launched against them in 1983. They formed factional alliances to protect each other, to oppose reform generally, and to exploit any opportunities that arose. A vivid example of their ability to cause the reformers embarrassment came in 1983–4 when Deng attempted to quell criticism that he was moving too fast, by initiating the campaign to oppose 'spiritual pollution. This was intended to be a limited drive against some of the unwanted developments which had accompanied China's opening up to the outside world, such as pornography. For a few months leftists in some areas were able to extend the campaign in a manner frighteningly reminiscent of the Cultural Revolution by, for example, attacking scientists for studying Western journals and women for sporting foreign 'perms' (Schram, 1984).

Hence in the 1980s there were various groups and many individuals who opposed the direction and speed of reform for a range of personal, political and ideological reasons. The intense questioning and discussion of virtually every aspect of China's economic and political arrangements which followed on immediately from the Third Plenum, and which found radical expression in unofficial journals and 'democracy walls', temporarily obscured the fact that change would be painful and that those likely to be hurt would strike back as best they could (Garside, 1981).

The reformers: unity and disunity

The heady atmosphere of the period also exaggerated the extent to which the reformers were agreed on a course of action at the policy level. In some respects there appears to have been a high level of unity in 1979 which persisted into 1987. The central goal remains the pursuit of rapid economic development based on the training and promotion of the technical intelligentsia, a greatly improved flow of information, and the maintenance of the 'open door'. It accepts the need for a combination of state direction and individual enterprise, the precise mixture varying from sector to sector. In contrast to the mobilisational style of Mao, development is to be based on orderly procedures and implemented by means of strong and stable institutions. It is to be recognisably socialist and conducted under the leadership of the Communist Party.

Agreement on such general objectives carried the reform group well into the 1980s without any serious friction. However, from 1983, tensions which had their roots in ideology began to mount. Although all leaders agreed on

China's continuing commitment to Marxism-Leninism and Mao Zedong Thought, they disagreed as to whether this was best served as a fixed menu or as an *à la carte* offering from which one could select.

A further source of controversy developed over how much legal and political reform was necessary. The need to create stronger and better institutions after the shambles of the Cultural Revolution was apparent to all leaders in 1979. But as the 1980s have progressed there has been a divergence of opinion as to how institutions should develop. In the general acceptance of the need for 'socialist legality' emphasis could be placed on the preservation of public order or the extension of the rights of the citizen. Similarly, the debate on 'democracy' could produce very different interpretations from those advocating it. Democracy could be seen as a way of strengthening effective Party control by improving communication and consultation between it and expert groups and lobbies with skills relevant to modernisation; or it could mean accepting that the Party should adopt a more low-key position, be more open to criticism, accept a measure of competition, and give citizens more choice.

In 1986 disagreement could no longer be contained. The debate on political reform aroused widespread and public discussion within the intellectual establishment and then permeated down to the student body. General-Secretary Hu Yaobang, and Zhu Houze, the Head of the Party's Propaganda Department, were either prepared to tolerate the expression of extremely heterodox views and a series of student demonstrations which accompanied them, or were indecisive in handling them. Other leaders were not. Deng himself criticised Hu, and in January 1987 both Hu and Zhu lost their posts, while a smaller number of individuals were stripped of their Party membership. A campaign to oppose 'bourgeois liberalism' was launched at the beginning of 1987 (see Chapter 4).

It is clear that these events were a setback for the cause of reform, but there is so far no hard evidence to sugest whether this is more than minor or temporary. Indeed, the Thirteenth Party Congress, held in autumn of 1987, showed the reformers to be in control.

There had been major personnel changes in the central institutions of the Party (Central Committee, Politburo, Standing Committee) in September 1985. These were now built upon to further change the political complexion and age profile of these institutions.

Ninety five new members entered the Central Committee which, with a total membership of two hundred and eighty five, was also reduced in size from the previous membership total of three hundred and forty eight.

One hundred and fifty members of the Twelfth Central Committee were not re-elected to the Thirteenth.

The Politburo was also reduced in size from a previous membership of twenty one to a new membership of seventeen, of whom six were new members. Eleven members of the old Politburo retired, including Deng Xiaoping himself. This overhaul was reflected in the Standing Committee of the Politburo, from which the 'old guard' of Deng Xiaoping, Chen Yun and Li Xiannian finally stood down. In their places were the new, younger cohort of Qiao Shi, Hu Qili, Li Peng and (slightly older) Yao Yilin – plus previous Standing Committee member Zhao Ziyang.

While there was much heated debate in the Thirteenth Congress about the concept of 'the initial stage of socialism', and while there was a certain caution about the pace of the process of political reform, the personnel changes seem to have been a fairly clean sweep, allowing the revolutionary generation to stand down and make way for the generation which is committed to China's modernisation to the year 2000 and beyond.

Note

1. In 1977 about 30 per cent of Central Committee members were from the PLA. In 1982 this dropped to 20 per cent. Of the full and alternate members elected for the first time in 1982, only 15 per cent had a military background.

2

Reforming the Political Structure

Tony Saich[1]

Reform of the political system has been on the agenda throughout the 1980s. By the middle of the decade a broad-based consensus had emerged on the need to undertake limited reform of the political system in order to prevent stagnation of the economic reforms. This consensus incorporated both the Party leadership and members of society. However, the degree to which reforms have been actively pursued has fluctuated, and considerable differences of opinion exist about how far the reforms should reach.

The removal of party General-Secretary Hu Yaobang in January 1987 indicated the extent of opposition to reform within the Party and military. But despite this opposition, and a degree of temporising, China has undertaken major changes to the 'Holy Trinity' of Party, state and army.

Development of the reform movement

In the period after the arrest of the Gang of Four, little attention was paid to the politico-administrative system. For the most part, such problems as were recognised were put down to the excesses of the Gang, the bad work-style to which officials had grown accustomed as a result of the Cultural Revolution, and the remaining influences of a 'feudal' way of

27

thinking. Increasingly, however, it became apparent that many of the problems derived not from attitudes but from China's political structure. The awareness that structural reform was necessary was reinforced by the emergence of a new development strategy at the Third Plenum of the Eleventh Central Committee in December 1978. The shift to a more market-oriented, decentralised economy reliant on officials who could give expert, technical advice was not readily served by a rigid, overcentralised political system dominated by the Party and staffed by people who felt at home hiding behind rules and regulations.

Deng Xiaoping and his supporters decided that an 'administrative revolution' was needed to shake up the system. The initial reforms dismantled the organisational system as it had developed during the Cultural Revolution, and whittled away other initiatives inspired by Mao Zedong in the previous decade. The major solution was to resurrect the political system that had existed in the mid-1950s – a much more Soviet-influenced system. By 1980 there was a growing recognition that the demands of a modern economy required a greater differentiation and clarification of roles for China's institutions.

In August 1980 Deng Xiaoping outlined the direction of subsequent reforms. In particular he highlighted problems that were hampering China's development, such as bureaucratism, the excessive concentration of power, patriarchism, life-long tenure in official posts, and abuse of privilege. These problems derived from faults in China's organisational system. Deng also alluded to the need to develop a high degree of democracy, arguing that it was important to make sure that the people genuinely had the power of supervision over the state in a variety of ways. In particular they were 'to manage the state organs at all levels, as well as the various enterprises and undertakings' (Deng Xiaoping, 1983).

Although this speech was not published at the time, it set the tone for subsequent discussions. Its more radical appeals to increase democracy were picked up and developed by reformers such as Liao Gailong (1981), while the more conservative party *apparat* concentrated on tinkering to eradicate the more obvious abuses of the system.

During the early 1980s a number of initiatives were taken to reform the political system, including the adoption of new Party and State Constitutions, measures to trim the bureaucracy, attempts to improve the quality of the cadre force, and steps to promote effective citizen participation (see Chapter 3). Although restructuring of the Party and state continued throughout the 1980s, a major overhaul was resisted, and the expansion of mass participation lost its earlier priority. The question of the Party's domineering role was not tackled, and many Party cadres balked at the idea of any curtailment of their power.

In 1986 more radical ideas about reform of the political system reappeared in the media. Moreover, it seemed that significant elements in the Party leadership were willing to countenance a reduction in the Party's power. Deng's August 1980 speech was dusted off and formed the starting point for discussions. The main reason for this renewed willingness to talk about reform was the fear among many that the economic reforms were in danger of reaching an impasse. Reform of the political system was seen as necessary for the development of the economy. Such thinking, while opening up the potential for reform, immediately set limits to the nature of that reform. Reform was seen as a tool for the development of the economy, so that the only political reforms necessary were those which oiled the wheels of economic modernisation. Some writers pointed to the increasing diversification of economic and social life as a reason for creating a political system able to deal with the growing pluralism of Chinese society. It is not, they claim, a mere 'subjective' whim to call for overhauling China's outdated political structure (see, for example, Wang Huming, 1986).

That political reform could return to the forefront of political debate was helped by the shift in the balance of power that occurred at the Special Party Conference held in September 1985 (on this see also Chapter 1 by John Gardner). This conference marked the consolidation in the top Party leadership of a group committed to reform, and a drastic reduction in members drawn from the more cautiously minded military. Major changes were also effected at the provincial level.

The old elite, drawn from those who joined the revolution before 1949, was largely replaced by a younger and academically better-qualified generation. For example, some 52 per cent of the Secretaries of provincial Party committees early in 1986 were graduates of higher education institutions. Their background, and their appointment within the last two or three years, indicated a commitment to reform.

While the need for reform was recognised, it was made clear that it would be limited, and implemented gradually. This stress on caution stemmed from the leadership's fear of spontaneous activity taking place outside Party control, and from a lack of consensus within the leadership about the precise nature of reform. In public pronouncements, for example, both Deng Xiaoping and Secretariat member Wang Zhaoguo were careful to stress that 'some reform of the political system is necessary to complement the current economic reforms' (see Deng Xiaoping, 1983, and Wang Zhaoguo, 1986). Political reform was becoming a divisive issue. A Hong Kong newspaper also referred to the uncertainty concerning political reform among China's top leaders. According to the report, in the summer of 1986 a meeting at Beidaihe had discussed the issue and some leaders had expressed the view that, on the whole, the current political system was basically suited to the needs of economic development and that reform could lead to the negation of the Party's leadership and of the 'four basic principles'. Disagreement on the issue led to the postponement of a decision until the Thirteenth Party Congress. This Congress convened in October 1987, affirmed the Commitment to 'political reform', and took a step in that direction by amending the Party constitution to restrict the power of primary Party organisations in enterprises or other institutions, and enlarge the discretion of officials and enterprise managers. The Party was to supervise, not administer.

But indicative of the opposition was the fact that the Sixth Plenum of the Twelfth Party Congress (September 1986), instead of discussing political reform, had passed a resolution on the need to improve work in the ideological and cultural spheres, issues identified with those who wish to limit the political reforms. Opponents of reforms perceived as too radical began to link them with 'bourgeois' contamination. In November 1986 Politburo member Peng Zhen warned against those who yearned for bourgeois democracy 'as if the moonlight of capitalist society were brighter than our sun'. To reinforce the view that the Party would remain firmly in command, Deng Xiaoping's March 1979 comments on the need to uphold the 'four basic principles' were widely publicised.

Three main opposition groups could be identified at the highest levels of the Party. First there were leaders such as Peng Zhen, Hu Qiaomu (who retired from the Politburo in November 1987) and Deng Liqun who were worried about the consequences of liberalisation for the social fabric of China. Second, there were those such as Chen Yun and Bo Yibo who represented the old state planning apparatus and were concerned about the economic consequences of current policy. Finally, there were senior military officers, many of whom were imbued with 'leftist' ideology and were worried about the integrity of Mao Zedong's legacy. All three groups sought to limit the scope of change and saw tight Party control, backed up by ideological education, as necessary (Saich, 1986b). While such a powerful lobby could halt reform for a while, it is unlikely that it will be able to reverse the process. More likely is a cautious period of reform with economic reform being detached from questions of political reform (for more detail on the reform movement and the student demonstrations, see Chapter 4 below).

The role of the party

The most important question in reform of the political system is that of the correct role of the Party and its relationship to other organisations in society. Any fundamental reform must lead to a decrease in its power. And such a reform will be much harder to achieve than economic reform because of the resistance of vested interests.

While Party hegemony is an unchangeable fact of life, significant changes have, nevertheless, taken place – although they are changes that do not challenge this hegemony. Having launched a development strategy that has created greater social differentiation and more interests to be brokered, Deng and his supporters have accepted that some reforms in the Party's role are inevitable. New institutions must be devised to mediate between the Party and the officially recognised and sanctioned sectors of society. The need to loosen the grip of the Party over other organisations in state and society has been consistently mentioned as a part of the reform plan. Having made this decision there remains plenty of ground for disagreement between acknowledging that the Party cannot control everything and defining what its role means in practice.

The overconcentration of power within the Party has been ascribed, by Chinese writers, to historical factors such as the need for a tight, highly disciplined, centralised Party during the long struggle for victory before 1949. The concentration of power in the hands of individuals is ascribed to the lingering influences of a 'feudal' political culture. Hence, it is widely propounded that power within the Party should be exercised collectively and that some functions should be redistributed within society. To quote Deng Xiaoping, 'unconditional power is the source of all unhealthy tendencies' (Cheng Hsiang, 1986a).

As a part of the reform programme, power is to be redistributed both horizontally to state organs at the same level, and vertically to Party and state organs at lower levels of the administrative system. To date, the Party has so dominated the legislature, the executive and the judiciary as to make their independence a fiction, although the Thirteenth Party Congress did vote to abolish 'leading party groups' in state and legal institutions at local and central level. To add to the problem, the Party has no effective regulatory mechanism. As a result, when the interests of the state, or of the individual, are infringed, the legal system cannot automatically intervene, since it is controlled by the Party. To remedy this situation it has been suggested that a separation of powers be established with clear guidelines laid down for each organisation. Some scholars have even suggested that a Constitutional Court be set up to adjudicate on decisions taken by central and local Paty and state officials (Su Shaozhi, 1986).

When the Party found itself in a weak position after the arrest of the Gang of Four, it seemed more willing to accept an increase in extra-Party, autonomous activities. However, in the 1980s, with its confidence restored as a result of economic success, the Party clearly demonstrated that it would set the terms of the debate. In particular it began to reassert its role as the guardian of ideology. That reform of the political system was not meant ultimately to reduce the Party's power is shown by Wang Zhaoguo's (1986) comment that 'reform must also be conducive to strengthening the leadership of the Party and be carried out in a planned manner', a point subsequently demonstrated in the reactions to the widening of the reform debate and student demonstrations in 1986–7.

Party-state relations

In all state socialist societies Party and state are closely entwined, with a dominant role for the Party. In China, during the Cultural Revolution any pretence of a distinction between the two disappeared. Thus, at the start of the Cultural Revolution the organs of Party and state, below the central levels, were identical (Saich, 1983). The revolutionary committee, which replaced the pre-1966 Party and state organs, initially combined the functions of both. Even following the restoration of the Party structure after 1969 there persisted confusion about the division of responsibilities between the Party and the revolutionary committees. To resolve this the post-Mao leadership abolished the revolutionary committees and restored the pre-Cultural Revolution system of local government. Further steps have been taken to tidy up the overlap between Party and state functions.

The 1982 State Constitution reflects the attempts to free the state sector from the grip of the Party. Unlike the more 'radical' constitutions of 1975 and 1978, the power of the Party is hidden in this Constitution. Reference to the Party as the 'core of leadership' has been dropped, as has the claim that it is the citizen's duty to support the Party. Mention of Party control only appears in the preamble, where its leading role is acknowledged in the 'four basic principles'. Yet even in official pronouncements ambiguity exists. While the new Party Constitution stipulates that Party activities must be conducted within the limits of the law, Hu Yaobang, in his address to the Twelfth Party Congress in 1982, remarked that it was the Party that leads the people in making the law and the Constitution which it must then obey. In the same address Hu made it clear that real power still lies with the Party. While the 'working people' were said to be the 'masters of the state', elsewhere Hu noted that 'our party is the leading core of nationwide political power' (Hu Yaobang, 1982).

At the basic levels of government, attempts have been made to improve economic efficiency. In the urban economic sector, more decision-making is to be placed in the hands of the enterprise manager, rather than the Party committee (see Chapter 7 by Lockett). In the rural areas the communes, where the will of the local Party too often reigned supreme, have been broken up and power redistributed.

These experiments, particularly in the urban enterprises, have met stubborn resistance from local officials. Conflicts have emerged between Party cadres who owe their position to their connections and their knowledge of the working of the old political system, and those who derive their power from detailed technical knowledge. While those with technical skills still push for greater autonomy, many Party officials have fought to exert greater control over the enterprise's work in order to protect their own jobs. As a last resort a Party Secretary can always invoke the ultimate authority of the Party to ensure getting his or her own way.

The Party itself seems confused about the separation of tasks, however. A state visit to Western Europe in mid-1986 was headed not by the Premier, nor by the President, but by the Party General-Secretary. Also, in September 1986, when a classroom roof collapsed killing eleven children in Henan Province, the school and the local Party Secretary were arrested for dereliction of duty. Yet since 1978, and even before, party committees have been told repeatedly that they should not get involved in routine day-to-day affairs. The fact that a local Party Secretary can be seen to be derelict in duty would suggest that they are still expected to concern themselves with more than just ensuring that the Party's line is being correctly implemented.

The best example of continued dominance concerns control of the military. With the stress on the need to separate Party and state work, and since the People's Liberation Army was the army of the state and not of the Party, it was rumoured that the Party's Central Military Affairs Commission would be axed from the 1982 Party Constitution. Its functions would be taken over by the newly formed State Central Military Commission. In fact, not only was the Commission retained, but membership of the two bodies was identical. According to Peng Zhen (1982), the Party's leading role in the life of the state 'naturally includes its leadership over the armed forces'. Hu Qiaomu, commenting that the personnel would be identical, stated: 'according to this idea, eventually there will not be two separate Central Military Commissions'. This, he felt, did 'not at all' contradict the stipulation that the State Commission is responsible to the National People's Congress, or its Standing Committee (Hu Qiaomu, 1982). These are two of the more conservative leaders, but it seems that even the reform group fears losing control over the military because of that institution's opposition to reforms. This is a case where the aim of separating Party and state work has given way to another principle – that the Party should command the gun.

Party structure

Reforms have also brought changes in the Party's organisational structure (see Figures 2.1 and 2.2), although they have not been as extensive as anticipated during 1980.

Democratic centralism creates a hierarchical pattern of organisation in the Party in the shape of a pyramid. In theory the top of this pyramid is the National Party Congress, or its Central Committee, which takes over the Congress's functions when the full Congress is not in session. In reality, power lies with the Political Bureau (Politburo), its Standing Committee, and with the Secretariat.

The system of secretariats (see the diagrams) existed before

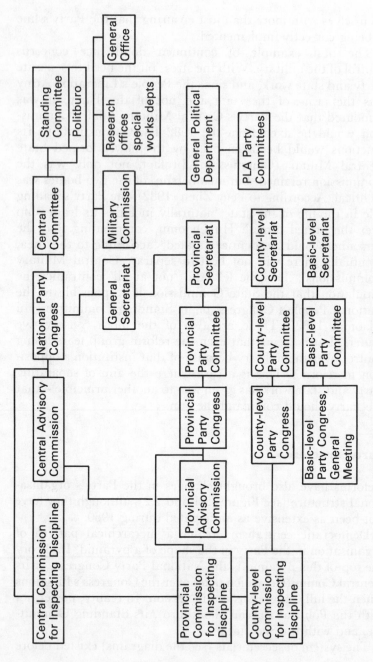

Figure 2.1 *Organisation of the Chinese Communist Party*

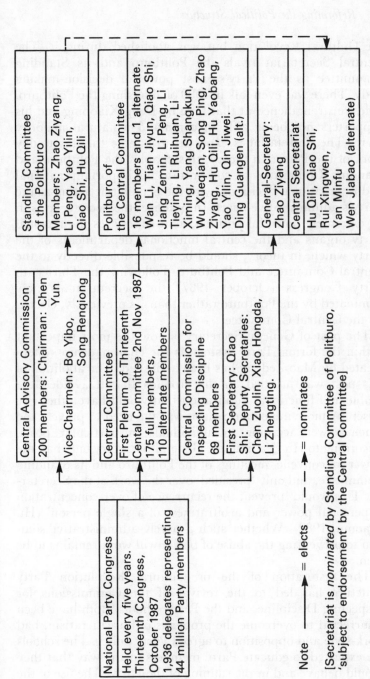

Figure 2.2 Central organisation of the CCP (simplified)

the Cultural Revolution but was abolished during it. The Central Secretariat rivals the Politburo and its Standing Committee as the Party's most powerful decision-making body. There was even talk in 1980 of abolishing the Politburo, a desire strengthened at that time by Deng Xiaoping and his supporters not being able to command a natural majority there. The Secretariat is expected to handle the day-to-day work of the Party. In theory, this enables the Politburo and Standing Committee to concentrate on important national and international decisions, with the Secretariat acting as the Party's administrative heart. In practice, the Secretariat is in an extremely powerful position, as it supervises the regional Party organs and the central functional departments of the Party which, in theory, should be responsible directly to the Central Committee and Politburo. Following the Thirteenth Party Congress (October 1987) the Secretariat is now nominated by the Politburo rather than, as previously, elected by the Central Committee.

The post of General-Secretary is now the most important within the formal Party system as the chairmanship system created by Mao Zedong has been abolished. The abolition of this post was justified on the grounds that it avoided the problem of functional duplication that would have otherwise arisen. A more important reason was the need to prevent too much power accruing to individuals in particular posts. According to Hu Qiaomu, the General-Secretary only had the power to 'convene' meetings of the Politburo and its Standing Committee, and only 'presided' over the work of the Secretariat. This would 'prevent the recurrence of over-concentration of personal power and arbitrariness of a single person' (Hu Qiaomu, 1982). Whether such a purely administrative solution to preventing the abuse of power will work remains to be seen.

The restoration of the pre-Cultural Revolution Party structure has led to the revival of the Commissions for Inspecting Discipline, and the Party schools. Both have been resurrected to overcome the problems of bureaucratism, bad work-style and opposition to agreed Party policy. The schools are expected to educate Party members in the way that they should behave and in the running of the Party. The use of the commissions is an important part of the attempt to re-establish a system for dealing with discipline and monitoring abuses in the Party. This system was to replace what the leadership saw as the arbitrariness and unpredictability of the Cultural Revolution. However, during the 1980s these com-missions have provided a power-base for those who are opposed to the full implementation of Deng's reform program-me, and who are worried about the rise in corruption. Deng and his supporters feel vulnerable on this question and have been reluctant to acknowledge any link between the growth of corruption and the economic reforms. However, to show that they take the matter equally seriously, a new three-person group was set up in January 1986 to take the lead in tackling the problem. The creation of this new body indicated that the reformers were going to take over the battle from the more conservative elements who had used the emergence of such 'unhealthy tendencies' to criticise various aspects of the reform package. Some more reform-minded writers have attacked the notion of a link between contacts with the West and increasing corruption. They see the corruption as arising from China's undemocratic political structures, heavily in-fluenced by China's autocratic political culture.

One further new body created at the Twelfth Party Congress was the Central Advisory Commission, with sub-ordinate commissions at provincial level. This was part of a ploy to relieve aged officials of their posts by shifting them aside, while still drawing on their expertise. Members of these commissions, who are expected to have a Party standing of over forty years, are to act as political assistants and consultants to the relevant Party committee. The commissions have been acknowledged as a 'temporary expedient' to deal with the problem of retirement. However, organisations once summoned up are notoriously difficult to wish away. Whether they are truly temporary depends on the establishment of a proper retirement system.

Reform of the state sector

Current policy has led to a revitalisation of the state sector, with a renewed stress not only on the state's economic functions but also its legislative and representative functions (see Figures 2.3 and 2.4). The National People's Congress (NPC), constitutionally the highest organ of state power, has begun to meet annually and has produced a steady stream of legislation. There have been reports in the Chinese press about policy debates conducted during its sessions. However, it is admitted that the Congress cannot realistically operate as described in the Constitution since it has too many delegates and meets too infrequently. It is now said that the NPC can 'only focus on solving some issues of basic importance in the life of the state' (Wang Shuwen, 1982). To solve this problem, rather than reduce the number of delegates or convene more meetings, it was decided to increase the powers of the Standing Committee of the NPC. Because of its smaller size, approximately two hundred people, it can hold regular meetings with comparative ease. The Standing Committee has been given legislative power and the power to supervise the enforcement of the Constitution. When the NPC is not in session, it can examine and approve partial adjustments to the State plan and budget. It is hoped that this will provide the state with flexibility and speed when reacting to problems in the economy. The Standing Committee's power of supervision over the state organs has also been increased.

The highest organ of state administration remains the State Council, which is the executive organ of the NPC. In theory it is responsible and accountable to the NPC and its Standing Committee and is, in effect, the government of China. The work of the Council is presided over by an executive board composed of the Premier, Vice-Premiers, State Councillors and the Secretary-General.

The revitalisation of the governmental sector has also breathed new life into the Chinese People's Political Consultative Conference (CPPCC). The Conference now meets annually, usually at the same time as the NPC. With the recent stress on social harmony, as opposed to class conflict, the CPPCC provides the Party with an important link to members of other political parties, and also to key personnel who have no party affiliation. As the main forum for co-operation with non-Communist Party intellectuals, it pro-

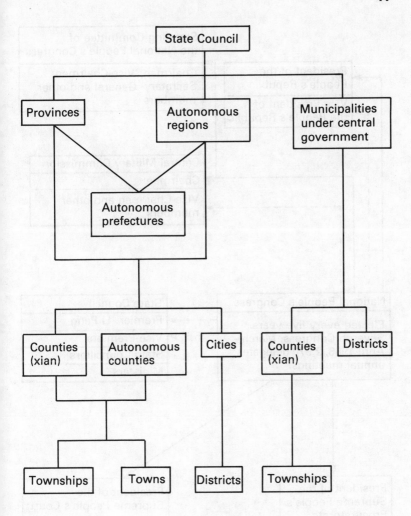

Figure 2.3 Levels of government under the State Council

42

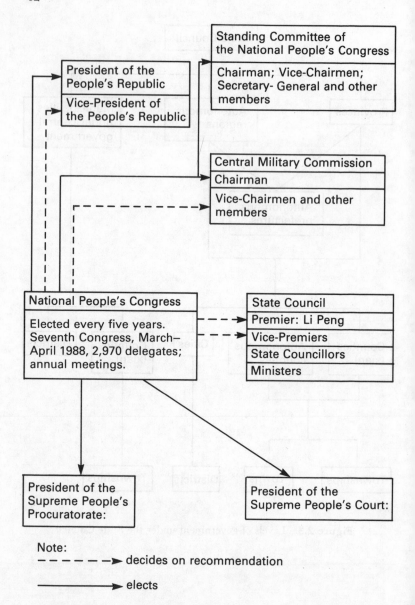

Note:
– – – – –▸ decides on recommendation

──────▸ elects

Figure 2.4 Central organisation of the Chinese government
as at April 1988

vides the Party and the NPC with expertise that is necessary for economic modernisation. For its members, the CPPCC provides influence on policy-making over a range of economic and social questions. Evidence suggests that proposals from the CPPCC do have some impact, although it should be pointed out that they do not deal with fundamental questions of policy or principle.

Despite the emphasis on increasing the state's representative functions, it is clear that the people's congresses at all levels are not fulfilling this role properly. In the words of Bao Xinjian, the key issue is whether government workers are 'servants of society' or 'masters of society' (Bao Xinjian, 1986); the latter appears to be the case. This has led to repeated calls to make the system more democratic by increasing the powers of supervision and curtailing the power of local officials. A number of steps have already been taken, such as ending lifelong tenure for officials, and extending the scope of competitive, direct elections. The commitment to the election of officials was shown by the abolition of the appointed revolutionary committees, and their replacement by elected people's congresses – directly elected up to, and including, the county level. Despite this commitment, the process of county-level elections has not been a success. Despite the intentions of national leaders and their willingness to order fresh elections where evidence of fraud was clearly demonstrated, the 1980 elections became bogged down in procedural complexity, electoral apathy, and abuse by local officials. This caused a delay in the subsequent elections while some of the teething problems were dealt with. In September 1986, the Standing Committee of the NPC announced that new deputies for county- and township-level people's congresses should be elected by the end of 1987, and in December 1986 revisions of the relevant electoral and organic laws were adopted (see Wang Hanbin, 1986, and Chapter 3 below by Benewick).

The non-central state apparatus has also undergone a number of changes in an attempt to improve its functioning. The powers of provincial-level congresses have been improved to allow them to adopt local regulations, and at above the county level, standing committees were instituted to carry out the work of the congresses on a more permanent basis. Furthermore, neighbourhood and villagers' committees have been written into the 1982 Constitution as the 'mass organisations of self-management at the basic level'.

Yet the most important change is that the people's communes, set up as part of the Great Leap Forward (1958–60), no longer functions as both a unit of economic and government administration. Now the township operates as a level of government, leaving the commune to operate solely as an economic organisation. This division of powers is not only designed to strengthen the state at the lowest level but also to improve economic performance. Under the old system, it was claimed that the Party committees interfered too much in the life of the countryside. With the decollectivisation of economic life throughout the countryside, the commune has begun to disappear altogether as an organisation of substance.

The People's Liberation Army

The biggest institutional loser in the reform of the political system has been the People's Liberation Army (PLA). The role of the PLA in the pre-1949 struggle (a role both political and military) has meant that, unlike armies in the West, it has been more than a professional standing army, and has had a wider field of operation than that of a bureaucratic pressure group competing for scarce resources. Since 1949 it has had a high profile within the Chinese political system, especially since the early phase of the Cultural Revolution, when Mao Zedong turned to the PLA to 'purify' the tainted ranks of the Party and state.

The current policies are aimed at limiting the PLA's multi-functional role, confining it to a purely military one. The rationale for putting the military back into the barracks is strengthened by the PLA providing a source of opposition, and a rallying point, for those disaffected with the reform programme. The PLA has harboured residual elements imbued with 'leftist' ideology, and many of its leaders have been particularly concerned about the erosion of Mao Zedong's legacy and the tarnishing of his reputation. Senior military personnel also appear to have been disgruntled about the low priority which the military has been accorded in the modernisation programme. Discontent surfaced among the rank-and-file peasant recruits when they saw new possibilities for making money opening up in the countryside. Most had joined the military to escape the poverty and drudgery of rural life. That the 'responsibility system' in agriculture provided a way of making a decent and tempting living is shown by the need to introduce a conscription law in 1984.

Faced with this opposition, Deng Xiaoping has been remarkably successful in neutralising it. In the space of a year he showed the military who was in control and, literally, cut them down to size. In December 1984, forty senior officers of the PLA general staff retired, the largest 'voluntary' retirement ever; in January 1985 budget cutbacks were announced; and in April, Hu Yaobang announced that troop levels would be cut by 25 per cent, around one million personnel, although by late 1986 only 300 000 had actually been demobilised. To neutralise its political impact, two crucial measures were taken. First, in June 1985 a meeting of the Party's Central Military Affairs Commission, chaired by Deng Xiaoping, announced a restructuring of the regional military command structure. This may well have been justified on grounds of efficiency, but it also had the effect of breaking up powerful regional ties of key military leaders. The restructuring reduced the previous eleven regional commands to seven, with a 50 per cent reduction in the total of senior officers and the appointment of younger officers with greater technical knowledge. A further reshuffle of senior military men took place in November 1987.

The second important measure was the shake-up of the Party leadership at the Party's special Conference, referred to earlier, which was held in September 1985. This saw a sharp reduction in military representation in the Politburo. Of the ten who 'resigned', six were military personnel. No military appointees were among the six new full members of the Politburo. The two remaining military figures on the Politburo are widely seen as supporters of Deng Xiaoping. The military establishment has, however, resisted one of Deng's desired personnel changes. It seems that he had wished to pass his post of Chairman of the Military Affairs Commission to Hu Yaobang. While the military appeared willing to bow ultimately to Deng's authority, they were not prepared to accept his protégé, and may even have been instrumental in the removal of Hu Yaobang as Party General-Secretary at the beginning of 1987.

Conclusions

Despite a considerable number of initiatives taken to reform China's political and administrative system, major problems persist. Fundamentally, the crucial issue of the role of the Party has not been addressed by China's most senior leaders. The Party's Thirteenth Congress, held in October 1987, produced much reform talk, but only preliminary moves to reform the role of the Party. The ingrained mentality of the superiority of the Party and the belief that the 'Party takes the lead in everything', combined with the resistance to change by those with a vested interest in the *status quo*, form powerful obstacles to far-reaching reform of the political system. The fact that for many of the Party leaders reform of the political system is seen in terms of its benefit to the economy also limits the scope for change. For many the reform of the political system is little more than a necessary evil, entertained only in order to progress with economic development.

Complaints in the Chinese press about continued Party interference in state affairs, over-concentration of power, bureaucratism and so on, all attest that reform has not yet met the limited goals set by the reformers in the Party. In mid-1987 the reformers took advantage of the occasion of the great forest fire in the Daxinganling region of North China to criticise continuing bureaucratic inefficiency, and to launch a campaign against 'bureaucratism', a simultaneous reminder of Deng's intentions and of the size of the problem. Even so, these modest gains may be too much for conservatives.

Much political activity takes place outside the formal political structures and is to some extent anti-systemic. Alienation from the political system is common, particularly among youths who grew up during the time of fluctuating policy directives from the centre. This surfaced in the student demonstrations of 1986–7.

In any further phase of reform, a political system will have to be devised that is not only managerially efficient, but also able to accommodate the demands of an increasingly complex society. The Thirteenth Party Congress made few obvious concessions to the anti-reformers, but the reform process seems likely to be undertaken at a moderate pace, and with caution.

Note

1. I would like to thank Dr J Unger for his comments on an earlier draft of this paper.

3

Political Participation

Robert Benewick

This chapter is concerned with an outstanding characteristic of post-liberation Chinese politics, political participation. It will focus on the objectives of political participation and the opportunities for fulfilling them. An attempt will be made to set forth what is meant by political participation in the Chinese context, to describe its purposes and functions, and to outline the forms it has taken since 1976. Particular attention will be paid to non-elite participation in the form of elections for people's congresses at the county level and the role of the congresses. While the constraints that are peculiar to the Chinese political system must be taken into account, in particular the dominant role of the Chinese Communist Party, it is nonetheless true that the Chinese have made efforts to encourage popular political participation since 1949, earlier through the mass campaigns of the Maoist era, later through the institutions of law and politics re-established by Deng Xiaoping.

It is important to bear in mind, however, that there are limitations to participation, particularly those imposed by established interests to block or minimise challenges to their authority and prerogatives. The power to influence decision-making, therefore, should not be used as the sole criterion for judging effectiveness.

The setting

China's reformers have accepted that their economic objectives cannot be achieved without changes in the political process. This recognises the complex interactions between economics and politics and between theoretical analysis and practical considerations. Deng Xiaoping (1983, p. 309) set the stage when he outlined the problems impeding modernisation: bureaucracy, over-concentration of power, patriarchal methods, life tenure in leading posts, and various kinds of privileges. More recently he provided the justification within the framework of the relationships between base and superstructure in Marxist theory. Commenting on the Seventh Five-Year Plan, Deng stated: 'During this time, comprehensive economic restructuring will affect every field: politics, education, science, etc.' (Li Kejing, 1986, p. 9).

The theme was taken up in several quarters. For example, in the symposium on 'The Political Restructuring of Socialist States' it was stated that it was incorrect to assume that political reforms would automatically fall into place with the achievement of economic reforms and, further, that the latter would not succeed 'without the co-ordinated and synchronised development of political restructuring' (Li Kejing, 1986, p. 11). At the same time the economic reforms, which are well advanced, particularly in the countryside, give rise to new interests which demand recognition, require accommodation and raise expectations. This takes place within the framework of a highly centralised political structure, party centrality and democratic centralism. At issue is how to arrange an acceptable fit. This in turn promotes conflict within the leadership over control of the extent, direction and pace of change. That the leadership is not prepared to permit open political conflict and unsanctioned change was made clear by its response to the debates and demonstrations of 1986–7 (see Chapter 4 below by Munro). Designated programmes of reform include streamlining the decision-making and administrative process, the separation of government and party functions, improvements in the legal system, and the development of 'socialist democracy'. The latter is based on what is described as the 'four basic principles': the socialist road; the democratic dictatorship of the people; the leadership of the Communist Party; and adherence to Marxism-Leninism and Mao Zedong thought. Socialism is further defined as 'socialism with Chinese characteristics', which allows the leadership to innovate, experiment, borrow, adapt and refine within the confines of the four basic principles and the political culture. Democracy refers to institutional arrangements and procedures. The further development of socialist democracy takes account of the need to improve the methods for the nomination and election of deputies to the people's congresses; to enhance the role of the congresses at all levels and of the consultative congresses, democratic parties and 'mass organisations'; to provide for the effective supervision of cadres; and to promote the responsibility and responsiveness of deputies to their constituents.

Different, though related, principles of participation are affected. These include the fundamental Chinese belief of a harmony of interests between the rulers and the people (Nathan, 1986, p. 228); the mass line which legitimates mass involvement and postulates the relationship between the Party and the people; Mao Zedong's version of citizens' supervision and control derived from Marx's view of the Paris Commune; and participation as mobilisation in support of the decisions and policies of the leadership and the Party. These have to be reinforced or reconciled with any new principles of participation which are in conflict.

The meaning of participation

An understanding of the nature of participation must take into account the following contextual influences: participation in Chinese political culture, the Chinese view of democracy, and the legacies of the Maoist period. At the level of ideology the importance of participation is enshrined in the mass line, while in practice it is circumscribed. It is understandable that there is no consensus among scholars. Participation has been approached in terms of the political culture (Pye, 1971) and as a 'distinct Chinese political style' (Townsend, 1967). It has been treated functionally as a means for political education, socialisation and policy implementation. Falkenheim (1978) empirically tested the impact of the mass line in the immediate post-Mao years by measuring involvement. His data suggested positive moves towards democratisation and opportunities for participation. More recently Saich (1986a) has examined participation within the framework of modernisation in state socialist societies, an approach which has particular relevance in view of the links between economic and political reforms.

In addition to a commitment to participation the post-Mao leadership inherited a tradition of democracy and a highly politicised society. It is common to think in terms of China lacking a democratic tradition and the Communist Party importing democratic centralism and adapting it to Chinese conditions in the form of the mass line. Nathan (1986) argues, however, that the Chinese have aspired to their own version of democracy for a century, claim to have possessed it for nearly three-quarters of a century, and 'have lived in one of the most participatory societies in history' for over one-third of a century. What is constant is the view of democracy as a means rather than as an end. The post-Mao leadership is determined to prevent a repetition of what is described as the 'Great Democracy' of the Cultural Revolution and has made clear its opposition to liberal democracy through its attack on 'bourgeois liberalism'.

The experience of the Democracy Movement, the deletion from the 1982 Constitution of the 'four great freedoms' – speaking out freely, airing views fully, holding great debates, and writing big character posters – and the hostile reaction to the 1986 debates and demonstrations, suggest democracy held firmly on a lead. The collar has been loosened as regards participation, however, and is likely to remain so. This is contingent upon the maintenance of the present economic strategies, but also as a consequence of changes in the functions of existing institutions or as a result of their decline in effectiveness.

The position of the Party (and more covertly the military) is crucial in this respect. As the Party withdraws from activities that do not involve major political issues, it will provide opportunities and set constraints for participation. The temptation to view reform or change as setting off a chain reaction should be avoided, however. A knock-on effect is likely, but as for participation, it will be differentiated and selective. For the present leadership a legacy of the highly politicised Maoist period – particularly the Hundred Flowers and Anti-Rightist campaigns, the Great Leap Forward and the Cultural Revolution – is the need to ensure stability and to promote economic development. This increases the pressure to direct and control the purpose, practice and pace of participation. The degree to which this is possible is subject to the politics internal to the leadership, Party and bureaucracy. What is notable is that just as the workforce during the Maoist period could be politicised and mobilised for increasing production, it has since been demobilised and 'depoliticised' to achieve the same end. The most prominent characteristic of political participation in China is still its collective nature. This does not rule out the representation and presentation of individual interests or elite recruitment. One of the tasks of the reforming leadership has been to incorporate new interests without threatening established ones. Even so, the dominant emphasis has been mobilisation for support, legitimation and policy implementation. This also involves arenas and forums for carrying out the mass line – that is, channelling information to decision-makers and providing political social-isation and education for the citizenry.

The often formal and expressive nature of participation needs to be qualified, however, in so far that issues and interests immediate to people at their workplace or residence are accommodated, suggesting an instrumental dimension as well. This will be examined in the following sections, but to summarise, participation is characterised by its selective, directed, controlled and largely collective nature. Participa-tion does, nevertheless, have an instrumental and develop-mental dynamic which can come into conflict with these characteristics.

Forms of participation

Before considering non-elite participation in any detail, it is useful to sample the range of available opportunities for collective participation. These include membership in the Communist Party, 'mass organisations', workers' congresses in industrial enterprises, residents' committees, and campaigns and dissent in the form of demonstrations. They can be designated for purposes of analysis as authorised or unauthorised, structured or unstructured. The Communist Party with its forty-four million members is the outstanding example of an authorised and structured form of participation. Its increase in membership in the 1980s is mainly the consequence of a policy to recruit intellectual and scientific personnel.

The 'mass organisations' are also a form of authorised and structured participation. They are under the leadership of the Communist Party, organised on the principle of democratic centralism, and implement and mobilise support for the policies of the leadership. Within this context of centralism, however, the degree to which they represent the interests of their members varies among the organisations. There has been a considerable effort to resuscitate the mass organisations. For example, the All-China Students' Federation and some of its branches achieved prominence during the demonstrations of 1986 by upholding the official Party position against the demonstrators. The Women's Federation, which includes all women at the local level, has progressively moved beyond mobilisation in support of government policies to the articulation of gender-related issues.

The workplace may provide the most potential for effective participation, with the re-establishment of workers' congresses, the extension of elections, and the growing status of the trade unions. Saich (1986b, p. 23) is correct in pointing out that the congresses should not be confused with workers' control or participation in management, and Walder (1983, p. 71) has argued that few meaningful decisions are made at this level. At the same time, the opportunity, although authorised and structured, for workers to discuss matters immediately important to them has instrumental and developmental implications.

Workers' (and staff) congresses were set up in the 1950s.

They were intended to be the main vehicle for participation but in practice had little influence. The post-Mao version, refashioned to conform with new industrial strategies, has more teeth, although in practice some may prove false. Essentially, a distinction has been drawn between the role of the director and that of the Party in state-owned industrial enterprises. The director has responsibility for running the enterprise, while the Party committee is no longer to be involved in routine administration and detailed production matters. Instead it has responsibility for political education and for the fulfilment of the state plan. The powers of the workers' congress have been enlarged. While many of these remain formal, those affecting workers' livelihood and welfare take on a particular significance with regard to profit allocation and in so far as the enterprise is also a living unit. In addition, the workers' congress has the right to arrange for the election of managers and has a watchdog brief over mismanagement.

Womack (1984, p. 427) distinguishes the current reforms from those of the Cultural Revolution with a similar content: 'elections are now seen as a democratic institution promoting the productive purpose of the enterprise in an orderly way rather than as an expression of egalitarian class control'. The reforms also have implications for the trade unions, which were disbanded from the beginning of the Cultural Revolution until 1973. The All-China Federation of Trade Unions (ACFTU) now claims 80 per cent of the urban workforce, and although membership is in principle voluntary, it includes all those eligible. As a mass organisation its main function remains the implementation and mobilisation of support for party principles and policy. Strikes are prohibited, and where they occur the trade union is expected to act as a state mediator. Yet the 1983 trade union constitution stipulates that unions 'do their work actively and independently' within the prescription of their role as a mass organisation (Lee, 1986, p. 164). At the enterprise level, unions act as the co-ordinating organ of the workers' congress, which should encourage them to work 'actively and independently', enlarge their representative function and promote issues of immediate concern to the workers. For the first time the new constitution specifies that unions at the basic level should look after the interests of women workers. The constraints are many, however. One set is derived from the priorities of the economic reforms including the state plan, the managerial responsibility system, scientific management to cope with the growing complexity of decision-making, and a more market-orientated approach which stresses 'efficiency and profitability'.

Workers' congresses and an increase in trade union autonomy are means for achieving these objectives, rather than democratic goals in their own right. A second set of constraints are political and refer to the reality of the withdrawal of Party cadres from the day-to-day managerial activities and the independence they are willing to grant to the workers' and the trade union in practice. This distinction leads to an uneven pattern of development. A third set of constraints is inherent in the nature of participation. Influence is subject to the possession of requisite skills, knowledge and experience. That they have not begun to fulfil their potential is suggested by a poll of one million staff members and workers undertaken by the ACFTU. Fifty-six per cent of the respondents claimed that their status in enterprises had dropped, and 70 per cent were negative or doubtful about the role of workers' congresses in examining major matters and supervising cadres. There were demands that the power of the congress be given legal status and that trustworthy people be placed in charge of enterprises. Moreover, the ACFTU demanded the right of democratically assessing cadres as well as electing and dismissing them (ACFTU, 1986). The poll followed the publication of three sets of regulations on the reform of factory leadership to be implemented from October 1986. These included a management committee to assist the director. The committee of nine is to include the Secretary of the Party Committee, the trade union President, the Secretary of the Communist Youth League Committee, an elected representative of the workers' congress, as well as the director and four managerial colleagues (An Zhiguo, 1986, p. 4).

Residents' committees (villagers' committees in the countryside) are urban basic-level mass organisations. In one sense residence determines membership, but in another sense the committee provides membership for those not otherwise organised and confined to the neighbourhood such as housewives, retired workers and unemployed youth. It has more to do with sweeping lanes than with sweeping powers, since the residents' committee is mainly responsible for the execution of policy handed down from above. The tasks are mainly political and information campaigns, and include the mediation of family disputes, social control and the provision of local services. There is, though, an unrealised potential for participation, given the relatively small numbers in a committee area and the likelihood of personal contact. The residents' committee is as yet unaffected by the economic reforms, although its role is under discussion (White and Benewick, 1986, pp. 64–5). The election of committee leaders is erratic, there is little turnover, and there is a lack of systematic evidence that the views of residents are transmitted to the higher reaches of urban government (Whyte and Parish, 1984, pp. 285–96).

Opportunities for participation are provided, however, for people who may not otherwise be able to become involved. Authorised movements and campaigns are characterised by mass involvement and mobilisation. In addition to their collective character they are directed and controlled. Neither has figured prominently in the post-Mao period, presumably because of the current leadership's priority of stability and order for development. The use of campaigns has not disappeared, although there was an initial reduction in their intensity. A stop-start campaign against 'bourgeois liberalisation' in 1981–2 merged into the 'spiritual pollution' campaign of 1983 which collapsed, and the recent Party rectification campaign has maintained a low profile. The 'double hundred' campaign of 1986 (marking the anniversary of the brief liberalisation of 1956, which took place under the slogan 'let a hundred flowers bloom, a hundred schools of thought contend') preceded the resignation of Hu Yaobang at the beginning of 1987, and although the attack on 'bourgeois liberalisation' has not constituted a mass campaign, it revived elements of the Maoist style.

Demonstrations can be authorised and structured when they are mounted in support of government policies. The right to demonstrate is set out in Article 35 of the Constitution, and unauthorised and unstructured demonstrations, although not necessarily unorchestrated, do take place, such as those against the Japanese in 1984–5. It is when demonstrations are viewed as expressions of dissent or threats of opposition that difficulties arise. During the student demonstrations of 1986 Articles 51 and 53 were wheeled out as limitations on Article 35. (Shanghai (City), 1986). Accordingly, the right to demonstrate may not infringe upon the interests of the state, society, collective or the rights of others, and citizens must abide by the Constitution and the law relating to public order. Cities in which the demonstrations took place promulgated regulations which in effect ban them. An immediate problem for the authorities, as with big character posters, is that such bans can be defied. In the longer term, victimisation is a deterrent.

Although the emphasis is on collective participation, this does not deny opportunities for individuals. They may speak out at meetings and there is a right of petition through letter and visitations. The latter is encouraged as a means of exposing corruption and abuse, and letters have appeared in the press. For the individual, there is a calculated risk as to whether critical intervention is worthwhile, as against the possible consequences if disfavour is incurred. Much may depend on the nature of the contact or the chosen forum.

County-level elections and people's congresses

It is in the countryside that the economic reforms of the post-Mao period have led to the most sweeping changes to the substance, institutions and political environment of collective participation. A nation-wide system of direct and competitive elections for people's congresses up to and including the township and county has been introduced. This in turn has contributed to the strengthening of these congresses, which have also benefited from the enhanced legislative role of the

National People's Congress and from their own institutional reforms (see Chapter 2 by Saich). Given the massive scale of this operation, with 96 per cent of the electorate of 540 million people voting in the 1980 elections, it is not surprising that there have been difficulties. In order to understand what has taken place, it is important to bear in mind that the reforms are neither a replacement for Party hegemony nor are they about policy formulation, but they do provide opportunities for the representation of immediate interests and the outlines of political control.

The 1979 electoral law revised the 1953 law to extend the direct election of deputies upwards from the township/commune level to include the people's congresses at the county level. In doing so there were a number of important innovations. The policy of one candidate for one seat was replaced by a policy which allowed for up to twice the number of candidates as there were seats to be won in a direct election. A successful candidate now needs the votes of more than one half of the electorate. In the indirect elections for the provincial people's congress there should be 20 to 50 per cent more candidates than the number of deputies to be elected. Candidates can be nominated by any organisation or individual and must be seconded by three others. If there are more candidates than stipulated, the number is reduced by a consultative procedure or through a primary election. The secret ballot which was optional under the 1953 law was made a requirement and it became permissible to campaign on behalf of a candidate. Electoral districts were organised to allow for registration at work units or, for those without a work unit, on a residential basis. A procedure for the recall of deputies was also instituted.

However, there is a marked urban bias, justified on the grounds of the leading role of the working class. A rural deputy represents a population four times as large as that of an urban deputy at the county level, while at the provincial and national levels it is five and eight times respectively. County-level elections were held in 1980, 1984, and 1987. The 1980 election was the first to be held for over thirteen years and, as indicated, the first direct elections for people's congresses at this level. Careful preparation was the order of the day. Two series of pilot elections were conducted in order to test the changes in the law, gain experience and establish workable procedures, and the election for the 2757 congresses was not in fact completed until the end of 1981. The intention in permitting campaigning was to inform voters of the qualities of the candidates, but there was no prohibition against candidates stating their views.

Furthermore, the elections were held against the background of the Democracy Movement. Nathan (1986, pp. 204–22) records that there were at least twelve elections in which Democracy Movement activists participated, the most spectacular, and for the authorities the most disruptive, of which took place in the election district constituted by the Hunan Teachers' College in Changsha.

Consequent upon the experience of the 1980 elections (abandoned unfinished in 1982) the election law has been revised. In particular, ambiguity about the right to campaign has been removed, and it is now restricted to nominators being allowed to brief group meetings. Accordingly, the 1984 election was a low-key affair notable for the absence of reported incidents (Nathan, 1986, p. 223). The 1979 law has been modified in other ways: the number needed to nominate an individual has been raised to ten; the minimum number of candidates exceeding the number of deputies to be elected has been dropped from 50 per cent to 33 per cent, and the possibility of holding a primary election has been dropped. Permanent registration has been introduced (National People's Congress Standing Committee, 1982, 1986a). Despite the experience of two direct elections at the county level, the electoral law as revised for 1987 still does not provide for direct elections at the level of the province. Nor has the bias in favour of urban areas been adjusted. The importance of direct elections for the immediate future may be primarily the acceptance of the electoral process by the leadership and the people as a legitimate channel for political expression and participation, however limited. Even within these limitations it has been subject to manipulation and corruption, although as Womack (1982, p. 269) has observed, this may be an indication of importance.

Allegations of manipulation and corruption were a trigger for the 1986 student demonstrations, and the Standing Committee of the National People's Congress admitted in January 1987 that there had been malpractice in some localities (National People's Congress Standing Committee, 1987). A confident estimate of the value of direct elections in China is further constrained by the quality of data available for systematic analysis. Electoral procedures are being tried and established, but it would be imprudent to pronounce on their effectiveness. The same reservation informs discussion of the people's congresses, particularly at the level of the county. Moreover, with over 2700 counties, development and practices will vary. Direct elections, however, should enhance the status of deputies, and the provisions for their supervision and removal should promote confidence in them.

There are ways in which the people's congresses can move beyond being a rubber stamp. Once elected, deputies not only choose their delegates for the provincial congress, but also elect their own officers, standing committee, leading members of the county government, court, and procuratorate, and retain the right of supervision and removal. The National People's Congress is giving a lead with its new propensity for lively debate. This is particularly true of its standing committee. Where the county-level congress normally only meets once a year, its standing committee meets at least once every two months. Provincial people's congresses and those of the large cities have been granted powers to enact local ordinances, but these have not as yet been extended to the county level. Delegates' motions provide the main opportunity for constituents' participation. These are local and immediate matters requiring attention and action by the county government. They are passed on to the relevant bureau and a response is expected. It is noteworthy, however, that where formerly such motions required three seconders, the new organic law specifies nine. This may be more an attempt to control the volume than to institute a curb. In any event, delegates' motions are a potential means for stimulating interest in the work of the congress and for judging and holding deputies accountable.

Summary and conclusions

It is important not to exaggerate the opportunities for effective participation in contemporary China. The reforms in the post-Mao period do not represent a shift in the power-base or a sharing of power. They do not authorise open opposition to the leadership, its policies or principles. Indeed, the charge of 'bourgeois liberalisation' can be viewed as an attack against those reformers and intellectuals who attempted to move from window-dressing to window-shopping.

Authorised, structured collective participation in China is about education and information. It is selective, directed and largely controlled. The unauthorised student demonstrations of 1986 were an expression of its limitations. At the same time the value placed upon participation enshrined in the mass line should not be underestimated. Direct elections, up to and including the county, have at the very minimum symbolic and ritualistic significance and, with the local people's congresses, are a part of a process which allows for the collective and individual expression of immediate interests. Workers' congresses and elections provide opportunities for participation on concrete issues. There has been a shift in style away from, although not eliminating, the authorised movement and to a lesser extent the campaign.

Mobilisation as a function of collective participation is viewed more subtly as a means of ensuring order and promoting stability. Political participation has been part of a programme of reforms that the post-Mao leadership accepts as necessary for its economic strategies. The proposed separation of Party and government and Party and economic management creates a new role for the Party but also provides a source of tension and conflict. To achieve these separations in reality will be a difficult and delicate task. Given the present leadership's commitment to, and endorsement of, political participation, there is unlikely to be a withdrawal of what has been achieved.

The priority, purpose, practice and pace of further extensions may well be disputed. More serious is that the future of political participation may be contingent upon changes in leadership which may advance or block it. The need for government based on laws is recognised, but there remains the question, based on American and European experience, whether rights and reforms have to be won rather than granted.

4

Political Reform, Student Demonstrations and the Conservative Backlash

Robin Munro

The wave of student demonstrations for greater democracy which swept through China's major cities in the winter of 1986–7 sparked off the country's most severe political crisis since the death of Mao Zedong. From the liberal reformist highpoint of the previous summer, China's political scene had by early 1987 undergone a drastic, unforseen lurch towards the Maoist left. A strident campaign against 'bourgeois liberalisation' began and Hu Yaobang, the protégé of Deng Xiaoping and the second most powerful man in. China, was abruptly forced to resign from his post as Party General-Sectretary. After more than a month of demonstrations, China's students discovered that their actions had precipitated a major counter-attack by certain senior Party and army figures against key political aspects of the reform programme of Deng Xiaoping and his associates.

The long-rumoured tensions and divisions between the more radical reform leaders, such as Hu Yaobang, Zhao Ziyang, Hu Qili and Deng himself, and their more traditionalist or doctrinaire counterparts such as Peng Zhen, Chen Yun, Deng Liqun and Bo Yibo, were suddenly laid bare. The widespread assumption that China under Deng had at last become a politically stable country engaged in a consensual process of steady, all-round reform was thrown seriously into question.

At the head of this political backlash stood a wide array of veteran Party and army leaders, most of whom were in their seventies and eighties. They included both 'conservatives' – those who identify most closely with the mainstream of Maoism of the mid-1950s or early 1960s; and also 'leftists', – whose concern that the reform programme might be leading China down the 'capitalist road' indicated the unexpected survival of rather more radical Maoist sentiments. Most members of these groups suffered as victims of Mao's Cultural Revolution, however, and the political thinking of neither group should be confused with the extreme leftism of the Gang of Four.

What were the issues which fuelled the crisis of early 1987 and what were its recent historical origins? Clearly the student demonstrations provided the unforeseen catalyst. But to find the underlying cause we must look further afield, in particular at the highly sensitive issue of 'political reform', which China's leaders began to debate in 1980. The economic reforms, which actually began in that year, have been contentious enough; but the question of political reform has proven much more so, for it concerns state power, and it impinges upon the rights and prerogatives of the Communist Party. It was above all the sudden and fierce renewal of the debate on political reform, in mid-1986, which inspired China's students to take peacefully to the streets in their own alternative push for democracy. The results, however, were far from what they had anticipated.

The post-Mao reforms: a discordant consensus

The reform programme was born at the celebrated Third Plenum of the 11th Central Committee in 1978. The 'tempestuous class struggles of the past' were declared to have come to an end, and economic modernisation and greater democracy were laid down as the main tasks of the coming era. Since then, economic progress has been steady

and often impressive, and cultural liberalisation has proceeded apace; but democracy has remained largely an
abstract ideal. The grassroots, semi-dissident Democracy
Movement was allowed to flourish for a while, and activist
Wei Jingsheng's idea of democracy as being a 'fifth modernisation' – the one upon which the official 'Four Modernisations' of the economy would ultimately depend – has
continued to resonate in China's political life. But with the
final suppression of the movement in 1981, and the sentencing
of its main activists to terms of up to fifteen years' imprison-
ment, the Party leadership signalled that democracy would
remain firmly in its own gift, to be granted as and when it was
ready.

In August 1980, in a major speech entitled 'The reform of
the Party and state leadership system', Deng Xiaoping for the
first time called for China to embark upon a programme of
political reforms. For many this speech signalled the green
light of liberalisation, and a forthright and wide-ranging debate
on the question of political reform and democratisation quickly
ensued among senior Party theoreticians. Unintentionally,
however, this gave fresh hope to the faltering Democracy
Movement, several of whose leaders proceeded to stand as
independent, non-Party candidates in local municipal elections in late 1980 (See Chapter 3). At the Hunan Teachers
College in Changsha, moreover, unlawful interference in such
an election by Party officials led to serious unrest, as students
boycotted classes, went on hunger strike and held public
demonstrations. These developments, which coincided with
the rise of the *Solidarnosc* free trade union movement in Poland,
greatly bolstered conservative opposition to the idea of further
political democratisation. The Democracy Movement was
finally crushed in spring 1981, and a brisk (though short-
lived) campaign against 'bourgeois liberalisation' followed in
that summer.

Political reform as such was thus put on the back burner.
Economic reform remained the more urgent and fundamental
task, and Deng and his reform colleagues channelled their
main energies into this area during the first half of the 1980s.
The first stage was in agriculture, where the institution of the
'responsibility system' gave free play to peasant initiatives,

culminating in rural decollectivisation and the abolition, in 1984–5, of the people's communes. Perhaps inevitably, however, such developments engendered suspicions among Party conservatives of a drift backwards towards capitalism, and these worries were not allayed by the burgeoning public interest in 'capitalist' life-styles and ideas which had arisen around the same time as a result of China's 'open door' policy of trade and co-operation with the West.

On the whole, however, even the more conservative leaders seem to have been persuaded of the necessity for economic reforms, despite their socially 'dangerous' effects, and so refrained from criticising them directly. Instead, from the early 1980s onwards, they began to espouse the cause of 'socialist spiritual civilisation', aimed at inculcating socialist values and communist ideals into China's citizens in a rearguard attempt to stem the more adverse social effects of the 'open door' policy. As this was an objective which the more reform-minded members of the leadership could also share, the project for 'socialist spiritual civilisation' initially seemed to represent an area of firm common cause, and to be relatively uncontroversial.

However, the vigorous revival of debate on political and ideological questions which took place in 1983, when senior Party theoreticians began advocating 'socialist humanism', talking openly about 'alienation under socialism' and again arguing in favour of real democracy, soon cast a very different light on matters. The Party conservatives reacted with startling ferocity, and in the winter of that year launched a formidable leftist campaign against 'spiritual pollution' from the West. With this chilling shift of context, which left China's intellectuals in a state of deep shock, the project for 'socialist spiritual civilisation' began to appear more as the ideological bastion of Party conservatives than as a common endeavour between both wings of the leadership.

The reformers again sidestepped the challenge by pressing ahead with accelerated reforms in the countryside: semi-capitalist 'social entrepreneurs' were encouraged, and the call went out for China's peasants to 'get rich quickly'. The conservatives were thus outflanked, as the reformers returned to the more consensual ground of the economy. This relative unanimity over the economic reforms was rendered more questionable, however, when in 1984 these reforms were extended to include the cities. The get-rich-quick ethos, combined with free-market ideas and creeping enthusiasm for 'bourgeois' lifestyles, proved a potent mixture for China's urban population. Consequently, the defenders of China's socialist purity have been required to make almost frantic efforts in the realm of 'socialist spiritual civilisation'.

It is probably the actual economic content of the urban reforms, rather than their adverse effect on socialist morality, which proved to be the most politically divisive for the Party. From about 1984 onwards the Party leadership has been instructing Party cadres to withdraw from economic affairs, and to leave them mainly to the enterprise managers and experts. Urban reform thus represents a direct threat to the power and vested interests of a large number of middle- and lower-ranking members of the bureaucracy. This makes it potentially subversive of social stability and harmony, since, for all its failings, the bureaucracy is still the only instrument of rule available to China's leadership, and its dissatisfactions must be taken seriously.

The first half of 1985 saw a determined resumption of the 1981 campaign against 'bourgeois liberalism' with both Hu Yaobang and Deng Xiaoping indicating their support. According to Deng, 'to practise bourgeois liberalism is to take the capitalist road. We must oppose any tendencies, words or deeds that take the capitalist road.' By September 1985, Chen Yun, the most senior conservative leader, was not only warning against moral corruption and lack of revolutionary zeal, but was openly criticising aspects of the economic reforms themselves, such as the relative neglect of grain production in favour of cash cropping. It must be said that the conservatives' misgivings about reform are by no means groundless. The extensive depoliticisation of society and general encouragement of consumerism in recent years has led to a number of fairly conspicuous social ills, ranging from mere selfish individualism to rampant official corruption. Equally, there have been serious failings of the reform economy itself, including a widespread and potentially disastrous neglect of infrastructural maintenance and investment in the countryside, and the massive 1984–5 overinvestment in urban capital construction, which sent foreign exchange reserves falling dangerously low. Finally, elderly Party and army dignitaries such as Peng Zhen, Bo Yibo and Wang Zhen are no doubt genuinely and deeply offended by the various, often highly visible, signs of China's gradual 'westernisation' – not least, perhaps, because of the memories that these evoke for them of China's former 'semi-colonial' subjugation and humiliation.

While both wings of the leadership place a high premium on the maintenance of 'stability' and 'unity', for conservatives this is unquestionably the paramount consideration. It is likely that they will have felt obliged to voice, at the highest level, the bureaucracy's various dissatisfactions and complaints about current economic reforms. In any event, when the economic reforms began to encroach upon conservative political territory, an impasse seemed to have been reached.

The political reform debate of 1986

In the summer of 1986, after an interval of almost six years, Deng Xiaoping renewed his call for the reform of China's political structure. The first half of the year had seen a spate of press reports describing cases of hindrance and even outright persecution of enterprise reformers by local Party officials. Sections of the leadership, headed by Deng himself, seemed to have decided that the only effective solution to this bureaucratic obstruction was a basic 'restructuring' of the political system. Whereas Deng's 1980 proposals had had little relation to the economy, and so could be put in abeyance, the reformers now argued that the economic reforms could themselves proceed no further without real political change.

Coming hard on the heels of a dramatic thirtieth anniversary revival of the 1956 'Hundred Flowers' policy of cultural and academic liberalisation, Deng's close linkage of economic and political reform was widely interpreted as the clarion call for wholesale, integrated reforms embracing most major aspects of society. An unprecedentedly bold and free debate among senior academics and Party theoreticians quickly ensued.

In general, senior Party reformers seemed agreed on the need to reduce what had become the Party's own stranglehold on power. The principle of the 'leadership of the Party' remained paramount, however, so there was a circle to be squared somehow. Proposals were many and varied, ranging from uncontroversial calls for governmental reorganisation and impassioned demands for true freedom of speech and democratic representation. Crucially the reformers themselves began publicly to echo (though without acknowledgement) Wei Jingsheng's theme of 'no socialist modernisation without democratisation'.

Among the more far-reaching ideas were those which called for the kind of freedom, choice and diversity implicit in current economic policy to be reflected in the political arena as well. The most controversial issue, however, concerned the extent to which the modernisation process should entail the absorption of values and institutions from the West – a persistent cultural dilemma for China in its 150-year-long struggle for national self-assertion in the modern world. In the 1986 debate, senior figures such as Zhu Houze, then head of the Party Propaganda Department, and Yan Jiaqi, director of the Institute of Political Science in the Chinese Academy of Social Sciences, stressed the need to borrow not only from the science and technology of the West but also from its culture and ideology – and even, where appropriate, from its political framework. These ideas were guaranteed to raise conservative hackles. On the whole, reformers of this more radical bent were merely calling for the dismantling of artificial barriers to the West, so that the requisite process of cultural selection and rejection could proceed unimpeded. Moreover, they patriotically affirmed China's cultural capacity firmly to withstand any 'unhealthy' influences from the West. They were later to be denounced by the conservatives as advocates of 'wholesale westernisation'.

In the conservatives' view a stiff injection of 'socialist spiritual civilisation' was called for to counteract the wider social effects of all this alarming ideological innovation and as an antidote to the apparently untrammelled growth of the political reform movement. In the event, at the Party's Sixth Plenum in September 1986, a major revival of the 'spiritual civilisation' project did indeed occur, but in the form of an apparent compromise, whereby the conservatives seemed to have lost ground. For despite the fanfare with which it was relaunched, the project was considerably toned down in terms of actual content, and as regards the specific requirements which it placed on the population. On the other hand, the Plenum omitted to place the task of political reform formally on the Party's immediate agenda. However, towards the end of 1986, the Party leadership confirmed that the debate on political reform would continue, and that an appropriate plan would be worked out and presented to the forthcoming 13th Party Congress due to be held in October 1987. Thus a serious breach had been made in the conservatives' ideological bastion, with little having been offered in the way of compensation.

Wary of raising popular expectations too far, Deng Xiaoping had warned cautiously that political reform would take 'at least a decade' and that it would be 'twenty to thirty years before national elections'. But debate did range far and wide, and student expectations soared.

The student demonstrations

Just as in 1980, when the official debate on political reform provoked an unintended street-level response, in the form of renewed Democracy Movement activity and independent student involvement in local elections, the 1986 debate was also to have serious and unforeseen social consequences. Only this time the sound from the streets was not a whisper but a roar.

The students who demonstrated in December 1986 had a number of more personal grievances, mainly to do with living and study conditions. But their main demands were political: democracy, free speech and freedom of the press. While these aspirations were not elaborated upon theoretically, as they had been by the earlier Democracy Movement, they were expressed with greater vehemence and by far greater numbers of people than at any time since the Tiananmen incident of 1976, when clashes broke out in central Beijing between the authorities and the many thousands of people who came to lay wreaths in memory of the recently deceased Zhou Enlai.

But what had inspired the students to act with such boldness and determination? There was probably a mixture of reasons. Primarily it was the heightened climate of reform in the latter part of 1986 which had fanned the flames of student unrest, and China's campuses proved to be the most sensitive focus for generally raised expectations of democratic change. But events at the international level – conveyed almost instantaneously by television satellite – may also have played a role. Student demonstrations in Paris, the anti-Moscow riots in Kazakhstan, the first ever multi-party elections in Taiwan, and Aquino's 'people power' revolution in the Philippines, must all have offered suggestive models to young Chinese interested in democracy.

The general desire for democracy merged with more directly personal concerns in the issue of free elections. As in the case of the students in Changsha in 1980, the several thousand who demonstrated publicly in Hefei, Anhui province, in December 1986, were protesting against high-handed bureaucratic attempts to ban students from standing in local elections. 'Down with sham elections!' and 'No modernisation without democratisation', their banners read.

The movement spread with extraordinary speed to Wuhan, Shenzhen, Kunming, Nanjing, Suzhou, Tianjin, Chongqing, Xian and Guangzhou – and above all to Shanghai, where at one point there were around 50 000 student demonstrators on the streets. The eventual participation of students in Beijing, however, marked both the culmination and the turning point of the movement's momentum. Their open defiance of a government ban by holding a New Year's Day demonstration in Tiananmen Square, was apparently the last straw for the Party leadership, which until then had been surprisingly tolerant.

In terms of overall political alignment of the students, there were a few 'extremist' calls for an end to 'one-party autocracy' and for a 'multi-party system', but the overwhelming majority stood firmly behind the Deng faction and sought only to promote the official moves towards political reform. In other words, the students' general strategy was very similar to that of the earlier Democracy Movement.

Much had happened since 1980, however. In particular, the traditional 'four great freedoms', allowing the use of wallposters and the carrying out of tempestuous street-level debates, had been declared illegal by the National People's Congress in the summer of 1980. All such methods of 'extensive democracy' have since come to be regarded by China's leadership as emblematic of the chaos of the Cultural Revolution. Therefore, despite the generally disciplined and good-natured way in which they were conducted, the students' actions in support of political reform were doomed to be at best ineffectual and at worst counterproductive.

The students showed a great deal of courage in confronting the police and the government – and also considerable altruism, for as prospective members of China's elite they had little to gain, and much to lose, by rocking the boat. But some of their more reckless activities also revealed a striking political naivety. In particular, the public ceremonial burning by Beijing students of copies of the *People's Daily* and *Beijing Daily* on New Year's Day, may have been an eloquent expression of their resentment at having been misrepresented by the domestic press, but as a political tactic it was probably the most 'inflammatory' – being directly evocative of the Cultural Revolution – that they could have chosen.

Government anxieties extended to the possibility of student unrest spreading to other sectors of society. In general, the recent urban reforms had increased the supply of food and consumer goods, but they had also brought higher prices and marked income differentials. Thus the government's greatest concern was probably to avoid any linkage occurring between student unrest and discontent among the workers. The spectral possibility of a Chinese version of the 'Polish August' was no doubt a remote one, but memories of the Cultural Revolution are still fresh in the minds of China's leadership, and alarm bells are easily set off.

Conservative leaders had already been worried about the social effects of economic reform, even before Deng raised the much more troubling question of political reform in 1986. The redefining of the 'socialist spiritual civilisation' project at the Sixth Plenum had then left them with a much weakened ideological power-base. However, the maintenance of 'stability and unity' in society constituted their ultimate trump card, as well as being the bottom line for the reform programme as far as Deng himself was concerned. By taking to the streets, China's students unwittingly allowed the conservatives to play that card.

The campaign against 'bourgeois liberalisation'

The conservative backlash initially took the form of a press campaign against the student demonstrations, but rapidly and with increasing confidence it broadened out into an attack on the more radical circles and ideas associated with Deng's movement for political reform. Ominously, a January 1987 *People's Daily* editorial said of the student demonstrations: 'They are the outcome of several years of an unbridled trend of bourgeois liberalism, and of the failure of some of our comrades to take a clear-cut stand and resolute attitude towards this.' Significantly, the main charge laid against those accused of 'bourgeois liberalism' was that of advocating China's 'wholesale westernisation'. By mid-January, the conflict was being defined in traditional Maoist terms as a struggle between the socialist road and the capitalist road – a clear sign that the biggest political showdown within the Party for a decade was underway. The 'four cardinal principles' (namely, adherence to socialism, Party leadership, proletarian dictatorship, and Marxism-Leninism-Mao Zedong thought) which were first enunciated by Deng Xiaoping in March 1979 in response to the political challenge posed by the Democracy Movement, now appeared as the fundamentalist creed of conservative leaders seeking to curtail any further 'creative development' of Marxist orthodoxy. The conservative opponents of 'bourgeois liberalisation' seemed firmly in the ascendant – and unlikely this time to be satisfied with mere ideological concessions in the realm of 'socialist spiritual civilisation'.

The principal casualty of this campaign was Hu Yaobang.

The fall of Deng's most senior ally in the reform leadership raised serious questions about the reform programme, and also about Deng's own previously unchallenged political dominance. Premier Zhao Ziyang, on his appointment as Hu's provisional successor, moved quickly to counter such doubts, claiming that Hu had been seriously at odds with Deng for several years, particularly over his failure to stem the growth of 'bourgeois liberalism'. Deng himself was soon being presented – and, more important, was presenting himself – as having been the most firm and resolute opponent of 'bourgeois liberalism' all along. This hat certainly fits Deng. His striking flexibility in the realm of economic policy does not encompass tolerance for even the slightest perceived threat to the 'leading role of the Party'. However, neither is there any doubt that Deng, wearing his other hat, was also the main architect of the controversial 1986 debate on political reform. Yet Hu Yaobang was a much more outspoken and conspicuous defender of that debate; his frank support of liberalisation served to give other Party reformers a false sense of security, and so helped to engender the growth of so-called 'bourgeois liberalism'. Deng, who had initiated but remained more circumspect about political reform, ended up being compromised by his own more radical wing, and Hu Yaobang, who for other reasons was widely unpopular within the Party's senior ranks, was then sacrificed to appease the conservatives.

The student demonstrations therefore left the political reform movement (and in particular its more radical and speculative neo-Marxist wing) dangerously exposed, as the most senior advocates of such reform headed strategically for the centre, the better to beat back the conservative offensive. Indeed, in an attempt to regain some of the initiative, the reform leadership itself took the lead in calling for reprisals. The first casualty was Professor Fang Lizhi, Vice-President of Hefei's University of Science and Technology, who had openly supported the student movement. Fang was dismissed and assigned to another post, and expelled from the Party, apparently on the order of Deng himself.

The bold and controversial writers Liu Binyan and Wang Ruowang, victims of previous political campaigns, were again singled out for attack, and both were expelled from the Party. Firm bureaucratic control was swiftly reimposed upon the publishing world.

While these and similar moves hardly constituted a purge, they sufficed to shatter the atmosphere of intellectual openness and confience, and to generate a deep sense of foreboding in liberal-minded circles. Thus 1987, the thirtieth anniversary of the notorious 'Anti-Rightist Campaign', which cowed the intelligentsia for a generation, had got off to a bitterly inauspicious start. After several years of incessant official exhortation to 'totally repudiate the Cultural Revolution', a moratorium was suddenly placed upon public analysis of that turbulent decade. On the eve of its publication, all copies of the first mainland Chinese history of the Cultural Revolution (by Yan Jiaqi and Gao Gao) were withdrawn. Troubling though such developments were for the intelligentsia, the leftist conservative backlash was directed in the main against senior 'rightist' theoreticians and policy-makers within the Party. All of the most outspoken advocates of political reform, such as Yan Jiaqi, were implicitly under attack, and some, including the Party propaganda chief Zhu Houze, were summarily sacked.

The implications of these events of early 1987 reached beyond China, as the West, which had finally begun to be persuaded that the 'open door' would remain so, was again visited by nagging doubts regarding the prospects for a China without Deng. While it remained most unlikely that the 'open door' would be drawn shut, renewed political in-fighting among the Chinese leadership had a damaging effect upon Western business confidence in China. Above all, it heightened the already considerable anxieties of the people of Hong Kong concerning their future after 1997. Aspects of foreign policy may also have been at issue (see Chapters 14 and 15).

But what of the reform programme itself? In a valiant attempt at damage limitation in early 1987, top reformers such as Zhao Ziyang stressed that China's previous policies would not be affected by the campaign against 'bourgeois liberalisation'. However, leftist ideologues such as Deng Liqun showed little sign of wishing to respect the limits set by Zhao. Reports soon emerged of negative effects being felt in both rural and urban economic reform, as peasants found themselves being re-educated in the old Maoist virtues of 'plain living, hard work and self-reliance', and as factory managers were once again required to share administrative power with their party committees. The renewed emphasis of January on more traditional economic concepts, such as 'taking grain as the key link' and increasing the role of central planning, gave a further intimation of likely areas of retrenchment in economic reform policy.

Indeed, certain major adjustments of policy were clearly called for. The drop in grain harvests in 1986, caused by the earlier decollectivisation of agriculture, provided a striking and serious example of how easily economic reform could misfire. Here, as in several other areas, the more conservative-minded members of the leadership were able to muster powerful arguments to support their misgivings about reform.

Adjustment or turnabout?

The demise of Hu Yaobang seriously imperilled Deng's assiduously constructed plans for an orderly leadership succession in the near future – a process dependent upon the 'second and third echelons' of younger reformers, which Deng and Hu had resolutely been building up over a number of years. The forceful re-emergence of the gerontocratic old guard, after several years of uneasy partial retirement, threw the leadership competition wide open again, as the possibility arose that these other senior leaders might have alternative 'echelons' of their own to champion.

The fall of Hu Yaobang also raised the question of the extent to which Deng was effectively still in charge. He was 83 years old, and the summary ditching of Hu (albeit ultimately at Deng's instigation) must have detracted significantly from Deng's political stature and influence. For the first time it seemed possible that the enormous hegemonic influence which Deng had exerted throughout the post-Mao era might finally have begun to wane. Certainly, in sheer confidence and stridency of tone, the political backlash of early 1987 smacked of outright disrespect for Deng the reformer – even as it applauded and elevated him in his alternative role as steadfast opponent of bourgeois liberalisation.

The primary contention of the 1986 debate had been that political reform was fast becoming the prerequisite for further economic advance. Problems thrown up in the course of the urban economic reforms, as a result both of bureaucratic obstruction and of insufficiently clear ground-rules, appeared fairly intractable, and there seemed to be little scope for purely economic solutions. According to the reformers' own logic, therefore, the conclusion had to be that although failure to push through political reform might not spell the end of reform as a whole, it could well mean its relative stagnation.

In the event, in March 1987 Deng informed a visiting Canadian dignitary that political reforms were, after all, still on the agenda, and that a tentative plan for such reforms would be unveiled at the 13th Party Congress in the autumn. This crucial intervention meant that Deng had at last bitten the bullet and begun, publicly and in full, to defend his original ideas. Having sharply distanced himself from the more radically democratic aims of the neo-Marxist *avant-garde* of the reform movement, and having further secured his rear by publishing a new volume of speeches showing his consistently tough line against bourgeois liberalisation, Deng apparently felt able to resume his earlier advocacy of political reform, one which would not endanger the Party's vaunted leading role.

This reaffirmation of basic goals, which was repeated in the following weeks, probably did much to restore Deng's overall political credibility, both within the Party leadership and in the eyes of the public. It helped to create the more balanced political climate which was so evidently needed, if the various social and economic problems which had been generated by the reforms were to receive the kind of direct, unhysterical attention they so pressingly required. However, the damage done to the reform cause by the recent campaign, and in particular the blow dealt to the confidence of the intelligent-sia, remained considerable. Deng faced an uphill struggle against leftist and conservative leaders who had recently captured much of the ideological (and some of the institut-ional) high ground – and who were continuing, moreover, from their somewhat improbable redoubt in the National People's Congress, to block key reforms of the enterprise management system.

At the April 1987 annual session of the National People's Congress, the first major meeting of the Chinese leadership since the fall of Hu, there emerged an apparent stand-off between conservatives and reformers, with both sides stressing their respective priorities while turning a blind eye to areas of mutual divergence. The underlying dispute, with political reform as its crux, thus remained basically unresolved.

Conclusion

What, then, was the long-term trend? Would the baby of reform eventually be discarded, along with the bathwater of bourgeois liberalisation? At the time of writing – some five months prior to the October 1987 Party Congress – such an outcome remained improbable, despite the recent leftist reversals, for the reformers had begun to recover from the demoralising setbacks which had been inflicted upon them in the wake of the student demonstrations. Collectively, they were insisting that the only real solution to the problems of reform lay not in conservative-style reversals of policy, but rather in a further 'deepening' of the reform process.

From a more detached perspective, however, it is worth recalling that the entire post-Mao programme has hinged, essentially, on the outstanding presence and commanding support of one man, Deng Xiaoping. This is not to imply that the reforms have lacked either public or official support: far from it. The point is rather that, without Deng, China would almost certainly not have undergone a social transformation remotely approaching in scale that of the 'second revolution' which he has so doggedly pursued over most of the past decade. Thus the reform process as a whole is deeply imbued with his personal charisma, in rather the same way as the Cultural Revolution bore the indelible imprint of Mao. While this parallel should not be overstressed, neither should China's proven ability to repudiate past verities be under-stressed. In order to guarantee the continuity of his policies, Deng – in the early summer of 1987 – needed above all to repair the damage which the untimely fall of Hu Yaobang had inflicted upon the reformers' plans and mechanisms for the leadership succession.

The political reform debate of 1986 represented China's most iconoclastic and creative development of Marxism since 1949. Indeed, much of the new Soviet policy of *glasnost* (openness) was apparently inspired by China's example, and the recent leftist reversals in China contained a most poignant lesson for Mikhail Gorbachev.

Perhaps the worst-case outcome of the bourgeois liberalisation crisis, one which is unlikely but which cannot be discounted, is of China after Deng slipping into a Brezhnev-style era of bureaucratic lassitude and conservatism, as the Leninist body-politic shrugs off the long-standing irritant of reform. Conversely, the best-case outcome would see Deng ensuring that the final act of his illustrious and turbulent career was to place China firmly back on the reform course, by acting as broker to the emergence of some new, less discordant consensus between the two wings of the leadership. Placed in this context, the 1987 campaign against bourgeois liberalisation would then appear as having been little more than a last boisterous celebration on the part of the remnant old guard of the Chinese Revolution – a senescent but well-intentioned reunion affair which went somewhat over the top.

This future consensus would ideally entail a delicate balancing of two main elements: firstly, concessionary policy adjustments intended both to resolve the emergent defects of economic reform and to allay ideological fears of a capitalist restoration; and secondly, a resolute programme of political change, with democratisation and decentralisation as its core, designed to complement existing reforms and to advance their momentum. On a cautionary note, however, it must be added that Deng's search for a species of genuine political reform which would in practice enhance, rather than undermine, the sacred leading role of the Party is, at bottom, problematic to the point of being almost self-contradictory. The intense controversy aroused by the reformers' plans to divest the

Party of its economic management role clearly illustrates this point.

Equally, however, Chinese socialism has long prided itself upon its Maoist ability to make a constructive virtue out of a contradictory necessity. China's 1986–7 winter of discontent was followed by a politically milder spring, with the promise of a hot but stormy summer ahead. The political reform 'contradiction' seemed to be firmly back on the Party's agenda for resolution, and veteran leftists and conservatives once again faced stiff competition, as old horse Deng (the long-time favourite) rejoined them in the vital race to the Party Congress.

5

The New Economic Paradigm: Towards Market Socialism

Gordon White

The post-Mao era has brought fundamental changes in official Chinese thinking about the nature of socialist economics and development. While few elements of the new paradigm are entirely new (they were already being discussed in the mid-1950s and experimented with in the early 1960s) they have developed in an unprecedented way to form a new orthodoxy for China's socialist development and have provided the theoretical basis of the programme of economic reform launched by the Third Plenum of the CCP's Eleventh Central Committee in December 1978. In the rest of this chapter I shall refer to this new thinking as the 'reform paradigm'.

The previous paradigm of socialist economic development

Until the death of Mao and the removal of the Gang of Four, thinking about economic development was essentially cast in this mould of traditional notions of a planned economy and 'socialist construction' derived from Soviet experience of the

Stalin period, although it was overlaid by certain distinctive
Maoist notions deriving from the experience of the Great Leap
Forward and the Cultural Revolution (White *et al*, 1983). I
shall begin by clarifying the main tenets of this previous
Chinese model.

Firstly, it was an economic development strategy which
rested on two principles: an emphasis on rapid industrialisation which required a high rate of capital investment, with
consequently fewer resources available for individual and
social consumption, and a decisive priority in the allocation of
state investment funds given to industry over agriculture,
heavy over light industry, and modern over intermediate or
traditional technology. The CCP espoused a principle of
national 'self-reliance' whereby international economic ties
played a relatively minor role in the overall pattern of Chinese
development, imports being seen as necessary to provide
modern technology for the industrialisation programme or to
plug temporary gaps in the domestic economy, and exports
mainly as the means to pay for them. Large-scale participation in the international economy was seen as potentially
harmful: foreign economic relations had to be strictly controlled and used only to strengthen domestic capabilities and
reduce dependence on the outside world (see Chapter 9 by
Cannon).

Secondly, it was a system of economic planning and
management which sought to bring most of the economy
under direct or indirect state control; this had been established along Soviet lines in the early to mid-1950s. In this
model – as it is supposed to operate, at least – planners take
the important decisions about the level and structure of
output, growth rates, relations between economic sectors, and
so on, and government officials relay these calculations in the
form of administrative instructions to productive units.
Within this 'command economy', markets play a relatively
minor role: the behaviour of economic actors (workers,
farmers, managers, traders) and economic units (factories,
farms, shops) is not based on commodity exchange and the
pressures of supply and demand (which the Chinese refer to as
the 'law of value'), but is subject to direction and control by
state agencies. As economic development proceeds, moreover,

the vestigial role of markets would decline still further.

This planning process operated within an ownership system predominantly 'socialised', that is, mainly state-owned, with agriculture mainly organised in producer collectives; the private sector was a very small and subordinate part of the economy. Moreover, the official conception of 'socialist economic transition' envisaged a process by which 'lower' forms of ownership (private and collective) would gradually be replaced by ever larger-scale units of 'higher' state ownership, with all enterprises eventually passing into 'ownership of the whole people'.

Maoism added certain elements to this system during the decade of the Cultural Revolution (Gray, 1973): the notions of 'the continuation of class struggle in socialist society' and 'politics in command' of the economy; the idea of 'walking on two legs' which gave more ideological prominence (but not state investment resources) to small-scale industry and intermediate technology; and a partially successful attempt to decentralise economic planning by transferring power from Beijing to regional and local governments. Despite these new elements, however, behind the ideological claims and political turbulence of the Maoist period lay a basically unreformed Soviet-style strategy of development and system of planning. This was to be the target of the economic reformers who rose to prominence in the late 1970s under the political sponsorship of Deng Xiaoping.

The reformist critique

Just what did the reformers have against previous modes of economic thought, whether the old-style 'Soviet model' of the 1950s or its Maoist successor? To some extent, the shift in economic thinking can be seen as a reflection of different stages of economic development. Command planning and Maoist-style mobilisation were probably more appropriate in the first stages of industrialisation when scarce resources had to be mobilised and basic structural changes instituted, particularly in an atmosphere of international threat (from the USA in the 1950s and from both the USA and the USSR in the 1960s). In the changed context of the 1970s (*detente* with the USA) and with the initial programme of industrialisation well under way, new economic conditions called for new economic thinking.

Certainly the achievements of the previous economic system had not been negligible. China had achieved high rates of industrial growth (about 11 per cent per annum between 1952 and 1978), creditable rates of agricultural growth (about 3 per cent per annum) and had been successful in establishing a reasonably comprehensive industrial and technical base while avoiding dependence on foreign countries. Industry's share of gross national product more than doubled (from 25 per cent in 1949 to nearly 60 per cent in 1977). Certain strategic heavy industries had developed very rapidly, notably machine-building, metallurgy, petroleum, chemicals and electric power. But these performance figures conceal basic problems which worsened during the 1960s and 1970s. The pace of economic advance was erratic, with periods of boom and slump. Marginal capital output ratios were deteriorating, which meant that high growth rates were being purchased at increasing capital cost (Ishikawa, 1983). While investment funds were being used more and more inefficiently, the cost of high levels of investment, in terms of consumption forgone, meant that people's income in both cities and countryside were either stagnant or rising only sluggishly (Nolan and White, 1984). Labour productivity in state industry was static or declining (Field, 1983).

These economic failings fed through into political discontent in the form of a growing backlog of popular frustration over the slow rate of improvement in living standards. It was to these basic deficiencies that the economic reformers directed their attention; in their view they were logical outcomes of the previous system of economic planning. In their opinion, certain basic changes – both strategic and institutional – were needed to create a more rational economic system which could bring greater efficiency and higher levels of popular welfare. While the previous planning system had achieved reasonable growth rates in an 'extensive' fashion by mobilising extra increments of capital and labour but using them inefficiently, the aim of the new economic system would

be to organise a process of 'intensive' growth which laid stress
on increasing the productivity of given factors of production.

The reform paradigm

The programme of economic reform ratified by the CCP
Central Committee in late 1978 embodied certain fundamental revisions in previous thinking about economic development (for Chinese overviews of reform thinking see Yu
Guangyuan, 1984, and Wei and Chao, 1982). First of all, the
Maoist insistence on the predominance of politics over
economics, indeed the denial of the existence of 'economics' as
a distinct sphere of society, was challenged. Reform economists such as Hu Qiaomu argued that there is a separate
economic sphere in society governed by its own 'economic
laws'; in the past, party and government officials had taken
'the will of society, the government and the authorities as
economic law which can be bent to political expediency' (Hu
Qiaomu, 1978). For Hu, the role of political leaders should be
more limited, 'to see to it that our socialist economic world
operates within the scope of objective [economic] laws'. The
'reinstatement' of the economy in turn led to the reinstatement of 'economics' as a distinct field of inquiry, as opposed to
the 'political economy' of the Maoist period; this in turn led to
the growth of a group of economists who set the theoretical
context for practical reforms and acted as policy advisers (Lin,
1981).

Though economists talked about economic 'laws', they
were in fact referring, in a rather vague and abstruse way, to
what they considered to be principles of sound economic
policy and the dangers of flouting these by arbitrary political
intervention as in the Maoist period (for a discussion of these
'laws', see Xue Muqiao, 1981, chap. XI). The following
discussion concentrates on these practical principles rather
than entering Marxian 'high theory'.

Changes in economic strategy

Reform economists argued that the previous strategy of
economic development had been imbalanced and was thus

irrational. Several strategic 'readjustments' were required, among which three were particularly important. First, the previously high levels of capital investment should be reduced to allow greater scope for meeting the consumer aspirations of the population. Second, policy priorities should be changed to favour light industry and agriculture which produce goods for mass consumption, which in turn act as incentives for increased labour productivity, and to devote more investment funds to improve welfare standards. Third, the potential benefits of the world economy should be sought by increasing international economic ties which could stimulate domestic output and technical change and increase employment. This led to an ever-widening 'open-door policy' which not only brought increased trade and foreign borrowing, but also joint ventures and 'special economic zones' (SEZs) (for a case study see Sklair 1985; see also Chapter 9 in this volume). These changes, it was thought, would establish a more rational economic structure which could create the virtuous circles on which economc growth depended (see Ma Hong, 1983, chapter II).

Ownership

Reformers have challenged the notion of a transition to ever 'higher' levels of ownership, arguing that this contravenes the Marxist economic 'law' that the relations of production must conform with the level of productive forces: that is, in China's conditions, large-scale collective or state enterprises often cannot be efficient, and the role of private, small-scale co-operative and various forms of hybrid or joint ownership enterprises should be encouraged for the foreseeable future. Though it is still thought necessary for state ownership to dominate the 'commanding heights' of the economy, this theoretical reorientation has led to a diversification of China's ownership system, with private enterprise gaining ground particularly in the commercial and service sectors.

Another theoretical innovation has been the separation of the juridical concept of ownership from the real exercise of control of economic assets. This means, for example, that the rural responsibility systems, which devolve actual control over farming to households, still operate within a context of collective ownership of land. Similarly, in industry, where there has been an attempt to enlarge the operational autonomy of state enterprises, reformers have argued that, though such firms are owned by the state, this does not mean that they should be run directly by state agencies.

Planning and markets

The central element of the reform paradigm is the attempt to reinstate markets as a central feature of socialist economic theory and practice. At the most abstract level, this implies recognition of the continuing role of 'the law of value': that is, the operation of supply and demand, the Marxist 'economic categories' (such as price, profit, interest, commodity) which Maoist theorists had seen as 'bourgeois' notions, and 'the law of distribution according to labour' which demands unequal pay for unequal work, challenging Maoist egalitarianism and underpinning new wage systems using piece-rates and differential bonuses.

This is a major theoretical innovation and has important implications for the future of state socialist economies. Unlike the traditional view of socialist transition in wich the role of planning will gradually supersede that of markets, the rehabilitation of the 'law of value', particularly in the more radical form of 'market socialism' or what the Chinese call a 'socialist commodity economy', means that, in the short and medium term at least and probably in the long term, it is the task of socialist governments (particularly in Third World contexts) to develop markets, not to replace them.

What does this mean in more practical terms? Developing the role of 'the law of value' has a number of aspects. Firstly, it involves the recognition that markets (including international markets) are not only unavoidable, since there is no way that a central planning apparatus can directly co-ordinate and control large areas of an increasingly complex economy, but also desirable since they provide the flexibility, dynamism and carrot and sticks which improve economic efficiency and welfare.

Secondly, it involves a reduction of the economic role of the state and a redefinition of the nature and functions of planning. Though reformers have different views on this

question, the central dilemma is how to establish a complementary relationship between state planning and markets.
There is a consensus that the state should be more selective
and restrained in its direct interventions, for example limiting
them to strategic sectors of the economy, and should
concentrate on establishing the macroeconomic context
within which relatively independent enterprises can go about
their business – for example, through fiscal, financial and
monetary policy. There is also a consensus that the state
should resort less to administrative fiat to enforce its
economic requirements (targets, quotas, and so on) and more
to indirect 'economic levers' (such as taxation, interest rates,
price policy) which influence the behaviour of enterprises and
individuals by changing the economic environment in which
they operate.

Internationally, this theoretical innovation implies that
China should take more active steps to discover and exploit
the economic benefits of international markets through
greater integration with the world economy. This implies
recognition that Ricardo's theory of international 'comparative advantage' is relevant even for a socialist country in a
capitalist global economic system (Yuan Wenqi *et al.*, 1980).

Finally, 'the law of value' implies that economic enterprises
themselves should have greater operational independence, i.e.
should have greater freedom from the bureaucratic shackles
of their superior state organs. They would thus operate more
(but not entirely, given the continued pressures of state
planning) in accordance with market rationality, measuring
their performance in terms of profitability, varying prices and
switching production according to market conditions, tying
wage payments strictly to performance, borrowing money
from banks and paying interest for it, and so on (Jian Yiwei,
1980).

These theoretical innovations have found expression in the
reform policies of the past eight years. In turn, the reform
programmes have reshaped Chinese society and economy,
though their impact has been far more pronounced in the
rural areas than in the cities, in agriculture rather than in
industry, in the collective rather than the state sectors. The
experience of the last eight years has been very valuable in

demonstrating the practical difficulties involved in imple-
menting the new orthodoxy and drawing attention to the
problems likely to occur as the Chinese leadership tries to
deepen the reform process in the late 1980s.

The future of socialist economic development in China: problems and prospects

The experience of reform between 1979 and 1987 raises
certain central issues which must be worked out, in theory
and in practice, if the reform programme is to move forward.
First, there is the question of how to define and organise a
mutually productive relationship between state planning and
market processes. The reformers differ among themselves on
this issue, with moderates such as Chen Yun favouring a
stronger role for planning and a more circumscribed sphere of
operation for the market. More radical reformers, particularly
certain noted economists in the Chinese Academy of Social
Scientists with the support of top CCP leaders, including
Premier Zhao Ziyang, wish to extend the role of markets and
roll back direct state involvement more decisively, under the
banner of establishing a 'socialist commodity economy'.
Future progress in the reforms will depend heavily on the
relative political influence of these groups.

Second there is a set of crucial issues surrounding the
question of ownership. Can the distinction between ownership and control be sustained if, as for example in agriculture,
control over land or livestock is converted into *de facto*
ownership? If state industrial enterprises increasingly operate
as independent enterprises, then what in practice will 'state
ownership' continue to mean? If the economy becomes more
diverse in its ownership structure and particularly if significant elements of private capital accumulation emerge, how
are relations between the different sectors going to be
managed?

Third, if enterprises become more market-oriented, how
will this affect relations of production *within* the enterprise,
especially between managers and workers? Does not China's
aspiration to the title of 'socialist' require, as in the Yugoslav
case, that a move towards 'the law of value' in relations

between enterprises be accompanied by a move towards worker participation and self-management *within* enterprises?

Furthermore, how successful has the open-door policy been in terms of achieving its stated aims, and can particular aspects of the policy (notably the SEZs) be sustained after their lacklustre performance? To what extent, moreover, can the beneficial aspects of foreign economic ties be obtained while filtering out any harmful effects, whether political, economic or cultural?

To the extent that the economy becomes more market-based, will this not bring consequences which clash with what the Hungarian Janos Kornai (1980) calls the 'ethical goals' of socialism, notably equality, solidarity and security? If so, how can such contradictions be tackled?

To what extent does progress in economic reform both generate and require concomitant political reforms? Since the reforms in effect are introducing a type of economic 'demo-cratisation', will this not spur continuing demands for political democratisation? If so, how can these be reconciled with a Leninist one-party system? (See Chapter 4 by Munro on this dilemma.)

At a more fundamental level, the rise of the reform paradigm poses certain basic challenges to the very notion of Chinese 'socialism' and the *raison d'être* of the Chinese Communist Party. In the realm of economics, to the extent that the reforms resurrect the 'economic categories' charac-teristic of capitalism, will Marxist economic theory (as opposed to 'bourgeois' Western theory) prove useful as a practical guide to action? Though the central elements of the reform paradigm provide general guidelines for the future of the Chinese economy, they do not as yet constitute a blueprint or precise guide to action. To that extent, the reformers are venturing into *terra incognita* without a clear idea of what a 'socialist commodity economy' would look like or how it would operate. While the previous conception of socialism has been discredited, and the notion of 'socialism with Chinese characteristics' has been put in its place, as yet the latter concept lacks clarity and significance. If deadlock or drift are to be avoided, the future of the reforms require a clearer and more cogent conception of this new form of socialism.

6

The Reorganisation of the Countryside

Marc Blecher[1]

China has probably had a more sustained, elaborated and generally successful experience with collective agriculture than any other socialist country (with the possible exception of Hungary). From the mid-1960s until the late 1970s it provided a model for many other countries, and a laboratory in which students of socialism have been able to analyse the possibilities for rural transformation. It has subsequently gone further than any socialist country in criticising collective agriculture and reforming it in the direction of individual farming. This also has important implications for practitioners and observers of socialism outside China, many of whom now conclude that socialist agriculture is a very questionable enterprise. China has, in other words, been both a positive and a negative model of collective agriculture.

Collective agriculture 1963-78

The collectivisation of Chinese agriculture proceeded gradually throughout the early 1950s, and then took a radical turn at the end of the decade with the infamous Great Leap Forward. Once the institutional and policy readjustments after the Great Leap were complete, collective agriculture settled down

91

to a fairly standard pattern for the next fifteen years, based on the commune. Within the three-tiered commune the lowest level, called the production team, was a small, face-to-face group averaging between twenty and forty households – roughly 100 to 200 people. Boundaries were drawn to conform to the pre-existing contours of civil society, sometimes taking in small hamlets, sometimes a small village, sometimes a neighbourhood of a larger village or town.

The teams were the 'basic accounting units', which meant several things. First, they owned the land and most of the basic productive resources. Second, they were the lowest level at which costs and incomes were accounted. Third, they were the unit of income-sharing among team members. That is, each peasant's income was a share of the net distributed income of the team, and not of the larger brigade or commune which formed the two higher tiers.

Income determination worked as follows. Each team member earned a certain number of work points each day, the amount of which was recorded by an official of the team. There were various methods for deciding how many work points each person had received. Sometimes teams set piece- or task-rate norms, and simply measured work performance against those norms to arrive at a work point total for the job. Sometimes they used 'time rates', which meant that each member was evaluated for skill, assiduity, strength, etc. and then given a rating of a certain number of work points per day. Teams were given considerable latitude to make their own decisions about which rating system to use and how to apply it. Since all team members had a direct stake in these issues, these decisions were made democratically at lively and sometimes acrimonious meetings.

At the end of the year, the total number of work points awarded by the team was divided into the team's net distributable income: that is, what it had left after paying taxes and other debts, and after setting aside funds for investment, next year's production, and welfare. This calculation produced the value of each work point. Each team member's annual income was then calculated by multiplying the work point total by the work point value, with the product recorded as a credit on the team member's account with the team. This credit could then be drawn on in the form of grain, other material commodities, or cash.

Thus each team member's income was a dual function of the number of work points earned and the value of the team's work point. Work point earnings were partly an individual matter; they depended on how much work the team member did, how well it was done, and how valuable the skill contributed. Though work performance was in some sense an objective fact, it still could not be translated into work points in a simple, objective way. This required evaluation of one's work by the team. So work point earnings were subject to some collective, and rather democratic, mediation as well as individual determination.

If the number of work points earned was partially mediated through collective decision-making, the value of the work point was almost completely determined collectively. That is, it depended on the labour organisation, skills, solidarity and entrepreneurship of the team. Each team member therefore had a direct interest in the economic results achieved by the team, and by extension in the way all other team members conducted themselves at work.

Thus, contrary to the stereotypical view that Maoist China relied primarily on moral and political exhortation to sacrifice for the larger good, a complex web of *material incentives* was built into the heart of collective agriculture: individual material incentives (the more one worked the more one could expect to earn) and collective material incentives (the more the team earned the more the team member would earn). Thus collective agriculture offered Chinese peasants two major ways to raise their incomes: they could work harder, or they could try to get others to work harder. The two were not mutually exclusive; on the contrary, since everyone faced the same individual and collective incentives, the two tended to reinforce each other.

Moreover, this system of incentives could promote collective solidarity and lively collective politics. Since all members knew that their incomes depended partly on everyone's efforts, they all had reasons to support each other's efforts as much as possible. And because each team member's income also depended upon successful decision-making in the team –

about management, planning, investment and innovation – peasants in general took a strong interest in collective affairs.

China's rural collectivism also had positive effects on economic equality within teams. Inequality resulting from ownership of productive resources was eliminated. Teams could find suitable employment for the elderly and the disabled which allowed them to earn an income. They could provide welfare benefits in the form of the 'five guarantees' to any family too poor to afford minimal standards of housing, nutrition, shelter, education and burial. Most inequality within teams was due to life-cycle stages: people with young children were poorer than those with none, or with grown children capable of participating fully in labour. To even this out, teams allowed their members to overdraw their work point accounts to pay for needed food and grain. They would repay their overdrafts in later years when their children were working and they had work point surpluses. In other words, the teams provided a way of equalising consumption without equalising income in the short run. Finally, they provided collective goods, such as inexpensive education and health care, recreation facilities and programmes, and in some advanced cases even housing, to team members equally.

It had been argued by the post-Mao leadership that collectivism hurt labour incentives and suppressed local economic entrepreneurship. This argument has been widely accepted by Western analysts, many of whom are prone to believe in the impracticality of socialism. In fact, little evidence has been adduced to support the claim that collectivism did hurt labour incentives. Moreover, good theory and evidence indicate the opposite. The economic model of rational behaviour under uncertainty suggests that the payment structure of Chinese collectives gave incentives to peasants to expend super-optimal quantities of labour. That is, since peasants did not know in advance how much their work points would be worth, they would have tended to work harder and longer than optimal from a labour-efficiency point of view (Putterman, 1983). Former peasants and rural cadres interviewed by numerous scholars in Hong Kong during the 1970s did not complain about indolence among the peasantry. Instead, their complaint was that the peasants worked very hard, as they always had, but did not seem to be reaping economic gains commensurate with their efforts.

The aggregate data on economic performance bear this out. Demands were placed on the teams to conform to state plans for agriculture, for example to emphasise grain production, often on land which was marginal or which could be made productive only at very great cost. This, combined with a reduced emphasis on specialised crops in which they had a comparative advantage, hurt productivity and income in many areas. Per capita output of food grain in 1978 was only 10.6 per cent higher than in 1952, and that of cotton and oil-bearing crops was actually lower. Meat and fish production were much higher, though. Rural standards of living grew just over 2 per cent per year from 1965 to 1978.

Restrictions on rural markets and other forms of commerce among teams made it difficult for peasants and collectives to obtain what they needed for consumption and production, while it also blocked the development of their entrepreneurial potential. In the absence of careful attention by the state to technical support and cost accounting, the emphasis on rapid, labour-intensive construction by rural collectives of infras-tructure projects such as dams, canals and reservoirs led to considerable wasted effort, as these projects piled up high costs or ultimately failed to produce the intended benefits.

But none of these problems was inherent to collectivism itself. There is every reason to believe that collectivism could have achieved much better economic results under a different set of state policies on commerce, planning and investment. Since the post-Mao leadership has made changes on all fronts at once – by eliminating some of the most extreme applications of the local grain self-sufficiency policy, en-couraging some specialisation in planning, freeing rural commerce, being more careful in calculating the costs of production and investment, and attacking collectivism – it is difficult to say for certain whether the impressive economic results that have been achieved in recent years are due to the new, less collectivist organisation in the countryside or to other factors. It can certainly be said that any claim collectivism had to be eliminated for economic reasons alone rests on very spurious logic. To the extent that the reformist leadership was aware of this, its reasons for dismantling rural collectivism would lie elsewhere – perhaps, we can hypothesise, in its desire to create a politically conservative smallholding peasantry.

The new agrarian structure, 1978 to the present

The agrarian structure which has replaced collectives has been regarded by many observers as capitalist, or at least as the end of collectivism. It has been defended by others, including the post-Mao leadership, as conforming to the basic definition of socialism. The truth lies somewhere in between.

The 'reform' of China's collectivist agrarian structure began in earnest in 1979. Scattered and often spontaneous local moves towards decollectivisation which occurred in 1978 gathered momentum after the triumph of the Dengist forces at the Third Plenum of the Eleventh Central Committee in December 1978. Official policy began to emphasise work groups or even households, rather than production teams, as units of production an accounting. It was argued that a closer link between work and reward would strengthen labour incentives and managerial efficiency. Small work groups or households would now contract with the production teams for the use of collective property. For several years peasants and local officials experimented with myriad forms of contractual relationships known as 'responsibility systems'. Some involved work points, which maintained collective mediation of income, and some revolved around a simple cash nexus; some were based on work groups and some on households. By the mid-1980s the vast majority of villages had adopted the most individualistic form of responsibility system known as 'household production contracting'. Under this system households contract for use of a plot of land, a piece of machinery, or even a workshop or enterprise, and assume full financial responsibility for operating it. Land contracts specify a quota of particular crops to be grown, which must be turned over to the collective partly as taxes and partly as a fee for the use of the land; contracts for workshops or machinery specify a cash fee. The peasant contractors keep all net profits, but also bear all losses. If they cannot meet their contractual responsibilities to the team, they have to sell off personal assets or take on debt.

In order to maximise the rational use of these productive resources, most restrictions on private commerce have been lifted: private markets have revived and now are virtually free of state controls. A further incentive to peasants was a 20 per cent increase in the state procurement price of grain in 1978, now purchased from the peasants through negotiated contracts rather than compulsory quotas. By 1984 the price had risen another 4 per cent. Other farm commodity purchase prices rose at about the same rate. To ensure that the responsibility systems would be implemented and that peasants would utilise them to the full, free of fears of political criticism, the state undertook a general depoliticisation of the rural economy. All 'class labels' were abolished so that enterprising and prosperous contractors could not be stigmatised. Economic and political administration were separated institutionally: communes were stripped of their political functions, which were vested in newly re-established township governments, and by the mid-1980s the communes were abolished altogether.

The relations of production of the new agrarian structure

How is this new agrarian structure to be understood? What relations of production does it embody? In formal terms collective ownership of land has not been abolished. This is no mere formalism. So long as contracting was done on a relatively short-term basis, as in the early 1980s, it was difficult for peasants to exercise a basic prerogative of land ownership – that is, to acquire income by selling or leasing their land. But this has begun to change with the rise of long-term land contracting, for fifteen to thirty years, which received state approval in January 1984. In some places peasants with long-term land contracts are sub-renting the land; land markets, rental payments and tenancy relationships have reappeared (Kelliher, 1986).

But even long-term contracts do not amount to unadulterated capitalist ownership. First, they specify not only charges for the land but also the crops to be grown on it. Second, contract terms are not really negotiable. Set by the collectives or the state, they do not reflect market prices or values. This creates serious non-market distortions even in the more spontaneous, unregulated sub-leasing markets. In some cases this has even led to land abandonment where profitable farming is impossible – a disturbing development in a country with such a severe shortage of arable land.

Land aside, from the outset of the reforms peasants have been permitted and encouraged to purchase their own capital goods, like trucks, tractors and other agricultural machinery, and even to establish their own non-agricultural enterprises. Those with such private capital equipment may hire labour to work it, a wage labour relationship associated with capitalism.

But here too there are new hybrids. In some places collective industries are sub-contracted to peasants. In others, peasants are forming joint stock companies with their collectives or with state enterprises. Some of these enterprises use wage labour and involve, at least partially, private appropriation of profit. But the terms on which these contracts are let, or under which these firms must operate – specifically prices and production plans – are not always set on market–based terms. They are still under considerable central or local government control. And even the resuscitated wage relationship is not always capitalist in nature. In Longbow village, Shanxi province, an old peasant has been hiring young people to work on the vegetable plot for which he has contracted (Hinton, 1986). Rather than specifying the wage in advance he promised only to pay what others paid or to give his workers some share of the crop when he saw how it came out – a labour relationship which is more pre-capitalist than capitalist.

What then remains of the collectives? In some places – including surprisingly parts of rural Guangdong, thought by many analysts to have had weak collective institutions – the collectives still appear to be functioning. Though land is sub-contracted, local enterprises are owned and run collectively, with their operations and profits under some form of popular control. These collectives continue to provide social services such as schools and clinics (Johnson, 1986). The fees charged by these collectives under the land contracts might even be thought of as membership dues or investment shares rather than rent.

In other places, however, the social services provided by the collectives have withered or been abolished, and collective enterprises have come under greater degrees of private control. The economic relationship of the peasant to the collective has become much more attenuated. It seems reasonable to hypothesise that the level of collective solidarity and the participatory character of village politics have declined as their existential and material bases have been undermined. Most Chinese peasants now spend their time working on family-sized plots leased from the team. They are in much less frequent contact with each other on an hour-by-hour, day-by-day basis. Since work points have been abolished under most of the responsibility systems, peasants' income is not collectively mediated as before. There is, in short, less opportunity for collective politics to take place, and less substance to it in terms of concrete economic issues. Yet occasionally lively politics have taken place around the terms of the contracts which the teams sign with their members (Lin Zili, 1983). Those terms affect the peasants deeply, and much of what is being leased is collective property which was produced by the accumulated labour of team members over many years,

Thus, questions remain about what the collectives are, what relations of production they embody, and what kinds of politics are engendered. Until these questions can be answered, it will continue to be difficult to evaluate the nature of collectivism in China, or to make confident pronouncements about the extent to which it still exists in any meaningful sense. The new agrarian structure is difficult to characterise in a simple or unambiguous way, since it combines elements of collectivism and state economic control with ones that have affinities to capitalism and even to pre-capitalist modes of production. Simplistic characterisations of the new developments in rural China as capitalist or socialist should be avoided, and efforts should be made to understand them as a new kind of hybrid with its own special characteristics and contradictions.

Characterisations of the new agrarian structure

To understand these contradictions, the economic, social and political effects of the reforms must be understood. Their aggregate economic results have been impressive. Per capita grain production grew at an average annual rate of 3.7 per cent from 1978 to 1984, compared to 1.2 per cent during the previous thirteen years. Rural living standards averaged a 12.3 per cent annual increase over the same period. This has been accomplished alongside significant diversification of the rural economy: between 1978 and 1984 per capita production of cotton, which had stagnated before 1978, rose by an average 18 per cent per year, oil-bearing crops 13.8 per cent, meat 8.9 per cent, and fish 3.6 per cent.

Nevertheless, the new growth has created new problems. One of the most important has to do with the distribution of the new prosperity. Little good, systematic data on this exists. Some areas whose economies were depressed during the collectivist period by the policy of 'taking grain as the key link' – including both rich areas which had previously grown cash crops and remote poor ones which had relied on grazing – have benefited now that they can once again exercise more control over what they want to grow. The economic gap between rural and urban areas has also been narrowed, as the state raised rural procurement prices and as peasants have been permitted to leave agriculture, and even to leave the countryside, for non-agricultural employment.

These gains in equality have been balanced by the very real, if not precisely quantifiable, unevenness of the rapid new growth within and between villages. The present leadership admits that this is happening and has adopted postures ranging from resignation (arguing that increased inequality is an inevitable result of development) to praise (arguing that it promotes incentives). Deng Xiaoping once replied to a question about growing rural inequality by expectorating and then stating that perhaps it would get the poor to work harder.

Growing inequality raises two questions: who is benefiting and who is not, and on what production relations are the inequalities based? To approach the first question, the various routes to prosperity under the reforms must be sketched. One is to become an officially designated 'specialised household', permitted to concentrate on a particular agricultural or non-agricultural activity at which it has proven itself especially efficient. These peasants are rich by definition: in order to qualify, a household's annual income must have reached a minimum in the neighbourhood of 3000 yuan (Kelliher, 1986). State policy entitles them to preferential supplies of credit and inputs in order, the leadership argues, to maximise the returns on these scarce resources – a strategy of building on the strong. 'Specialised households' comprise 10–15 per cent of rural households, which gives some idea of the economic inequality involved.

A second route is to engage in specific lucrative activities, including individual handicraft or sideline production, trade or rural or urban service provision, even if not as a 'specialised household'. Here peasants are benefiting from opportunities presented by the structural separation of urban and rural economies dating from imperial times, and by state controls on rural-urban economic interchange during the Maoist period. For example, in the past the state monopoly of commerce resulted in shortages of consumer goods in many places, so today peasants can make small fortunes by engaging in trade. Or because of the urban-rural income gap they can provide urban services such as haircuts, tailoring or transportation more cheaply than the state-run service enterprises. This suggests that the economic gains experienced by peasants under the reforms are to some extent a one-off result of readjustment in sectoral balance which, though perhaps sorely needed, cannot provide a basis for sustained rural economic growth.

A third route to wealth is to form businesses, euphemistically known as 'economic associations', in conjunction with other peasants or even with rural collective or state-run enterprises. These are proliferating with extraordinary rapidity and dizzying diversity (Watson, 1983; Howard, 1986).

Who is using these channels to wealth? Former cadres of the rural collectives have been well positioned to take advantage of the new economic opportunities. In a survey of Shansi province they comprised 43 per cent of those who have prospered most under the reforms (Oi, 1986). Their success can be partly attributed to the same personal qualities and skills which helped them rise to leadership positions in the first place, or which they later developed on the job. It also has to do with connections they have developed outside their villages in the course of attending meetings and dealing with suppliers and buyers. These are helpful in collecting timely market information, procuring inputs, and identifying potential business partners. Another factor is the power of local cadres to contract out to themselves or their relatives or friends the best collective property, including not only land but also machinery, and even whole enterprises. For example, in Xintian village, near Wuhan, the fish ponds – highly lucrative operations employing one worker per pond and netting ¥5000 to ¥7000 annually – were all contracted out to the village cadres by 1986.

Of course, not all local cadres have taken advantage of the economic opportunities presented by the reforms. Many are revolutionaries, committed socialists or communitarians who suffered mightily under the pre-revolution systems of private property and trade, and are ideologically opposed to privatisation and the market forces nurtured by the recent changes. Some local leaders, concerned that the reforms undermine their institutional and political bases of power and prestige, have devoted their energies to blocking their implementation. Others have even found ways to benefit from the reforms while opposing them. There are frequent reports of local officials levying all manner of *ad hoc* unauthorised taxes and fees on private entrepreneurs or, more simply, demanding a cut of the profits. They have also begun to drop in, unexpectedly and uninvited, for dinner at the homes of the most prosperous villagers. This gets them a meal and, in the context of Chinese political culture, is a way of reminding the reluctant 'hosts' of the cadres' politial power over them.

Several other groups have been able to prosper in the reform period. In the early 1980s, when land contracts were first being let, households with large numbers of workers relative to total family size were able to secure the largest plots, since distributions proceeded on a per-labourer basis. So for many the fortuitousness of timing – since family size tends to rise and fall over the household life-cycle – made a difference. But non-random factors have been at work too. Those with education or technical skills – including many students and demobilised soldiers – have done well. So have those with connections with influential or strategically located friends and relatives, which they can use to identify market opportunities, procure inputs and locate sources of finance.

This last point raises a very important but largely unexplored question about the role of private finance. Private enterprises and joint private/collective enterprises have proliferated. But there is little information on where the investors have obtained their funds. In some cases they have managed to secure loans from state-run banks, either because of the potential merits of the enterprise or because of connections with bank officials (or both). But rarely are such enterprises financed completely on bank credit, and often little or no credit is involved. It appears that significant private funds have been used to finance these enterprises. One can only wonder at the sources of these funds: overseas relatives, previously accumulated savings, incomes from profitable enterprises formed in the early reform period and, of course, illegal activities such as smuggling and embezzlement, widely reported in the Chinese press. Whatever their provenance, it is clear that a small but growing number of sizeable private fortunes are being accumulated. This development was significant enough to cause alarm to many Chinese leaders, who have muted the effusive praise given in the press to 'ten thousand yuan' (annual income) households.

Exploitation

The question of the productive relations on which the new inequalities are based raises thorny issues. So long as the reforms involve increasing latitude for self-employment, on a household-sized plot of land or in a sideline enterprise, they could be conceptualised as embodying *petit bourgeois* productive relations: that is, mainly self-exploitation. And since, as shown above, these reforms occurred without formal private ownership of the means of production, one could – and the Chinese leadership did – make an attempt to present them as complementary to, and not necessarily contravening, the socialist relations of production. In these relations of production, inequalities among producers arise either from the unequal productive capacities of their labour power, which is fully consonant with socialist productive relations, or from the unequal productive resources at their disposal. The latter may result from regional differences or from the way the contracts were let. Neither of these is consonant with socialist principles, but nor do they arise from direct exploitation of the labour of others.

Yet some of the inequalities in rural China are based on productive relations that are unambiguously capitalist or pre-capitalist. As we have seen, wage labour has begun to proliferate again, both in agriculture and in rural industrial and service enterprises, and has received state approval. It often takes the form of seasonal or full-time migrant labour, as peasants from land-poor, labour-flush villages seek work in areas with a greater demand for labour. They often earn subsistence wages of one or two yuan per day, or simply receive food and shelter. Some private enterprises employ hundreds of wage labourers and realise profits reaching six figures (Kelliher, 1986). In a particularly vicious recidivism, migrant labour gangs run by gang bosses have also reappeared.

Other exploitative practices that had been eliminated by the Chinese revolution and the collectivism that followed have also been revived. One is usury. Private lenders are charging rates of up to 80 per cent per annum. Another is tenancy, involving up to 10 per cent of cultivated land in some rural counties, at rents of up to 40 per cent of the harvest. Some of this is innocent in motivation: a household which undertook a long-term contract for a large plot of land because it had a large supply of labour may need to dispose of some of it as its dependency ratio rises, for example if the daughters marry off, or the main breadwinner becomes disabled or dies. But in other cases peasants who contracted for large plots of the best land and made high incomes then use the proceeds to undertake non-agricultural occupations, while still retaining the land. In such instances the new 'landlords' are already the wealthiest in the village. Official policy has been to treat the rent they receive not as exploitation but as the just desserts of the most enterprising peasants (Kelliher, 1986).

In contrast to the essentially *petit bourgeois* relations of production involving mainly self-exploitation which appeared at the outset of the reforms, wage labour, usury and tenancy clearly involve economic exploitation, and as such are more difficult to justify within a framework informed by Marxism. This is not to say that the present Chinese leadership has not tried to do so. The word 'rent' has been shunned in favour of 'transfer', for example. Criticisms that these phenomena indeed amount to exploitation have been met with tortured, unconvincing ideological rebuttals. Can it really be, for example, that rich households who have left agriculture must be allowed to collect rent on contracted land they no longer cultivate so they will contribute to the development of the productive forces by operating, and profiting from, their lucrative businesses? There can be little doubt that many of the inequalities that exist and may be growing in rural China are based on relations of production that are not socialist and are not necessary complements to socialism.

Social conflict and its politicisation

These new inequalities, and the exploitation on which they are based, engender social conflict along several lines of cleavage. One is urban-rural. Peasants who come to cities and towns to pursue their businesses are meeting with considerable opposition from urban workers to whom they provide competition. For example, drivers employed by a state-run bus company in the city of Harbin drove into a private bus owned and operated by a peasant migrant; a month later they beat him up. Opposition to peasant competition with the urban state sector is felt and expressed by state officials, too. For example, food shops run by peasants are often permitted by urban officials to operate only on side-streets, to help protect the state-run shops (Zweig, 1985).

Another cleavage is between local leaders and peasants. In some cases, as seen above, local leaders are resentful of the newly prosperous peasants, and are taking steps to block their economic activities, or to appropriate some of the proceeds. In other cases, local cadres are the ones getting rich; and where they have done so by taking advantage of their positions they have incurred the wrath of the peasants whose collective interests they were chosen to represent, protect and nurture.

Still another cleavage is that between rich and poor peasants. In many cases, the newly prosperous peasants come under intense social pressure from their fellow villagers to share their wealth. This is what is behind many of the reported instances of 'philanthropy' and 'community-spiritedness' – contributions to village libraries or clinics – which are regularly lauded in the Chinese press. But resentment of the newly rich by those left behind has also erupted in violence. Reports of vandalism against property contracted for by prosperous peasants often blame 'hooligans' who learned their bad behaviour in the Cultural Revolution. More likely this is a protest against a peasant who is using a valuable piece of property, built originally by the collective, to make personal profit.

The new productive relations have been accompanied by political changes which make it all the more difficult for opponents to express their views: grassroots political institutions have been gutted, and supporters of the collectivist policies of the past silenced. There has been debate on the need for greater democracy, and even some tentative practice with the formation of people's congresses and contested elections up to and including the county level (see Chapter 3 and Womack, 1982). But there are countervailing tendencies. In the collectivist period policy implementation relied largely on non-formal methods known as 'winds', which included propaganda campaigns, political study programmes and political 'movements'. Precisely because these 'winds' lacked, and indeed shunned, regularised administrative procedures and legal force, localities had considerable room to manoeuvre, which they used to resist, evade, distort or ignore certain policies (Zweig, 1986). The present efforts to extend 'legality' and to formalise governmental institutions and administration – in the name of preventing abuse and extending democracy – may actually have the effect of circumscribing the political power and manoeuvrability of the grassroots.

This will, of course, help reduce the power of the left opponents of the present policies. It may also depoliticise the social tensions caused by those policies. One of the key goals of the post-Mao leadership is the establishment of political stability. The reasons given are the demands of economic modernisation and the widespread desire of so many not to relive the difficult and anarchic days of the Cultural Revolution. Less explicit, but probably no less important a motivation, is the desire of the present leadership coalition to maintain itself and like-minded successors in power.

But the strategy may backfire. By blocking the politicisation of discontent with the rural reforms, the present leadership may be hampering its ability to become aware of, and to ameliorate, social tensions in a timely fashion. Confident pronouncements of the present leadership to the contrary notwithstanding, rural political conflict is not over. To be sure, the leadership coalition has the upper hand. It has successfully dealt with opposition by dispersing it, depriving it of an institutional base and organisational opportunity, and undercutting it with an economic programme that has been successful, at least in the aggregate. But everything we know about Chinese history and about the political effects of rapid economic development suggests that eventually the social tensions produced by the reform programme must find expression.

Note

1. Thanks to Frances Pinter, Publishers, for permission to use some passages from my book *China: Politics, Economics and Society – Innovation and Iconoclasm in a Revolutionary Socialist Country* (1986).

7

The Urban Economy

Martin Lockett

Introduction

The most important feature of China's urban economic policy in the 1980s has been the move away from central planning towards economic reforms which have introduced a limited degree of market forces and competition. To understand and assess these changes, it is necessary to know something of their background and rationale. The chapter therefore begins with a summary of the economic planning system developed between 1949 and 1978. The problems encountered during this period and the rationale for economic reform are also analysed.

Urban economic policy over the last decade is then outlined, with a particular emphasis on the course of urban reform. While reform is seen by the Chinese leadership as the goal, progress towards this is still limited and uneven. However, economic performance has been good, and there have been significant structural changes in the urban economy, though not as great as in the countryside. China's future goals are outlined, together with the Seventh Five Year Plan (1986–90) which is seen as a crucial stage in their realisation. Finally, difficult issues for China's urban economy are discussed.

China's planned economy

The development and consolidation of an economic planning system, with its associated problems, was the clearest change in China's urban economy between 1949 and 1978.

Socialist transformation and the ownership system

For the first few years, the major task was restoring the economy to its previous state. There soon followed a rapid transition to socialist forms of ownership. This involved moving from a predominantly individual and privately owned urban economy to one in which state and co-operative forms of ownership prevailed. Initially it was foreseen that this process would take ten years or more, but the major transformation had taken place by 1957 as a result of political pressures. By the late 1950s four-fifths of the urban workforce was in state-owned enterprises, a fifth in co-operatives, and about 2 per cent in individual self-employment.

During the Great Leap Forward (1958–60) many urban co-operatives were converted into collectives. The difference between these two forms of ownership is that in a co-operative, the workforce owns and controls the enterprise, whereas in China's collective ownership system, the workforce officially owns the enterprise but in practice effective control is in the hands of various levels of local government. So while in theory the collective sector in China has been owned and controlled by its workers, in practice the system is more like municipal ownership. A further distinction was made between 'big collective' and 'small collective' enterprises, with the latter being tied to local districts and neighbourhoods. The former were run in a way similar to state enterprises, while the latter grew through the formation of neighbourhood and other small-scale enterprises, often staffed mainly by women.

The wage and social welfare system

With the socialist transformation of the ownership system came the establishment of national wage scales for urban workers in the state sector. These varied between sectors, with pay in heavy industry higher than in light industry. There were also regional differences based on living costs and sometimes special allowances for bad working conditions or other factors. For workers there were eight grades, with separate scales for technical and administrative staff. Within an enterprise, typical differentials were three or four to one between the highest and lowest paid. While, at various times, bonuses were paid based on performance, during the Cultural Revolution these were abolished and all workers received a flat rate salary. In addition, a social welfare system was set up giving workers substantial benefits, especially by comparison with other Third World countries. These included sick pay, maternity leave, retirement pensions and other benefits such as housing, provided by many state enterprises. As a result, the work unit (*danwei*) is central to the life of most Chinese urban residents.

These changes established a high degree of income equality, even by the standards of other socialist economies. In urban areas China was one of the most equal countries in the world. Within the state sector, much of the pay differential depended on length of service. Jobs in the state sector were secure – an 'iron rice bowl'. Thus while state sector employees had low pay by international standards, they had comparatively high levels of welfare provision and job security.

However, wages were substantially lower in 'small collectives', contributing to sexual inequality in wages. In addition, 'small collective' and individual workers were not covered by the state welfare scheme, were not usually entitled to other benefits, notably housing, and had less job security.

The planning system

With substantial Soviet assistance, China established an economic planning system in the 1950s. While there have been changes in the details of the bodies involved, the basics of this system remain today. The most obvious change was the establishment of the State Planning Commission to draw up plans for the economy as a whole and a State Economic Commission to oversee their implementation. These are linked to a range of ministries which control particular sectors of the economy – for example, the Ministry of the Textile Industry. In addition there are other bodies responsible for policy which may cut across ministerial boundaries, such as the State Science and Technology Commission. While this system is essentially similar to that in the USSR, a significant difference is the relative influence of provinces and major cities. The bodies mentioned above had their equivalents such as a Provincial Economic Commission or Municipal Textile Bureau. In theory the textile industry may be planned in Beijing, but in practice provinces and cities have much more influence than in the USSR.

Until the recent reforms, an individual state enterprise had little autonomy, except on day-to-day matters. Investment plans had to be approved by the relevant bureau in line with state plans, and the enterprise would then be given a grant for approved expenditure. Prices were set by the state, with everyday necessities at low prices and luxury goods at high ones. Inputs were allocated by planners and the products allocated to customers by the state. The profits earned by the enterprise were handed back to the state, providing a significant source of revenue.

The enterprise was run by a Party Committee, officially elected by the Communist Party members in the enterprise, but in practice usually appointed from above by higher level Party bodies. The factory director was responsible to the committee, and in practice the Party Secretary was usually the most influential figure. Trade unions were under Party leadership, performing an ambiguous role of promoting state and Party leadership policies, while to a limited extent representing workers. In practice unions were often most concerned with welfare issues. Enterprises were production, political and welfare units without significant decision-making autonomy.

Problems of planning

Between 1952 and 1978, China's urban economy expanded rapidly. Industry's gross output in 1978 was sixteen times that of 1952. Heavy industry had grown over twenty-seven times, light industry almost ten times. Sectors which hardly existed in the past such as oil, chemicals and motor vehicles had been created. Thus with a planning system China had successfully achieved a significant level of industrialisation.

This success was accompanied, however, by a growing range of problems, typical of planned economies. First, planning became more difficult and complex as the number of enterprises and range of their products increased and their inter-relationships grew. Second, where in a market economy prices are used to regulate supply and demand, in China this adjustment relied on changes in plans, as enterprises neither had the autonomy to change what they were making nor did they receive signals through the price system. Third, many goods were of low quality, as the main target for enterprise management was the volume of production, while their customers could not switch their source of supply if it was of bad quality. Fourth was lack of innovation, both in new product development and the upgrading of existing products, a consequence of ineffective incentives and insufficient investment in improving existing enterprises. Fifth, while it can be argued that labour is so abundant in China that its productivity need not be a major concern, the efficiency of use of capital, energy and other scarce resources was low, often due to weak incentives at enterprise level for both managers and workers.

While these problems may result from the planning system itself, others arose from the lack of effective planning. A number of bottleneck sectors had emerged, notably energy, transport and building materials, which constrained further economic development. More generally heavy industries such as steel had been given priority, while light industries had lagged behind. This was reflected in the rationing of goods such as bicycles and cotton cloth. Overall, the Chinese people did not receive as much benefit from industrialisation as production figures indicate. Average urban wages were more or less static between the 1950s and the mid-1970s. In addition, the service sector was seen as largely non-productive, so that retailing, restaurants and repair services were neglected.

Overall, therefore, while there had been major achievements resulting from the planning system, systemic problems became increasingly serious.

Between 1976 and 1978 there was an unsuccessful attempt to achieve rapid growth based on heavy industry, through the import of advanced foreign technology and financed by oil exports. Ideologically, it was assumed that after the fall of the 'Gang of Four' the major blocks to rapid growth had been removed. The problems soon became clear. First, oil export revenues were not as high as expected due to stagnation in oil output and increased domestic demand. Foreign loans, the alternative form of hard currency finance for technology imports, were disliked for political reasons. Second, the import of heavy industrial plants exacerbated the existing bottlenecks in the economy. Third, the balance between investment and consumption was problematic. To gain political support and increase incentives, significant wage increases and bonus payments were introduced. At the same time the level of investment was soaring, leading to macroeconomic imbalances and inflationary pressures. Fourth, the supply and quality of consumer goods was often insufficient for increased wages to act as an effective incentive.

The rationale of reform

To resolve these problems, some Chinese economists advocated a major change in the direction of economic policy. They argued that the problems of the planning system were fundamental and that greater enterprise autonomy and elements of a market economy were needed. The reformers argued that without substantially greater enterprise autonomy, many of the problems of the planning system would persist and increasingly constrain economic growth. The state should move from direct administrative methods of planning towards indirect economic ones, and give enterprises substantial decision-making power. They argued that profit rather than output should be the main target of an enterprise, as this would better reflect efficiency in the use of resources. Enterprises in most sectors should be free to choose their suppliers and market their own products, with competition acting as an incentive for efficiency and innovation. In addition, finance for investment should come from bank loans, with interest payments made by enterprises to encourage efficient use of capital. To make the system work, prices would have to reflect current costs of production as well as supply and demand.

While all this implied a substantial influence for market forces, it was argued that the state should still plan the overall direction of the economy and guide its development by means of economic levers such as interest rates. Some key sectors, such as energy, would still be controlled centrally, as would their prices. The aim was to obtain the benefits of both plan and market through economic reforms.

Urban economic policy 1978–86

Readjustment, reform and consolidation (1978–81)

The shift in official policies came with the Third Plenum of the 11th CCP Central Committee in 1978. Economic policy shifted towards a phase of 'readjustment, reform, consolidation and improvement' lasting until 1981. Readjustment meant shifting priorities from industry to agriculture, from heavy industry to light industry, and focusing attention on bottleneck sectors. Industry reform moved towards the types of reform suggested by economists and already implemented in Eastern Europe, notably in Hungary. Such reforms give enterprises greater autonomy in decision-making; use profit as an incentive and allow enterprises to retain part of their profit (for use in production, bonuses and welfare/housing); introduce limited competition among enterprises and some direct marketing of their products; and grant increased but limited flexibility in labour management. Initially these reforms were concentrated in a small number of experimental enterprises, notably in Sichuan, but were then extended through a variety of economic responsibility mechanisms.

Reform in the background (1981–4)

These 'reform, readjustment, consolidation and improvement' policies led to a move towards urban reforms. But there were significant problems. The first was a conflict beween readjustment and reform. The former required central control over investment and related decisions, while the latter implied giving enterprises greater financial and decision-making power. Second, the combination of enterprise profit retention, readjustment, decentralisation of financial responsibility to lower levels of government, and urban food subsidies led to a major state budget deficit through falling income from industrial profits and rising expenditure. Third, as a result, inflation rose significantly – a politically sensitive issue. Fourth, there were further problems, such as enterprises shifting to products made profitable by anomalies in the price system as well as tax evasion and fraud. These were problems seized upon by those threatened by reform, notably in the middle ranks of the Party and managers without technical or professional skills.

These problems ushered in a second phase from mid-1981 to mid-1984 in which urban and industrial reforms were slowed down while the rural reforms continued at a fast pace. In industry more attention was paid to profit-sharing systems between state and enterprise which clearly benefited the state. More generally the focus shifted from institutional reform of state-enterprise relations to 'consolidation'. Improvement of internal management was seen as the key to growth and efficiency. There was greater emphasis on the power of factory managers, management training, and economic responsibility systems within enterprises. However, those in favour of reform saw a need to move faster, given that readjustment had been basically accomplished.

Renewed urban reforms (1984–)

A third phase began in late 1984, with the October Central Committee decision on urban reform. Attention was focused on urban reforms, with the aim of creating a 'socialist planned commodity economy with Chinese characteristics'. Again enterprise autonomy was emphasised, with planning shifting towards a guiding as opposed to a directive role. A shift to a tax system for enterprise profits was also finalised, though in practice this is subject to administrative adjustment given a still 'irrational' price system. However, price reform was seen as an essential component of the reforms, though how this was to be implemented was less clear. A first step was to let many food prices float in urban areas in 1985.

Change in the wage system was also advocated, to bring pay more into line with enterprise and individual performance. The enterprise director's role was to be strengthened through the introduction of the 'factory director responsibility system' in which power was to shift from the Party Committee to the factory director. There was also encouragement of the private individual sector, which has grown rapidly, especially in commerce and services.

In the final quarter of 1984 industrial growth rates shot up, but the economy was overheating. Inflation rose, especially in cities, as a result of the decontrol of meat and vegetable prices. Both investment and consumption rose rapidly, fuelled by internal bank credit, wage rises and a rundown of foreign exchange reserves as the import of consumer and capital goods increased sharply. It was necessary by late 1985 to attempt to cut back investment, especially that outside the state plan, and to impose stricter control of foreign trade. Zhao Ziyang stated that 1986 was a year in which to 'consolidate, digest, supplement and improve reform'. The pace of growth consequently slowed and further reforms were made, usually on an experimental basis: for example, particular enterprises issued shares to their workers and others.

Finally, despite the political shifts of early 1987 and the fall of Hu Yaobang, the target of urban reform was reaffirmed.

Assessment of China's urban economy

An official Chinese assessment of the economy was given in 1986 by a Vice-Minister in charge of the State Commission for Restructuring the Economic System:

Although our all-round economic structural reforms have only just started, a favourable situation has been created. A series of profound and revolutionary changes has occurred in the economic operational mechanisms and management system in our country, and our national economy has entered the most vigorous and dynamic period since the founding of the PRC.

How justified is this view?

Economic reform

By early 1987, urban and industrial reforms were still limited and partial. The planning system still exerts a major direct influence, especially at the provincial and municipal levels. According to a leading Chinese economist, Xue Muqiao, 'all these reforms are still at a transitional stage and have not been basically completed. We have also failed to co-ordinate these reforms sufficiently and satisfactorily.' The clearest example is the price system. Enterprises still receive signals from the price system which go against efficient resource allocation and give rewards which are not necessarily based on efficiency or on satisfying consumer demands.

Overall, the rural reforms are much more radical. In comparison with other socialist economies, the Chinese reforms have not yet gone as far as those in Hungary, while the USSR has more freedom for workers to change jobs. So while reform as a strategy has been adopted by the top leadership of the Party, in practice much of the old central planning system remains a powerful force.

Further, the urban reforms are in certain respects contradictory. In particular, further decentralisation to provincial and lower levels of government has come into conflict with enterprise autonomy, undermining reforms aimed at improving efficiency through competition and profit incentives. There has been a growth of 'local protectionism', with local government erecting barriers to trade with other provinces and regions.

Economic performance

China's economic performance in the 1980s has been good, especially in comparison with most other Third World economies, and particularly so in agriculture. In China's 6th Five Year Plan period (1981–5), real GNP growth was an average of 10 per cent a year. Industrial gross output grew by 12 per cent a year, with light industry growing somewhat faster than heavy industry. The problem of major central budget deficits was also reduced substantially, but re-emerged to some degree in 1986. While growth was relatively fast, it was subject to significant fluctuation, particularly in heavy industry, as a result of the changes in policy outlined above, especially 'readjustment' in 1979–81.

An important feature of reforms has been the shift away from the state sector towards collective and private ownership. Private ownership is still limited in scope, being primarily individual or household enterprises with strict, though not always enforced, limits on the number of hired workers. The collective sector has increased in importance, particularly in the generation of new employment and in growth areas of the economy such as consumer goods and services.

In industry the state sector is still dominant, producing three-quarters of output in 1985 compared with over four-fifths in 1978, but in other sectors the situation is different. In retailing, the shift from 1978 to 1985 was dramatic, with the state sector's share dropping from over 90 per cent to under half, with collectives taking an almost equal proportion and the private sector a tenth share compared with a negligible proportion in 1978. Urban private sector employment has increased dramatically, though it is still small compared with the state and collective sectors. The record in job creation is also quite good, with the urban unemployment problems of the late 1970s substantially reduced though not eliminated.

But the previous bottlenecks still exist. Energy is still a major bottleneck, especially electric power in south China where there are regular power cuts. Transport still causes major problems. Growth in raw materials and semi-processed goods production has trailed behind the demands from processing industries. Shortages also appeared in other sectors as a result of the rapid demand growth of 1984–5. Only the difficulties with building materials appear to have been resolved to any degree. Thus despite a good overall economic performance, underlying structural problems remain. Furthermore, it is questionable whether some of the gains in the last few years can be sustained, as they may be 'one-off' results of the changes in economic policy. Future economic performance depends on whether reforms can continue to stimulate new dynamism in China's enterprises.

Issues in the mid-1980s

The rapid growth of the Chinese economy in 1984–5 accentuated some of the bottlenecks in the economy. As these blockages were in sectors with relatively long lead times between investment and results, notably energy and transport, such high growth rates were not sustainable. So while the new reforms boosted growth, they also increased the need for medium- to long-term planning in key infrastructure sectors. In addition they reinforced the sellers' market characteristic of most sectors in the Chinese economy as well as raising a range of other important issues which could threaten future economic development.

The relaxation of direct planning controls was not accompanied by effective indirect controls over the domestic economy. According to an official source, 'macroeconomic factors went out of control in varying degrees in the fourth quarter of 1984 and the following period'. In particular, credit was provided freely by the banking system to enterprises and others for investment, whether within or outside the state plan. Often little attention was paid to the likely economic returns from projects, and banks did not exercise real control over this lending. Wages rose rapidly, though these increases were partly eroded by inflation from price rises. While some of this inflation was a deliberate result of reform, in particular the decontrol of prices of non-staple foods such as pork and vegetables, much was the result of lack of macroeconomic and financial control. The political impact of inflation in China is significant, as one of the Party's claims to legitimacy in the past was stable prices. Groups adversely affected, including many state and Party employees on fixed incomes, could move towards opposition to reform.

A final issue is that of corruption. In 1985 over 200 000 cases of economic crime were tried in China. Most have been cases of outright fraud and bribery, often by Party members. While these have always existed to some extent, the opening up of China to the outside world has increased the opportunities for such corruption, especially in the Special Economic Zones, as has the general shift in policy and attitudes towards profit-seeking. But many of the cases arose from loopholes in reform combined with inadequate regulation. Moreover, police investigations were often obstructed by the protection of those involved by superiors who might themselves be implicated.

The shift towards enterprise profit retention and the use of taxation to raise state revenue as opposed to administrative control provided great opportunities for tax evasion. This was made easier by weaknesses in the systems for auditing and tax collection. Some cadres and Party officials set up their own businesses for private gain, using information and contacts obtained through their official positions. Throughout China, problems of petty corruption became more pervasive. For example, cadres used official trips to dine out and buy cheap local goods; truck drivers traded their rationed petrol for eggs at the roadside; and a black market in foreign currency grew. Many of these problems can be explained as a result of the partial nature of reforms. If reforms are to work effectively, then relaxation of administrative controls must be accompanied, or preceded, by the strengthening of indirect ones. At the same time reforms must be co-ordinated to ensure that the incentives generated are consistent with overall goals.

The future: the 7th Plan and after

China's strategy for future development is based on the 7th Five Year Plan, which covers the years 1986 to 1990. It represents the first step in a longer-term strategy. This is recognised explicitly in the Plan itself, which sets three main tasks:

1 To create a favourable economic and social environment for economic structural reform . . .
2 To maintain sustained and steady economic growth . . .
to prepare the required capability for continued economic
and social development in the 1990s.
3 On the basis of the development of production and
improvement of economic results, to continue to improve
the living standards of urban and rural people.

The Plan suggests two phases: the first in 1986–7 and the
second in 1988–90. During the first phase the focus will be on
macroeconomic control to remedy current issues as well as on
'invigorating' state enterprises and developing lateral economic ties between them. In the second phase there will be
greater emphasis on pushing forward with structural reforms
and faster growth.

The targets for economic growth are higher than those set
out in the 6th Five Year Plan (1981–5) but lower than the
growth achieved in the early 1980s.

The targets imply a shift in direction as the service sector is
to assume a larger role in economic growth. Compared with
other countries. China's service sector is at present underde-
veloped, and this provides opportunities for both economic
growth and employment generation at relatively low capital
cost per job. The service sector is expected to grow much
faster than industry or agriculture. Among the areas targeted
for growth are tourism, posts and telecommunications. There
is also strong emphasis on shifting industrial investment from
creating new plants to upgrading existing ones, with investment in this area growing fast.

Living standards are expected to increase at 5 per cent a
year, with a somewhat faster improvement in rural areas than
urban ones. Only a limited improvement in diet and higher-
grade clothing is foreseen. The growth of domestic electricity
demand is another concern, and the production of energy-
intensive electrical goods, in particular heaters and air
conditioners, will be constrained.

One of the major innovations in the Plan is an explicit
regional policy which divides China into three main areas: the
Eastern Coastal Region, a Central Region and Western

Region. This marks a further move towards differential economic development. The Eastern Coastal Region is designated as the major export base, with attention concentrated on the upgrading of existing enterprises, the creation of new 'knowledge- and technology-intensive' industries, and the expansion of the service sector. The Central Region is to be the base for extractive, power and materials industries. In more advanced cities there will also be some features of the Eastern Coastal Region's form of development, but, if anything, energy and materials-intensive industries will be transferred from the Eastern Coastal Region. In the Western region, the focus will be on agriculture, with industry often based on technology transfer from the military to the civil sector. The political implications of this in the future are substantial, both domestically and in foreign relations.

While the Plan's targets are probably achievable, they do depend on progress in the critical bottleneck sectors of energy and transport. The Plan implies a commitment to reform to achieve the goals of higher efficiency, as well as ensuring that economic growth will be political priority. This in turn has major implications, as the focus on economic improvement will lead to higher expectations which must be satisfied to maintain support for, and the legitimacy of, the Chinese leadership and also of management.

Long-term goals

The best known long-term goal is that of achieving the 'Four Modernisations' (of industry, agriculture, science and technology, and defence) by the year 2000, a goal put forward by Zhou Enlai in 1964 and again in 1975, but also closely associated with Deng Xiaoping, who argued for it in policy documents in the mid-1970s. However, the central idea of 'bringing China to the ranks of advanced industrial countries by the year 2000' was quickly seen as unrealistic. As a result, more concrete and less ambitious targets have been adopted to guide China's longer-term development.

The most immediate target is quadrupling the 1980 gross agricultural and industrial output value by the year 2000. This would bring China into the middle ranks of the Third

World, rather than being 'in the front ranks of the world' as in the original formulation of the Four Modernisations. More concretely, there is a target of US$800 (at 1980 prices) per capita gross national product for the year 2000. The World Bank sees these Chinese targets as well above their expectations for the Third World as a whole. Some countries such as South Korea and Japan have exceeded them in the past, as did China in the 6th Five Year Plan, but for the overall targets to be met, economic performance approaching this level must be maintained for the next fifteen years without significant faltering.

Looking beyond 2000, the targets are less precise but still ambitious. The next stage is to reach the level of an 'intermediately developed country' by 2020 – around the 100th anniversary of the founding of the Chinese Communist Party. Finally, by 2050, about the 100th anniversary of the People's Republic, the goal is to have 'come close to the level of economically developed countries'. This implies continued growth at a slightly slower pace than that foreseen for the rest of this century, but still high compared with expectations for the rest of the Third World.

Future issues

Given the reform strategy of the Chinese leadership and the economic strategy proposed in the 7th Five Year Plan, there are controversial issues which will arise over the next decade in the urban economy.

The ownership system is the most controversial. Since 1978 there has been a major reappraisal of the idea that socialist economic development involves continual moves towards both larger-scale enterprises and 'higher' levels of ownership, from individual through collective to state forms of ownership. Instead it has been recognised both that small enterprises have a continuing and even increasing role, and that state ownership and control is often inappropriate, particularly for smaller enterprises.

A related change has been the growth of individual capital stakes, especially in collective enterprises. These are no longer rejected ideologically, and are seen as methods to raise funds and develop worker commitment to the enterprise. While there is some agreement that individually owned private business should be confined to being a supplement to state and collective sectors, moves towards individual ownership and capital stakes in businesses pose a set of difficult choices for Chinese leaders.

The major blocks to future growth, notably transport and energy, will have to be removed. In both of these sectors expanding output requires heavy capital investment, with benefits accruing mainly in the long term. Choices between alternative projects are both complex and uncertain, posing major planning problems and the need for a strategy going beyond the 7th Five Year Plan. For example, if reforms succeed in encouraging specialisation and breaking down existing barriers between provinces, the demand for transport will increase substantially.

Other problems include the planning of the level of investment and its direction into priority sectors. Currently when direct administrative controls are relaxed, the greater freedom of enterprises and the lack of indirect controls through the banking and credit systems lead to a loss of macroeconomic control. Without the development of effective indirect controls economic policy will swing between relaxation and administrative intervention, with the former leading towards chaos and the latter to rigidity and inefficiency.

Current urban reforms must be more consistent if enterprises are to be guided by consistent and rational incentives. The key is the price system, which gives enterprises economic signals still based on historic costs and previous pricing policies, rather than on current costs and demand. While the necessity for price reform is accepted, no clear plan has emerged, especially on how prices are to be fixed in future. In the meantime, enterprises are given irrational incentives if they profit-maximise, loopholes are created for corruption and semi-legal deals, and administrative intervention is needed in areas such as the tax system in attempts to remedy these problems.

Reform of the wage system is another important issue. Urban China has been exceptionally equal compared with other societies, including other socialist ones. Current policy is to link wages to individual and enterprise performance. However, this will create new patterns of inequality and may restrict employment in well-off enterprises. Creation of a labour market is one suggested policy, which would probably increase differentials between skilled and unskilled workers significantly. All these possibilities are likely to increase social tensions as some groups benefit while others lose out.

Another issue is that of unsuccessful enterprises, given that in theory they are now responsible for their profits and losses. In practice, according to a leading Chinese economist, 'Everybody knows that our state enterprises now bear only the responsibility for their profits, but not for their losses.' In 1986 a bankruptcy law was formulated, to be applied experimentally at first. However, the experience of other socialist economies demonstrates the difficulties of implementation of such laws.

China must also improve the skills of managers if urban reforms are to succeed, particularly in new fields such as marketing. Western and Japanese management techniques are now being lauded, but it must be asked whether they will be effective within a Chinese culture, and whether they fit into a socialist economy. The internal organisation of enterprises is another controversial issue. Recent moves towards strengthening the authority of factory managers relative to Party committees have run into substantial opposition, as the power of less professionally skilled Party members is threatened. Worker participation in management also remains undeveloped (see Chapter 3).

So the goal of a 'socialist planned commodity economy' will require further reforms, especially in the price system. These changes will have adverse effects on some groups and will form a basis for political opposition to the reform programme.

Conclusions

This chapter has shown that since 1978, the Chinese leadership has had a long-term strategy of economic reform. The 7th Five Year Plan which runs from 1986 to 1990 is seen as the period which lays the foundation for a period of rapid growth and institutional reform in the 1990s. But while this long-term reform strategy has fairly clear outlines, the actual mechanisms for a transition from the present state of China's economy are more vague. The 7th Plan gives some indications of this but does not give clear answers to many of the issues raised. In particular this chapter has highlighted the lack of development of effective mechanisms of indirect economic control, such as prices and exchange rates, as well as the conflicts which may be caused by the simultaneous decentralisation of power both to enterprises and to lower levels of government.

Progress towards the realisation of this reform strategy depends on a combination of economic and political factors. There are a number of obstacles which must be overcome if there is to be relatively rapid and sustained economic development, notably the bottlenecks in energy and transport, where long-term investment is needed.

Success in the economic strategy will also be dependent on the handling of political conflicts. Opposition will form if elements of the Party and state administration with access to political power can take advantage of economic problems to forge an alliance between themselves and groups adversely affected by reform. The previous experience of both China and other socialist economies shows that this could well happen. The result of such a political blockage would be to restrict the reform strategy to a series of unco-ordinated and contradictory adjustments to a planned economy.

8

Technology and Economic Development

Richard Conroy[1]

Economists have had great difficulty in measuring accurately the contribution that 'technical progress' has made to measured growth in industrially advanced countries. This is largely due to the nature of the process. Technology in its strict sense is the body of knowledge about the industrial arts, applied science, engineering and so forth. Used more loosely, it encompasses both the knowledge itself and the tangible embodiment of that knowledge in an operating system using physical equipment. This knowledge is generated in a number of ways, but increasingly the new and improved products, processes, materials and systems which are the ultimate source of economic advance originate in large-scale research and development (R&D) institutions. Obviously not all R&D, or the application of the results, has an effect in economic terms. New products and processes have to be adopted to have any economic impact. The whole innovation process is usually described as the technical, industrial and commercial steps which lead to the successful marketing of new manufactured products and/or to the commercial use of technically new processes and equipment. In market economies, therefore, technological change is intimately connected with the concepts of competition, profit and the private possession of knowledge. In centrally planned economies, some

127

factors influencing technological change are rather different, as are the actors in the innovation process.

Theoretically, there is no compelling reason why a centrally planned economy should perform any worse than a market economy in utilising a given amount of scientific and technological resources and generating more products and processes. There could, though, be different priorities resulting from differing social and political objectives.

Many would argue that centrally planned economies by their very nature allocate and use human, financial and material resources ineffectively, and that their economic organisation and administration in general militates against innovation. Some evidence supports this view, and most centrally planned economies have, since the early 1960s, attempted to introduce specific reforms to stimulate technological change, with varied success (Poznanski, 1985). China has been no exception to this general trend, and is in some ways going further than the Soviet Union and most Eastern European countries have done in reforming the fundamental principles governing the allocation and use of productive resources.

Although technological change has always been considered to be extremely important in modernising China's economy, a number of factors have combined to reduce its contribution to economic growth. By the late 1970s it was conceded by the Chinese leadership that its production facilities were largely obsolete. As a new modernisation strategy gradually emerged, the issue of how to stimulate rapid technological change became one of vital interest to Chinese policy-makers, so much so that science and technology are today seen as the key to the long-term modernisation of agriculture, industry and national defence.

In economic terms it is planned to quadruple the total 1980 industrial and agricultural output value by the year 2000, and it is expected that half of this increase will come from 'technological progress' rather than increased inputs of capital and labour using existing production methods. One crude but important illustration shows the dilemma China is in. In 1980 China consumed the equivalent of over 600 million tons of coal. The most optimistic estimate for energy output by the end of the century is around 1.2 billion tons of coal equivalent. In this situation, unless China's product mix is changed and its energy utilisation rate and production technology levels are substantially improved, the whole modernisation process will grind to a halt, and economic performance will fall far short of the projected targets.

This chapter investigates the production technology levels of the late 1970s and the reforms introduced to stimulate technological change. The role of foreign technology in China's economic development is then examined. The relationship between technological progress and economic development in the context of wider social, political and economic changes is surveyed to identify areas where concomitant reforms may be needed.

Production performance and reforms to stimulate new technology

One way to measure relative levels of economic development is by reference to 'technological gaps' between different countries. Chinese economists commonly estimate that the country is currently twenty to thirty years behind industrially advanced countries in the field of production technology. A major aim of the 7th Five Year Plan (1986–90) is to reduce this gap to between ten and twenty years by 1990, depending on the particular sector. While it is extremely difficult to define and measure such gaps, a number of partial indicators highlight China's relative technological stagnation. If trends in labour productivity are examined it is found that while in industry output value increased thirty-six-fold in state-owned enterprises between 1949 and 1981, labour productivity only improved three-fold. Another measure is the relative vintages of industry's equipment and end-products. The machine-building industry is a good sector to examine, given its pivotal importance for other industrial sectors. Of the 27 000 products manufactured by the sector in 1982, most were of 1950s design and performance, with 12 000 needing urgent updating and 4000 scrapping completely. Apart from this, the sector could not manufacture over 10 000 products urgently needed for modernisation.

A range of statistics detail other aspects of backwardness: depreciation rates are so low that much equipment has a standard life expectancy of twenty-five years, and over one-quarter of all industrial fixed assets in 1981 were operating beyond their set service life. If skill levels of the industrial workforce are examined, 80 per cent had not achieved a junior high school educational level, and the proportion of qualified technical and engineering staff was around 3 per cent. China's domestic industrial standards in the early 1980s were well below international levels (Conroy, 1985).

A 1984 survey of over 3500 research institutes estimates that less than 10 per cent of their scientific achievements were being applied to production. In terms of investment in R&D as a proportion of total output value, a recent survey in four major industries indicated proportions of 0.5, 1.1, and 1 and 5.5 per cent for the metallurgical, chemical, machinery and electronics sectors respectively, significantly below investment rates in the same indusries in industrially advanced, and many developing, countries. Chinese economists have estimated that between 1952 and 1982 technological progress contributed just 11.6 per cent to increased industrial output value, with significant variations over time (Conroy, 1988a).

It is not just the level of technology that affects performance. The skill levels of the workforce and the organisation and management of production also count. However, there are limits to the performance of any given technology which no amount of reorganisation or improved management will overcome. The generation and application of new technology to production has gone hand in hand with a wide range of initiatives aimed at restructuring the economy, reforming the economic system, and changing social and political attitudes.

The reforms have interacted in a complex manner but, to keep the discussion within manageable limits, the following only examines major issues. Even though China's new leadership in the post-1976 period recognised the crucial role of science and technology, this was not at first acted on in any coherent way. By 1978 two national development plans had been formulated to cover the period to 1985, one covering the economy and the other science and technology (S&T) development. Both were unrealistically ambitious and were never implemented, but more importantly neither was co-ordinated with the other. In 1979 a policy of economic readjustment was introduced in the economic sphere to start redressing structural imbalances, but it was not until 1981 that a set of guidelines was agreed which defined the role of S&T in the modernisation strategy. The major element was the insistence that S&T activities be closely tied to economic needs, with basic research relegated to a minor role. These guidelines were given an operational form by the publication of the 6th Five Year Plan (1981–5) in late 1982, in which for the first time a medium-term plan for S&T development was co-ordinated with the economic development plan. The interaction was only partial, however, as detailed technology policies for twelve key economic sectors were only published in September 1986. These formed the basis for the policies and targets contained in the 7th Five Year Plan (1986–90).

A second key component of technological change has been the shift from investing in new production facilities to an emphasis on renovating the equipment in existing factories. This is intended to save on investment, to introduce innovation into existing processes, upgrade the quality of existing products, and permit re-tooling for new lines. Combined with increased budgetary allocations for S&T, this policy of intensive development has resulted in more funds being available to finance technological development.

The third area involves making the maximum use of human resources. The scientific and engineering community have, since 1949, been regarded by the Party with suspicion and hostility. This has been tempered by the need to tap their expertise. Policy has therefore sought to improve their standing and devise ways of maximising their expertise.

Linking expertise with production

Until recently R&D was largely carried out within the formal research sector rather than in industrial companies, and R&D institutes were financed mainly through the central or local government budget. It would therefore be expected that few problems would arise in formulating research projects which address economic or sectoral needs. This has not been the case, and a major reason for the low rate of transfer of research results into production has been the lack of linkage between the supplier and the user, resulting in new products ånd processes that cannot easily be put into production or for which there is little need. Part of the problem lies in the nature of the research process, which is inherently risky and does not lend itself easily to planning. In the past, projects have been chosen by administrators with little reference to the opinions of either those who would be doing the research or using the results. The pressure to get results has often led to the adoption of untried technologies with consequent economic losses.

Reforms have been introduced to rectify these problems. While most S&T resources are still allocated according to central or local plans, the scientific community has been progressively co-opted into the decison-making process, resulting in less arbitrary decisions over R&D investment. To improve the work efficiency of R&D personnel, research institutes have been given greater control over managing and organising their activities, including limited autonomy in the important areas of finance and staff. They also now have the right, on condition that they fulfil state assignments, to initiate their own projects and undertake a wide variety of activities by contract with other organisations, from local governments down to small, collectively owned workshops. Although still in the early stages of implementation, the rapid emergence of a 'market' for technology in which vendor and buyer negotiate directly is potentially of great significance.

Where economic benefits cannot be readily measured, such as in basic, medical and environmental research, these activities will still be funded by the state, but through contracts for specific projects with an element of peer appraisal included in the project allocation process. By the end of 1985 over 1900 of the 4760 independent R&D institutions were carrying out some work under contract, and some 360 of these were economically fully independent.

At a more general level, linkages have been developed in other spheres. The significant research capacity of the defence sector is now being used in the civilian sector. There have also been attempts to stimulate flows of technology from the more advanced regions along the eastern seaboard to the central and western provinces. This is being done through factory-to-factory tie-ups, as well as through more general technological co-operation agreements between cities (Conroy, 1988b).

The stimulation of demand for new technology by the production sector

New technology will only contribute to economic development when it is readily adopted and diffused throughout the production sector. Policy has focused particularly on improving incentives to take up new technology in the basic production unit. The initiatives are intimately linked with overall economic reform, as many of the causes of slow technological change in the past were not technological in nature but fundamental to the working of the command economy itself. A major constraint has been the system of pricing. Over the years prices have less and less reflected scarcity values. Industrial inputs have tended to be underpriced, while capital and consumer goods have been overpriced. In addition, differentials within sectors have not been tied to differences in quality. The net effect has been both to distort technological innovation patterns and remove the pressure on the production sector to adopt new technology, as little or nothing is gained by reducing costs, improving quality or increasing output. Overall, price reform has been introduced very cautiously, as it is such a complex and sensitive issue (see Chapter 7).

Ultimately, the key to improving incentives to introduce new technology at the factory level depends on the resources available to develop or buy new equipment, processes and so on, and the economic benefits accruing to the management and workforce. Traditionally, funds provided to upgrade the technical base of industry have been either misused or used inefficiently. This situation may be changing, with factories being allowed more control over their investment programmes on the one hand, and grants for technical innovation being replaced by repayable loans on the other. While the combination of such carrot and stick methods is bound to have some effect, it does not appear that the huge investment in technical transformation made since 1978 has up to now given reasonable returns in terms of improving production technology. Part of the problem is the lack of interest shown by large production units in technological change compared to small and medium factories. As the former often account for a large proportion of total output in many sectors, and also virtually all of China's more technologically sophisticated products, their slow rate of introducing new technology is having a significant knock-on effect on the whole economy.

Human resources

The effective utilisation of the S&T workforce is a key factor in successful technological change, as knowledge is ultimately created by individuals. The environment within which the S&T community has worked in China has left much to be desired. Their political rehabilitation and elevation in social and economic status has been a major focus for reform, but one in which results have been slow. There is still widespread aversion to giving intellectuals more power, and they are still one of the poorest groups in urban society.

But the major short-term issue has been how, and to what degree, to introduce mobility into the personnel system. This is traditionally a jealously guarded preserve of the Party, and introducing greater mobility tends to loosen its control. After years of debate and tentative but largely unsuccessful attempts to tinker with the personnel system, a certain amount of mobility has been approved by the leadership, and research and production organisations can participate more directly in the limited S&T labour market. An associated and even more contentious issue is the extent to which S&T personnel can take on part-time work. Although this practice has been officially condoned, it raises fundamental issues involving the private appropriation of knowledge, and unfair exploitation.

A final issue, hotly debated since the late 1970s, is the degree of intellectual freedom to be accorded to the S&T

community. Freedom of academic enquiry and discussion is considered by most Western commentators to be an essential component of a healthy R&D system and, by extension, a vibrant economy. While such an atmosphere is promoted in China, administrative and political interference still intrudes and limits intellectual freedom, even though under Deng it has been frequently said that S&T has no 'class character' and that there is no such thing as ideological contamination in this area.

Imported technology and economic development

Many of China's modern industrial sectors owe their existence to imported technology (Conroy, 1986). While in the 1950s the assimilation process was rather efficient, the failure to sustain the scale of imports after the Sino-Soviet break was not compensated by increased domestic R&D capabilities. The virtual self-sufficiency operating in the 1960s was relaxed in the 1970s when a number of complete, advanced factories for heavy industry were imported. The decision in the late 1970s to expand economic relations with the outside world had two important objectives: to gain access to funds to increase the rate of growth and to acquire advanced technology to speed up economic development. It was quickly recognised that the past strategy of 'turnkey' imports (the purchase of complete industrial plants) concentrated in a few sectors had resulted in little transfer of technological know-how or improvements in domestic S&T capabilities.

The 1981–5 period saw a significant shift in technology import policy. Attention is now focused on the selective acquisition of key equipment and technical know-how. The renovation of small and medium plants has been emphasised, and special consideration has been given to the light industrial export sectors as well as machine-building and the electronics sector. Investment in imported technology has tended to flow to the old industrial bases along the eastern seaboard, with the aim of eventually creating an economically advanced coastal zone which will absorb foreign technology, adapt it to Chinese conditions and transfer it to the hinterland and also become a base producing increasingly sophisticated goods and services for domestic distribution and export.

Apart from increasing the direct purchase of foreign technology, a new mode of acquiring technology introduced since 1979 has been through direct foreign investment. But hopes here have not been realised because of a reluctance on the part of foreign firms to transfer advanced technology to China through this mechanism (see Chapter 9 for details). The Chinese authorities for their part have progressively introduced incentives to attract foreign investment, especially for projects involving the introduction of foreign technology.

The economic impact of the investment in acquiring technology from abroad is difficult to guage accurately as the process is dynamic, with a considerable lag between investment and effect. The undeniable waste caused by poor co-ordination, unclear strategy and extensive duplication of essentially assembly-line imports in some sectors is being corrected. As little attention has been paid to the complex and expensive task of assimilating the technology already imported, the effect on domestic S&T capabilities has undoubtedly been less than originally planned. In a few sectors such as textiles and electronics, however, the level of production technology in existing plants has been raised significantly, and a number of new capital and consumer products have resulted. Increased flows of foreign technology are vital to increase the overall level of exports and develop import substitution more intensively. How to achieve this without resorting to a strategy of debt-led growth is a major current problem with no simple solutions available.

Summary

While the Chinese leadership's faith in S&T as the key to future economic development and prosperity remains undiminished, it is recognised that the relationship between technological change and economic growth is complex and not simply a matter of changing domestic resource allocations or buying from abroad. Chinese policy-makers see no dilemma between generating technology domestically and acquiring certain types from abroad; and there is no fear of becoming 'dependent' as imports can never supply more than a small amount of the total volume of technology needed. It is conceded, though, that imports will continue to play a vital role in promoting development in sectors using advanced technology, and that their effect will be disproportionate because of the increasing impact that sectors such as computers and biotechnology will have on the economy, enabling China to leap-frog certain stages of development. This is only true in so far as foreign technology is assimilated to improve domestic capabilities, an assumption that is by no means certain.

It is probable that the 'slack' in the economy will provide opportunities for some time to apply new technology which will create significant economic returns with bearable social and political costs. As the modernisation process continues, however, the social and political dimensions will intrude more and more into the decision-making process. Issues such as employment and equity are two of the more obvious.

At a more general level, increasing reliance on technological change as the motor of economic development means that certain groups may appropriate knowledge and use it to exercise power and privilege. These issues were, of course, preoccupations of Mao Zedong, whose attempts at resolving such contradictions were not noticeably successful. The current leadership's attitude is implicitly, if not explicitly, deterministic − that is, it assumes there is some inner dynamic in modern industrial technology that results in broadly similar social consequences. The assertion that technology in a socialist society will necessarily be used for the good of all is too simple, unless the relationship between socialism and inequality is redefined.

Note

1. This chapter was written when the author was Visiting Fellow at the OECD Development Centre, Paris. The views expressed are the author's own and do not necessarily reflect those of the OECD.

9

Opening up to the Outside World

Terry Cannon

China's place in the world

It is hard to imagine the mystery which China evoked less
than ten years ago. Visiting the country was rare, whereas
today travellers to the 'middle kingdom' are numerous, and
have become part of China's strategy to earn the dollars that
are used to purchase foreign technology. Visitors are now also
likely to find themselves sharing a hotel with people from all
over the world who are in business and doing deals with
government departments or directly with enterprises.

China's post-Mao leadership, determined to modernise the
country, has for the last decade promoted business links with
the capitalist world which were unthinkable before the
overthrow of the Gang of Four in 1976. The mainstay of the
new policies, the 'open door', is typical of the pragmatic,
undogmatic and, some would add, anti-socialist, new leadership. This chapter explores the consequences of the new
trading policies, of China's decision that in order to modernise
it must import more goods, finance and knowledge from
abroad.

Communism and self-reliance

For a period after the establishment of the People's Republic in 1949, the new government suffered a trade embargo imposed by the West, which severely hampered attempts to overcome the legacy of decades of war, and consequently forced the country into reliance on the Soviet Union. At the same time we must take account of the traditional Chinese belief that contact with the outside world is harmful to their culture and civilisation, if not unnecessary. This is a belief which has often restricted China's interaction with the rest of the world and one which to a degree reinforced more conventional Marxist anxieties about subjugation to capitalism and its denomination of the world economy.

China used to proclaim proudly that, having paid off its 1950s debts to the Soviet Union, it neither borrowed money nor permitted any foreign investment in its economy. Furthermore, its trade was miniscule by comparison even with other, much smaller countries. The 'ultra-left' leaders of the Cultural Revolution period held the view that capitalists could not be trusted, and that buying their products or letting them invest in China was a danger to socialism. The policy of self-reliance, 'relying principally on our own efforts and resources', they decided, ought to be a policy of self-sufficiency too. This was not just an exclusion of foreign 'evil influences', but an assertion to the world of the superiority of the Chinese socialist system.

Modernisation after Mao: import needs and expanded trade

China's trade has expanded rapidly since the Cultural Revolution, and foreign loans and direct investment from abroad have been welcomed. Economic growth is now the means by which the lives of the population are to be improved, and thus income differentials have been allowed to widen, and to a limited extent the control of capital, enterprises and commerce has passed into individual hands. Previously, the goal of economic growth was subordinate to the political criterion of collective control of social resources. While growth was slower than it might have been, it compared favourably with that in many other Third World countries. However, the reforms, which have increased the availability of consumer goods, enjoy widespread popularity.

Foreign technology

The reformers have decided that more modern equipment must be purchased from abroad; it is the perceived relationship between modernisation and consequent economic growth that is the driving force behind the 'open door' policy.

Equipment chosen for import includes industrial technology, for example machine tools, which enable China to produce a wider range of its own equipment and expand its own technology, and machinery for producing light industrial and consumer goods. This is an important aspect of a well-organised trade strategy; through the careful selection of imports, items previously imported or unobtainable in China can be manufactured domestically. Such an 'import-substitution' strategy can enhance a country's self-reliance, although initially it might raise the import bill.

Importing such foreign technology almost invariably means purchasing equipment that is capable of providing the same amount of output with less labour – it is more 'capital-intensive'. Whether employing such technology is actually cheaper than employing labour in China is a question which has yet to be analysed. Just when policies for the countryside are likely to shed up to 30 per cent of the rural labour force, importing labour-saving equipment may be a problem.

There are other problems too. For instance, now that individual factories are free to decide the prices of products, and each state-owned enterprise is expected to be profit-seeking, imported technology may undermine existing industry. Previously, a price took account of the costs of all enterprises manufacturing the same product. Now, with each producer seeking reductions in its costs which can be passed on in lower prices, new equipment which reduces those costs may make other enterprises 'uneconomic'.

Further, to benefit from technology, unfamiliar imported equipment needs to be properly used and maintained, and be part of a well-managed enterprise. Providing such operating conditions for new equipment is difficult when educational levels and management skills are below those of the economies which produce the equipment. The training of scientists and managers who will form the human resources essential to modernisation requires a much expanded tertiary-level education system. The interchange of scientific, technical and other personnel with universities and research institutions around the world is impressive compared with a few years ago. The flow is in the opposite direction, too, with a large number of Western teachers going to China to help train personnel and students, as well as overseas Chinese who wish to make a personal and patriotic contribution. But this exchange, even though still somewhat limited, worries the 'old guard' in the Party and bureaucracy who are concerned about the erosion of socialism through increased contact with the outside world.

Foreign ownership in China

A great deal of effort has gone into increasing imports of technology. Since outright purchase is expensive, new trade strategies have been adopted to encourage foreign interest and involvement in the economy, and to obtain new equipment and expertise. These schemes reflect deep changes in political outlook and direction. Thus not only can Chinese and foreigners set up 'joint ventures' in China, but, under certain conditions, complete foreign ownership of enterprises on the Chinese mainland is now permitted, something which would have been anathema to the previous Maoist leadership. Yet there is hardly a flood of investment into the country. This partly reflects some of the controls on investment imposed by China, but also the anxieties of potential investors that their capital might serve Chinese aims more than their own objectives. There is also the fear that China may suddenly change its policies, which could threaten foreign assets.

Early plans to attract foreign investment suggested China's concern about the 'polluting influence' of foreigners. Four

Special Economic Zones (SEZs) were set up in 1980, with tax and other incentives. These effectively restricted the territory in which foreign investors could set up their businesses. The largest of these zones, Shenzhen, borders Hong Kong and is only a few hundred square miles in area. But the others, Shantou, Xiamen and Zhuhai, are much smaller. Moreover, the biggest investors in these zones have been 'overseas' Chinese, particularly from Hong Kong and Macao, who have not installed the up-to-date technology that Beijing sought. Their priority has been to use cheap, unskilled mainland labour in the assembly of garments, electrical goods and toys.

Initially cautious about foreign investment, this attitude was relaxed soon after the SEZs were set up. Provinces were allowed more autonomy in foreign trade, and soon many local authorities were also trying to attract their share of foreign capital. Overseas Chinese in particular seem to have been welcomed in, and more willing to go to, other parts of China, especially the southern provinces of Guangdong and Fujian where they may have linguistic and family connections.

The next most significant investor is Japan. Here too cultural similarity helps, although Japan's 'second invasion' has encountered some resistance. In December 1985 there were student demonstrations against Japan in some cities. The protesters, not old enough to have experienced the horrors of Japan's occupation of much of China in the 1930s and 1940s, seem to have had some support from leaders at higher levels who did.

It is clear that China has not acquired a great deal of modern technology from outside, both because of the failure to attract capital on a sufficient scale, and because of the type of equipment brought in by investors. Moreover, a considerable amount of finance has gone into the service sector rather than manufacturing, for example into the construction of hotels which will accommodate tourists, with their valuable foreign exchange.

Whatever the source, foreign investment is still less than anticipated. For example, China's investment in fixed assets – that is, buildings, machinery and equipment – came to roughly US$50 billion in 1985, while in the same year total foreign investment, excluding loans, was only US$1.87 billion, or about 3.7 per cent (*Beijing Review*, No. 12, 1986).

Borrowing capital to finance purchases

China's most significant foreign borrowing ever was from the Soviet Union in the 1950s. It provoked great concern about the control the Russians might exercise over the economy and led the Chinese to be wary of loans from abroad. The severe debt repayment problems of several other Third World countries in the 1980s also evoked caution in China. Even so, the willingness of China to borrow at all, as it has since 1982, is an extraordinary shift in policy. In doing so, however, China has been able to call the tune on borrowing to a significant degree, given that many companies from indust-rialised nations want access to the potentially huge Chinese market. Foreign governments and companies know that concessions on interest and repayment periods are what win contracts, not necessarily the quality or price of the goods on offer.

Thus, in general, the countries that have done best at selling to China are those whose governments or corporations have been most willing to allow credit, or whose banks have offered 'soft' loans – that is, at low rates of interest, and/or with favourable time limits. Part of the reason that Britain is a minor exporter to China is the UK's restrictive attitude to such 'soft loan' facilities. Japan has been ahead in its willingness to provide credits and bank loans at very favourable rates and thereby win contracts for building new plants or selling equipment.

Loans from banks and financial consortia also provide foreign exchange and bridge the payments gap, which allows China to import goods when it is not possible to pay for them by rapidly expanded exports. But as for any country, borrowing creates a future repayment burden, one that must ultimately be funded by new exports. In 1985 the total borrowed for the year was US$2.43 billion. This compares

with the total value of exports for the same year of
US$27.36 billion (*Beijing Review*, No. 12, 1986), which means
that were China to borrow at the same level for ten years, all
its exports in 1997 would be used up repaying loans. It is
extremely difficult to judge how much new foreign exchange
earning capacity can be created. As with other aspects of
trade imbalance, problems in expanding exports can result in
goods which might otherwise be consumed in China being sold
abroad instead. This applies whether it is goods consumed
directly, or indirectly as with the materials used to build a
new hotel for tourists. In all, the country owed a total of
US$6.87 billion to foreign countries as of September 1986,
compared with foreign exchange reserves of US$10.37 in the
same month. In 1987 there was growing concern at the
pressure on these reserves from growing trade deficits and
rapidly increasing borrowing.

International agencies, especially the World Bank, the
International Monetary Fund (IMF) and the Asian Development Bank, have become significant sources of funds, and are
likely to grow in importance as China asserts its role in the
international economy. Again, the political turnabout in
which China entered the World Bank and the IMF is
extraordinary, such institutions being regarded by many
communist and Third World governments as the epitome of
the world capitalist system. World Bank money is being
borrowed to ease the two main bottlenecks in the economy:
energy and transport (see Chapters 7 and 8). Unless more
energy can be produced and more electricity made available
to industry and agriculture, updating equipment which is
then subject to power cuts is wasteful.

Paying for foreign technology by increasing exports

A balance-of-trade problem can arise either through exporting far more than is imported, or from an inability to export
sufficiently to match the level of imports. The latter problem,
which is usually much more serious, has already affected
China. To some extent, expanding the services sold to

foreigners, invisible exports, can make up for the inability to export enough. The rapid expansion of tourism in China indicates the use of such a strategy.

Under certain circumstances a balance-of-payments crisis will arise if, for instance, there are no reserves of foreign currency (or gold) to cover purchases. So far China has had adequate levels of foreign exchange, and large gold reserves. Sometimes borrowing from abroad can cover such a payments gap, and is preferable to draining reserves. But as noted above, such measures merely delay the need to increase exports.

If the value of imports continues to rise, and is not matched by a rise in price or quantity of exports, then there will be a serious rundown of currency or gold reserves, or a pressing need to borrow. Conversely, if the value of a country's exports falls for reasons beyond its control, then again a balance of payments can occur when other exports cannot suddenly be increased to make up the gap. In the mid-1980s, for example, oil prices plunged, affecting China's trade position with Japan, which buys Chinese oil and in return sells high technology. Cut-backs in the amount exported (to try and hold up the world price of crude oil), combined with the lower price, meant that in 1986 China's oil revenue was reduced to US$3.08 billion, compared with almost US$7 billion the previous year.

It can therefore be seen that increased participation in the world trade system makes a country more vulnerable to forces beyond its immediate control, and China has already felt the chill winds of such exposure.

This highlights one of China's key problems in modernising through increased imports of foreign technology: finding ways of paying for them by exporting is difficult. The obstacles to expanding exports are not of China's making alone: there has been a long-running dispute with the United States over the imposition of import quotas on textiles and garments into the USA. In the mid-1980s China responded by seeking to import wheat from producers other than the USA.

China does have exportable raw materials other than oil. Coal is one example, but coal exports are also sensitive to price fluctuations, since in many energy applications oil is a substitute. Thus exporting raw materials and primary products can be precarious in terms of price variations and buyers' control of the market. It is a delicate matter to balance the benefits of buying the products from abroad with the costs to the economy, and the possible political objections to exporting domestically useful commodities. Moreover, to boost exports China must either expand existing manufacturing capacity or create new industries which can sell all or part of their output abroad.

Some of the trade and investment arrangements set up under the reforms are intended to resolve these problems. The willingness to accept foreign investment, and even ownership, in industry has been at least partly motivated by the potential boost to exports. The SEZs on the south coast offer a wide range of incentives to potential investors, as also, to a lesser degree, do the fourteen 'open cities' opened up to foreign investment in 1985. The financial incentives they offer are designed not only to bring in advanced production techniques, but also to encourage the making of manufactured goods for export. However, as seen above, foreign investors have been more enthusiastic about the potential gateway into the Chinese market which such production bases on the mainland might afford them, and this has given rise to a conflict of interests.

Other measures adopted by the Chinese government link the acquisition of technology from abroad with payments in kind from the goods which it produces. In such 'compensation trade' arrangements the Chinese specify the equipment they want to acquire and, once it has been installed, it is paid for not in cash but from the returns on exporting the products over a fixed period, say ten years. In this way China may import technology without using valuable foreign exchange, though the equipment may well be outdated (if not worn out) by the end of the contract period.

Consumerism and the cultural pollution factor

So far I have assumed that China's increasing trade derives from a modernisation policy which has raised the demand for imported technology. The pursuit of growth has promoted the 'open door' policy. But given, additionally, the 'liberalisations' in the domestic economy, it is inevitable that a proportion of foreign trade will be channelled through, and support and serve, local and individual interests. State enterprises which earn foreign exchange from the export of their products are now permitted to retain some of these earnings in order to buy their own equipment from abroad.

One unintended consequence of this is indicated by the many anecdotes about the importation of equipment which is either inappropriate or misappropriated. Inevitably, managers are subject to pressures from foreign sales personnel eager to gain contracts. Added to this, the economic reforms have significantly increased the availability of consumer durables, many initially only available from abroad, at a time when many Chinese have more income at their disposal. As a consequence, in 1984–5 there was something of an important boom in 'high-tech' consumer goods such as cassette players, televisions, cameras, motor bikes and the like. This used up much foreign exchange, but since the government wanted to demonstrate the virtues of its policies, this consumerism was not stemmed. The glamour associated with this boom, and with a worship of 'things foreign', is seen by 'conservative' leaders as harmful importations of Western decadence which unduly influence young people. The 'spiritual pollution', or distortion of the ideals of socialism, associated with the 'open door', has been a significant factor in the opposition to the reformist policies from these conservative elements in the Party, who prefer a more traditional and less outward-looking economy. In the clamp-down on 'bourgeois liberalisation' which followed the student demonstrations of 1986–7, workers and peasants have been urged again to serve national rather than personal goals, and there is evidence of a retreat from foreign investment and trade deals.

Modernisation dictates a continued commitment to the importation of foreign technology. But it is unlikely that the economy will be able to generate the level of exports needed and also cope with the increasing range of imports arranged by enterprises themselves, together with the consumer goods that ordinary people now demand. So there is likely to be increased pressure for borrowing, and recurrent balance-of-payments problems if exports cannot rise rapidly over the next decade. The alternative is a significant rise in the level of central control over imports, accompanied by a slowing down in the rate of modernisation.

10

Health and Medicine in the 1980s

Sheila Hillier

In 1948 China was described as having the greatest and most intractable health problems of any nation in the world. Less than forty years later, many of these problems have been dealt with. Life expectancy for adults and infants is approaching Western levels, and China's ramshackle health-care system has been expanded and improved to produce rapid growth in medical facilities and personnel. Nutritional and sanitary improvements, together with economic growth, have accompanied these changes and augmented and consolidated their effects.

Evolution in health care policy: the background

Health priorities were spelt out at the 1950 National Health Conference: to promote an accessible system of health care for all, to incorporate traditional practitioners into this system, and to emphasise preventive medicine both as a necessary response to shortages of doctors and beds, and as an effective long-term method of disease control.

Early efforts at prevention included mobile medical teams to deal with epidemic outbreaks, and mass 'patriotic health campaigns' to improve environmental sanitation. Together with the rapid growth of maternal and child health centres, these methods produced major gains in saving infant lives and wiping out epidemics. Early limited growth in rural health-care facilities was speeded up during the Great Leap Forward (1958–60). Attempts were made to make the communes the fundamental economic unit and the basic source of free health care, based on commune and village clinics. Mass campaigns were extended in an all-out attack on the major parasitic diseases.

But policies to deal with the rural disease burden still remained inadequate and, in 1965, Mao Zedong attacked the Ministry of Public Health for its urban bias and inattention to rural problems (Mao, 1965). From about 1968 concerted attempts were made to produce a decentralised health service in the countryside based on the production brigades, staffed by rapidly trained peasant doctors and financed through brigade co-operative medical insurance. One-third of urban medical workers were transferred to the countryside. These measures led to an important expansion in basic-level facilities and personnel. By 1973, there were approximately two 'barefoot doctors' (health workers with basic medical training) per production brigade, a co-operative medical system in about 70 per cent of brigades, and commune hospital beds amounted to about almost 40 per cent of the growing national total, as compared with 17 per cent ten years previously (Hillier and Jewell, 1983). However, this basic-level expansion was offset by the closure of medical schools during the Cultural Revolution, leading to a shortfall of 130 000 medical graduates, and a simultaneous attack on scientists and research work.

Health policies after Mao

In the early 1970s policies which had been founded on decentralisation and deprofessionalisation came under scrutiny, both in regard to the quality of health care and the stability of the system of local financing which depended on local agricultural conditions.

Since 1979, a new set of policies affecting agriculture and

industry have emerged, which are described in other chapters. In the medical field, changes have been both a reflection of, and response to, the economic reforms. Modernisation and new investment in science and technology have produced an emphasis upon the quality of care and the promotion of fundamental research into disease. Changes in the rural economy, in particular the responsibility system, have altered the system of co-operative funding for medical care, and the growth in rural incomes has increased demand for more and better quality medical facilities. Although the state continues to provide a planned amount of resources for health-care facilities, there is increasing pressure on new hospitals to be 'collectively' owned and run, and for all hospitals to be responsible for their own survival. There is also official encouragement for private hospitals and practice (Cui Yueli, 1984), and a tendency to regard health care as an aspect of consumption rather than social accumulation. This is reflected in the rapidly evolving view that curative health services should be paid for, whereas the state's responsibility is to provide basic preventive services. The system of medical training has moved to a more professional model, with expansion of training for all grades of health worker.

Some policy continuities remain: the priority given to prevention and public health; and the basic organisational and referral structure of health care – village and factory clinics for primary care, township (commune) or district hospitals for more serious illness, and county or specialist municipal hospitals for the gravest or more unusual cases. Traditional medicine remains a crucial aspect of health care, and there is a continued commitment to population control.

There has also been a continuation and expansion of some initiatives promoted in the early 1970s, for example a burgeoning of research into cancer, and a continuing attempt to control the increasing problem of environmental pollution. Essentially, however, the means of achieving these goals have been altered. There have been four Ministers of Health since 1976. This rapid turnover is an indication of initial policy uncertainty, the search for safe and well-tried solutions, and a commitment to changes which incorporate the objectives of the new economic policies.

The achievement of economic objectives is not, however, the only consideration. China is the world's most populous country and is far from wealthy. It faces the problem, despite stringent control measures, of a population which will continue to increase for years to come, and of whom 75 to 80 per cent live in the countryside. There is a continuing need to ensure accessible health-care facilities for the rural areas, to develop preventive services and provide clean water for the 40 per cent of rural people who lack it (Jamison *et al.*, 1984).

Health policies also have to come to terms with the changing pattern of disease. Many parts of China, particularly the cities, are experiencing the 'epidemiological transition' – the causes of sickness and death begin to resemble those of a developed country. Instead of parasitic and infectious diseases and high rates of infant death, the longer living population increasingly suffers from chronic complaints like heart disease, cancer and hypertension. These diseases affect not only the elderly but also the middle-aged working population. A survey of seventeen cities and thirty-eight counties in 1980 showed the three main causes of death, in order, to be stroke, coronary heart disease and malignant tumour (Jamison, *et al.*, 1984). For example, in Beijing the mortality rate from coronary heart disease increased from 71 per 100 000 in 1958 to 141 per 100 000 in 1979. In China as a whole, cancer is the cause of death in 11 per cent of males and 8 per cent of females, and is the leading cause of death in the 35–54 age group (Li and Li, 1981).

Although the medical technology to deal with infectious and parasitic disease was fairly well established when the Chinese first applied it nearly forty years ago, the same cannot be said of measures to deal with heart disease and cancer where, with the exception of smoking, causes are less clear and methods of prevention largely untested.

Additionally, China's population now contains a large number of elderly people, at present 6 per cent of the population, rising to over 7.2 per cent by the end of this century. This is a group of over 70 million people with particular medical needs.

These are challenges which must be met while the health-care system is itself undergoing treatment.

The organisation of health-care facilities

In-patient facilities

In 1984 China had 2.11 million hospital beds, an average of 2.07 per 1000 population. In total there are 66 284 hospitals, of which 6500 are in cities with 41 per cent of the beds (4.3 per 1000): the 59 per cent of beds in the countryside gives a ratio there of 1.5 per 1000. It is clear that rural dwellers are relatively less well served in terms of in-patient facilities, and compared with developed countries there is a general shortage of hospital beds. Remedies to improve the supply have been two-fold: the first is the treatment of patients in their own homes wherever possible. Over 500 000 patients have been treated since the 'family sick bed scheme' was introduced in 1982, the year the Minister of Health proposed two million of these beds over five years. Far more important, however, has been Minister of Health Cui Yueli's pronouncement that

> for a long time, our principle of monopoly has affected the development of public health services ... it is necessary to discard this principle and fully arouse the people's enthusiasm for building hospitals. (Cui, 1984)

Essentially this means the need to stimulate local 'collective' ownership, producing independent, self-financing hospitals. These measures are aimed at decentralising the organisation and financing of health-care facilities by placing the onus upon localities, institutions and enterprises to invest their own money and develop hospitals as a profitable sideline (Wu Shouzhan, 1984). Hospital medical workers are now employed on contracts with bonus incentives. They now work longer hours, which is expected to improve efficiency, shorten waiting times and increase patient turnover. Hospitals derive income from taking on contracts with factories or suburban townships to treat their patients. This has the advantage of providing a pre-paid stable income, with no individual or enterprise default on payment (Hillier, 1986), and simplifies complex accounting procedures.

Though the full impact of all these changes is not yet clear, hospital beds increased by 3.1 per cent in 1984–5, compared with 2.8 per cent in the previous two years and 1.8 per cent in 1981–2. But advantages that flow from a greater level of provision can be attenuated by poor and patchy distribution. It is likely that those areas best able to undertake enterprises of this sort are ones which are already relatively well provided. While availability may be increased, accessibility may not, and the existence of an effective referral chain is important. The 'three-level network' linking village clinics to township and county hospitals has always been a feature of health-care organisation and has been reasonably effective in parts of China's vast rural areas. However, it has been suggested that referral to large, specialist hospitals is easier for the urban than the rural resident (Parker and Hinman, 1986).

The initial thrust of recent rural health policy has been to upgrade selected county hospitals and commune health centres, using state funds and a World Bank loan. One-third were to be improved by 1987, the remainder by the year 2000. The idea was that the county, sensitive to the needs of a particular locality, should be the focus of state investment and health planning, set standards in curative medicine, and be responsible for planning preventive health care. It appears, however, that at least some county hospitals are to be removed from this programme, to be developed as independently owned facilities.

A World Bank analysis of China's provincial health data confirmed a finding noted in many other countries, that improvements in life expectancy bear little relation to the number of hospital beds or health staff (Prescott, Jamison and Birdsall, 1984). It is therefore questionable whether the direction taken, while concordant with current economic policies, is going to make a great deal of difference to mortality.

Primary medical care – rural areas

For a successful answer to the problems of accessible, good quality medical care, an effective system of primary care is essential. Inefficiencies at this level may mean poor or delayed treatment, with people trying to bypass the primary level. Defects were apparent during the early 1970s when, despite expansion, commune hospital beds remained underused because peasants preferred the better equipped, if over-crowded, county hospitals.

The village, formerly brigade, medical centre is the point of first contact. While poorer villages have generally received state support, the majority of village clinics until recently have been supported by a co-operative system of funding: a prepaid insurance system to which all members contributed. Funds varied substantially according to the wealth of the production brigade. In 1975, 85 per cent of brigades were operating this system. However, low fees and erratic accounting meant that many were overspent.

The introduction of the production responsibility system, by weakening collective organisation in the countryside, has also affected the mobilisation of shared resources to meet health needs. Eighty-seven per cent of villages have some form of clinic, but only about 40 per cent operate the co-operative system: a further 40 per cent are the new 'collectively' owned clinics, and about 11 per cent are owned by groups of self-employed doctors, including ex-barefoot doctors working as private practitioners. Latest figures estimate about 125 000 private doctors in China. This is a small proportion of China's 4.5 million medical workers, but numbers jumped 63 per cent in the period 1983–5. The rate of increase is now slower, probably 6–7 per cent per year, but the development will continue, as there is active government support. Nearly 80 per cent of private practice is based in the countryside, and in the southern province of Guangdong 10 per cent of patients use private doctors (Nie, 1987). All practitioners are licensed, and fees are regulated (Zhuang, 1985).

These changes have important implications. A solution has to be found for the practical problems of providing a good quality, accessible system of curative care, and it now looks as if the government is seeking to fund this from individual fees or insurance schemes. Increased rural incomes mean that richer peasants may have raised expectations and demand better quality care. Poorer peasants, however, may be unable to afford treatment which was previously financed by their brigade, even though there was variability in the amount different brigades could afford. While it is hoped that market forces will produce more and better quality services, these could well result in individual overspending on medicine, and warnings have already been sounded to doctors that they 'should in no way deceive the masses in order to make financial gain' (Zhuang, 1985). The move towards a market in health care is unlikely to provide an important solution to the problems of rural health-care provision.

Urban areas

In towns, fee-for-service practice also flourishes, as does a variety of specialist traditional-medicine doctors to treat particular ailments. Factory clinics are now being developed to provide better primary care and to take the load off the hospital out-patient departments. Factories are also reorganising their systems of health insurance. Instead of blanket coverage, they are offered fixed per capita sums. If less than 60 per cent is used, the employee keeps the balance, the remainder going into a collective fund (Tan, 1984). The relative prosperity of cities obscures the facts of intra-urban disadvantage. There are about 35 million contract and temporary workers in joint ventures and small collectives, as well as the unemployed who enjoy no welfare benefits and must pay for health care. As the costs of medicine rise, and the contract system begins to take hold, their situation worsens, and it is readily admitted that their problems 'have not been solved' (Liaowang, 1985).

Preventive health services

Preventive health services in the past have been organised in two ways: horizontally, by integrating environmental sanitation, vaccination and immunisation with the curative services at village level, in the work of barefoot doctors (World Health Organisation, 1984); and vertically, through a nationally organised system of epidemic prevention stations and maternal and child health centres.

Basic preventive work in the villages is undoubtedly

affected by the responsibility system, since tasks which might previously have been carried out by voluntary labour – for example, digging wells – now have high opportunity costs for peasants. In order to encourage the continuation of previously free services such as childhood innoculation, health check-ups and sanitation work, fees will now be charged. Before these changes, barefoot doctors were often overwhelmed by the demands for their services, spending up to 68 per cent of their time on home and out-patient visits (Gong and Chao, 1982) and only 12 per cent on preventive work. The introduction of fees is therefore an incentive to them. Specialist preventive health workers are to be trained and employed on contract by the village or county public health department, with greater technical input from the county's epidemic and sanitation experts (Wang Haiyun, 1984; Zhao, 1984). Groups of health workers have been contracted to immunise 85 per cent of China's children by 1990. There is still a considerable urban-rural gap in infant mortality rates, with rural rates three to four times higher.

The decentralisation of curative medicine is balanced by the limited centralisation of public health and prevention, although there are apparently more organised procedures for the surveillance and notification of infectious diseases. There has been a 53 per cent increase in sanitation and anti-epidemic stations since 1981–4. The rationale for the strengthening of the preventive network is the continuing need to attack endemic parasitic disease (Guo, 1987).

Efforts to deal with the 'epidemiological transition' are less likely to benefit from these attempts to tighten up the public health network. Although better organisation at county level may help in the more thorough execution of cancer-screening programmes, many of these have now been carried out and, rather than further uncovering the scope of the cancer problem, the search has begun for causes. This work is clearly regarded as a job for the laboratory scientist or epidemiologist. The policies most likely to make an impact are those carried out nationally to alter behaviour – for example, to reduce the excess salt in the Chinese diet (connected with hypertension) and smoking. But the political climate is likely to be resistant to such measures, which some consider to smack of ultra-left puritanism. The emphasis, moreover, is upon consumption even at the expense of health. Nowhere is this clearer than in the case of the tobacco industry. China is the world's largest cigarette producer, and the state monopoly produces a prodigious 8 per cent of national income, with little being done to discourage China's 330 million smokers.

Medical personnel

In 1984 there were 1.3 doctors per 1000 population and 118 medical colleges in China. The ratio of senior (that is, graduate doctors of Western medicine) to population is 0.8 per 1000. The early 1980s saw a 20 per cent increase in the number of senior Western-trained doctors, but their distribution is uneven 2.4 per 1000 in urban areas, and 0.5 per 1000 in rural areas (Hsiao, 1984). Historically, it has been difficult, even during the enforced rustication of the Cultural Revolution, to persuade senior doctors to work in the countryside, and evidence suggests that it is still difficult to do so despite the incentives offered for private practice. A balance has to be maintained in the possibly inefficient use of skilled doctors performing tasks which could well be carried out by less highly trained personnel, and the need to raise standards of rural health. Only a 10 per cent expansion of medical graduates is planned in the 1980s, which just keeps pace with population growth.

One of the most interesting features of China's health-care system has been the attempt to incorporate traditional Chinese medicine into the structure of health-care provision. Although this has occasionally been a source of conflict with Western-trained doctors, traditional medicine is now well established. The late 1970s saw attempts to regularise the training of traditional physicians, either through college or apprenticeship. There are now 303 000 traditional doctors and 140 000 traditional pharmacists, reversing the decline of the early 1970s. Just over half the physicians, and 70 per cent of the pharmacists, work in rural areas in commune and village clinics (Hillier, 1986). The remainder work in China's 1343 specialist traditional hospitals or in hospital departments of traditional medicine. Expansion is planned to ensure that by 1990 every village has at least one traditional practitioner and that there is a traditional department in all Western hospitals.

In 1984 there were 1.28 million barefoot doctors in China, an average of two per production brigade. Their numbers fell by a third in the period 1976–82 (Rogers, 1980) due to the occasional bankruptcy of medical services, the opportunity of more lucrative alternatives offered by the responsibility system, and criticisms of their skills. There has been an attempt to improve and extend their training, and those who are successful are upgraded to 'rural doctor'. Villages which employ a certified barefoot doctor must guarantee job security. Certified barefoot doctors may aso set up their own practices, singly or jointly. The future expansion of numbers may depend more upon the ability of a locality to pay, rather than the health needs of its population. And incentives to doctors to establish their own practices may encourage the development of a solely curative service, at the expense of the development of basic-level preventive health care.

Conclusions

The experience of China since 1949 has provided valuable lessons for developing countries. The Chinese pioneered important innovations in the organisation of public health and rural health services, but China is now attempting to come to terms with economic development and its impact on health care.

The gains achieved in infectious disease control and the consequent dramatic effects on life expectancy by reducing infant deaths cannot be as readily replicated in those diseases which affect the middle-aged and elderly. Western experience has shown expensive high technology curative measures to be relatively ineffective at the national level. The Chinese could again choose to be innovators if they chose to bypass such solutions and commit substantial resources and organisational capacity to the prevention of chronic disease, or the evaluation of cost-effective curative medicine.

There are fears, however, that the unplanned growth of

health services may prove to be an expensive luxury, and fail to benefit those most in need.

The questions facing China now are, should government investment be targeted on poor areas which are unable to exact the best from the reforms in agriculture, or should it support the development of richer rural areas and the cities? The latter policy is likely to be less cost-effective and to sustain inequality. At present, the state does provide support at a minimum level for poorer villages and families, but there is an overall policy of 'self-reliance' which it is hoped will provide the necessary medical facilities. There seems to be a commitment to the idea that most people are able and willing to pay for curative health services. There is some indication, however, that people are less willing to undertake collective ventures in medicine, and that expansion of the collective sector and progress in reforming the state sector has not been as swift as expected. Equally, many rural hospitals are still in a poor condition and are not being modernised.

It is doubtful whether the new economic policies applied to health care can provide the sole answer to China's health problems. The mushroom growth of hospitals geared to profit, without a system of control and evaluation, is a nightmare with which Western nations are familiar. In-appropriate medical treatments offered on a fee-for-service basis is another. A decline in co-operative systems of funding is a negative result of the new policies, not only because this affects the worst-off, but also because local co-operative financing of public health measures is unavailable. This is only partially compensated by the consolidation of Ministry responsibility for public health departments, which although now relatively well equipped to deal with infections and parasitic disease, are less promising regarding plans for chronic disease and an ageing population.

Health, however, is not just a matter for health services. It is claimed that economic policies have improved living standards, diet and income, reduced unemployment, and raised educational standards. It remains to be seen whether these effects will be sufficiently equitably distributed for China to continue to improve national health and provide a decent health service for all its people.

11

The Household, Family and Reform

Elisabeth Croll

One of the most important dimensions of the recent rapid and radical reforms in China has been the new interest in and focus on the household or the family as an economic, political and social unit. From the yellow mud-baked villages of the north to the long, low white terraces or individual one- or two-storey brick houses of the south, or the low-level, old-style grey and white courtyard city houses to the new concrete high-rise flats in the cities, the reforms have wrought fundamental changes in family size, structure and function.

Before the reforms the household or family unit in the People's Republic of China was distinguished by the reduction of its traditional socio-economic and political functions and its incorporation into new collective units of production, consumption and welfare. The household or family was defined as largely a caring and sharing unit organised primarily for the support and welfare of the younger and older generations. Its definitions omitted any reference to a property base or the socio-economic functions which characterised the traditional domestic group in China and which underlie the usual sociological definitions of the family unit. Although informally the household, and particularly the peasant household within the rural collectives, was a more important unit of production, consumption and welfare than was generally allowed for within socialist ideology, it has now become the most important socio-economic and political unit in rural China and an increasingly important unit in the towns and cities. The reforms have in effect separated political and economic authority, redefined responsibility for production, altered the balance of production for the state plan and for the market and the balance of public and private forms of resource allocation, and have made new demands on the individual household. In both city and countryside the household is expected to undertake a variety of new functions to do with production, consumption and welfare for which it requires new skills, resources and facilities. Perhaps the most immediate and obvious change in China in the past few years has been the decline of the rural collective, with the simultaneous emergence of the peasant household as the dominant unit of production. In the growing number of small towns and the cities, too, there has been an increase in the number of small enterprises based on the household.

The household and production

As a result of the new rural production responsibility system, land has been contracted out to the peasant household and the control of the processes of production has passed from the production team to the peasant household (see Chapter 6). Although it is officially stated that land has only been contracted out to the household for a period of fifteen years and is not subject to private ownership, the peasant household has acquired *de facto* control over the land in that it is encouraged either to invest in and accumulate land or to sub-contract it in return for annual cash sums or payments in kind. There has thus been a major change in the relationship of the peasant household to land resources, with an increase in control of the peasant household over its utilisation and production. The reassignment of responsibility for production to the peasant household also demands that it take charge of all field management, from sowing to harvesting, of the costs of production, including the hire and exchange of labour, animals and small machines, and of the disposal of its products.

In 1985 the state abolished the mandatory purchase of crop quotas which marked another significant step in the overall reduction of state planning and controls. Increasingly, the market is likely to constitute the main determinant of the types and amounts of crops produced, and act as a redistributive agent. The reforms not only allocate new responsibilities to the household, but they also encourage households to diversify their activities to include other agricultural and non-agricultural activities.

The diversification of the rural economy is one of the major new policy platforms aimed at broadening the previous and narrower emphasis on grain production and developing animal husbandry, cash cropping and – in particular – small industries and commercial activities within the rural economy. To encourage peasant households to produce a wide variety of goods over and above, or instead of, those necessary for family subsistence, the government has arranged for new inputs and expertise to be made available to them, and it has re-established rural fairs and markets where goods, foods, local handicrafts and other daily necessities can be exchanged between producer and consumer at negotiated prices set according to local supply and demand. Foreign trade offices have also arranged for the production and purchase of local industrial and handicraft goods for export.

As a result of such policies, peasant households have generally followed one of two trends. They have either simultaneously diversified their activities so that 80 to 85 per cent of the peasant households operate a mixed economy. Thus they may cultivate responsibility lands and undertake a variety of sidelines such as vegetable production, the raising of livestock, household industries and the provision of services for their local community. Alternatively, in a new and important development, they have moved outside of agriculture to specialise in forms of commodity development. These 'specialised' households mark the beginning of a new type of household economy, one that is 'small and specialised' as opposed to one that is 'small and complete'. Probably as many as one-fifth of China's peasant households now belong to this new category, although the proportion is probably much higher in the fertile well-developed and industrial coastal and plain regions. In regions adjacent to small towns and cities, where there are numerous opportunities for employment outside agriculture, peasant households have increasingly directed their members into full-time employment off the farm, but at the same time they have usually remained resident in the villages and continue as spare-time farmers.

As a result of the rural economic reforms, the types and range of production operations undertaken by the peasant household have broadened dramatically. Peasant households have become complex economic organisations responsible not only for arranging and undertaking the process of production itself, but also for procuring raw materials, purchasing their own means of production, and searching out markets for their products.

In towns and cities, too, urban households have increasingly become the base for new and individual enterprises. For the first time since 1949 urban residents have been encouraged to set up their own individual enterprises in the cities either to manufacture products or to provide services. After an interval of some thirty years or so, individual handicraft workers, street stalls and peddlers have again become a common sight in the towns and cities. To develop the production and service sector of the urban economy, provide employment and increase state revenues and export earnings, municipal authorities have been encouraged by the government to register and support individuals and households who can produce small goods, foods and services for urban dwellers. Some of the more common individual enterprises in the streets and lanes include repair facilities for bicycles, shoes, electrical goods or furniture, and purveyors of small goods such as handicrafts, watch-straps, combs, newspapers, specialities brought from other regions and snack foods. Officially there are limits on the numbers and types of employees in individual enterprises, and most individual operations – whether restaurants, shops or workshops – employ family workers and are household-based. Indeed, they have been referred to as 'Mum and Dad', 'brother and sister' or 'parent and child' operations. Although the majority of urban residents are still employed in the state and co-operative-owned enterprises, the number of individual household-based enterprises have been increasing steadily.

An allied development which has increased the number of home-based workers in the cities is the widespread introduction of the 'putting-out system' or the contracting out of processing or finishing work by factories to home workers. In most cities it is now common to see individuals or small groups of workers (often women) sitting labouring in the streets or in the courtyards or doorways as in the countryside, where outwork has long been a practice.

Where the peasant or urban household has become the major unit of production, the degree to which it has been able to meet the new demands upon it and take advantage of the new policies and opportunities to expand its economy and diversify or specialise in a new range of income-generating activities has been dependent on access to material and labour resources. The basis of any household strategy to expand and develop its economy has been primarily dependent on its ability to generate sufficient capital to invest in fixed assets, tools and transport. The primary material resource for most peasant households is still land – 'responsibility lands', private plots and fodder or waste lands – but there are limits to the means by which land or indeed any other material resource can be accumulated. The generation of capital has been limited by the absence of inherited capital and the prohibitions, before the reforms, against the accumulation of material resources, which have meant that the major, if not only, means by which households have been able to expand their material resources in the past few years has been through savings from the incomes and wages of its members. Although surveys of both urban and rural incomes suggest substantial rises in per capita and household incomes in the past few years, much of the surplus income has been allocated to consumption rather than production, and many households still find it difficult to generate sufficient surplus cash for investment.

In any household the accumulation of capital is likely to be dependent in the first place on the accumulation and distribution of labour rather than material resources. The correlation between economic livelihood and welfare of a family unit or household and its labour resources is not a new characteristic of the Chinese economy. Even before the reforms and within rural collectives, the demands of the rural economy had required that individual households continue to mobilise their labour resources in order to undertake collective and domestic production and the transformation of materials for consumption. In China before the reforms, labour formed the major part of the total means of production, and because the individual or private hiring of labour was prohibited by law, the accumulation of, and control over, family labour within the household was the major source of its economic support and welfare, and also of income differentials. Although the maximisation of family labour resources may not be a new demand on the peasant household, it has been greatly exacerbated by the economic reforms, which actively encourage family units to expand and diversify their income-generating activities. Now that households have once again become units of production, one of the factors inhibiting their expansion and diversification is very often their limited labour power, and one of the immediate responses of households has been to intensify the demands on the labour of its existing family members. Moreover, the decline of the collective organisation of labour and the relocation of family labour to the household-based production unit has enabled the household to adopt this strategy rapidly. For instance, in peasant households and urban household-based enterprises the economic reforms have altered the ways in which family members structure their working day. In interviews they have repeatedly and quite spontaneously contrasted their working patterns before and after the reforms (but see Chapter 6 by Blecher for a contrasting view). In the past, production team and factory cadres allocated work tasks each morning, and the work points or wages earned were directly related to and dependent on daily attendance in the fields or enterprise. Now, work is done only so long as the production process demands, and for most it means greater flexibility and control, but also more production activities and longer hours. Interviews in peasant households and urban enterprises suggest that they work harder than before and that all family members, including grandparents and children, have been pressed into some form of income-generating activity.

The new demand for family labour is also confirmed by the declining rural school rolls, especially at post-primary levels and among daughters (see Chapter 12). Where the peasant or urban household has become the major unit of production this may affect the control, organisation, and division of labour within the household. Whereas in the past it was the production team or enterprise which controlled production, it is now the head of the household who will in all probability have assumed this responsibility and arrange for the distribution of tasks and rewards. The degree to which the household head exercises these controls depends on the size and structure of the household and the division of labour within it. For instance, in many multi-functional households where not all family workers are engaged in the same activity, individual workers have frequently commented on the new degree of flexibility, control and autonomy which they now have over their own working patterns. However, it it also evident that where several members of the household have engaged in the one family and home-based enterprise, they may experience the loss of many of the previous advantages associated with entry into social production, such as visibility of labour, individual remuneration, and a reduction in the power of the household head, and therefore of age and gender hierarchies.

The household, consumption and welfare

The new status of the household as the dominant unit of production in the countryside and as an increasingly important unit of production in the cities has contributed both to the greater economic interdependence of family members and to the importance of the family or household as the dominant unit of consumption and welfare. The individual household remains the chief unit of consumption primarily responsible for meeting the basic needs of its members.

In the countryside the reorganised rural economy continues to demand that the peasant household provide housing, non-staple foods, clothes and other basic necessities for its members. It is also newly responsible for procuring its own staple food supply now that the distribution of grain by the production team no longer takes place. Likewise in the cities, the urban household is responsible for meeting the basic needs of its members, with the exception of housing, which is allocated either by the municipality or the large state factory.

The ordinary care and servicing of family members also continues to make demands on household labour. As in the past, the production, purchase and processing of foods for consumption can alone take up to three to four hours per day in addition to the laundry, household cleaning and child care. In many households there have been substantial improvement in the facilities and conditions of servicing as a result of the explosion of peasant investment in new housing incorporating new cooking stoves and water pipes. In the cities and richer rural regions, the practice of employing domestic servants, which is encouraged to reduce unemployment, and the introduction of appliances such as washing machines and refrigerators should reduce the labour time involved in domestic servicing. Although such changes may have a limited impact for some years to come, there has nonetheless been a substantial nation-wide increase in leisure interests and activities.

In many regions one of the most interesting and obvious changes is the new interest in consumption and the marked alteration in consumer habits. A distinguishing feature of the era of reform has been the degree to which the government has raised expectations and generated a demand for consumer goods. Prior to the reforms there had been few surplus foods, durables or services available for consumption beyond those necessary for basic needs – and even some of those had not always been satisfied. There were frequent reports and complaints of shortages, and the long queues so characteristic of other planned economies were evident in the towns, while in the countryside many necessities were simply not accessible to peasant households. One of the aims of the reforms has been to adjust the previous emphasis on capital accumulation, production and construction in favour of giving priority to light industry, consumption and the raising of living standards, both in the interests of developing the economy and providing incentives to greater productivity. As a result, a wide range of new foods, clothes and consumer durables and services has become available at prices within the means of many. Shops and markets are crowded as households and individuals, even in the rural regions, acquire the means of greater leisure and pleasure. Shopping itself has become a favourite pastime, and current patterns of expenditure reflect the new interest in labour-saving devices and the increase in leisure activities including television, listening to tapes, reading, photography, dressmaking and various sports and hobbies.

Many of the objects of consumption and the leisure activities are based on the household and family use, but what is also characteristic of the new consumer trends is their attraction for the individual. Where consumption takes the more individualised form of styled and fashioned clothes, tapes and records and other leisure activities likely to appeal especially to the younger generation, competing claims on the budget may cause tension within households. Younger members are increasingly likely to question the management of a common household budget which gives priority to accumulation in the interests of production or common household consumption, and which may deny them some share or choice. This is most likely to occur where the household operates a singe activity, there is little division of labour and remuneration is made according to the output of a household. The operation of a single budget may mean that it is as difficult or even more difficult than in the past to identify the contribution of, and therefore remuneration due to, each household member. On the other hand, where individual members work outside the household enterprise and earn an individual wage it may be more difficult for accumulation to take place at the household level. A new pattern of budgeting may develop which resembles that already characteristic of towns and cities, where individual incomes are earned and accumulated separately by each family member, who then contributes a negotiated sum to the common household budget. At present it is probable that there are different patterns of budgeting and negotiating household incomes and expenditures which mediate the new individual interest in consumption and leisure and the greater economic interdependence of family members in their responsibility for production, consumption and welfare.

The household is expected to take responsibility for the economic support and welfare of its dependants, including its young unemployed, elderly and disabled, or otherwise hand-icapped members who are not able-bodied enough to be in full or part-time employment. The peasant household is no longer aided and subsidised by collective structures and services to the same extent as before. For instance, previously the collective team absorbed all village residents into its labour force in some capacity or another, so that they all earned work points. For those entirely dependent on welfare, the cost of the 'five guarantees' of food, shelter, clothing, fuel and burial expenses was met out of the common welfare funds of the collective. Since the decline of the collective, however, those without full labour power must either be incorporated into the income-generating activities of the peasant household or be supported out of the earnings of its other members. The persistence of even the basic welfare provisions formerly provided by the collective is uncertain and probably varies very much according to the level of economic development of the region, the wealth of the new village and township governments, and their will to maintain welfare funds and services. The government has recommended that local com-munities establish committees to 'aid the poor' by maintain-ing regular contact with them and helping to plan and develop new income-generating activities. This solution is more informal and *ad hoc* than in the past, and it is likely that welfare provisions in rural areas are increasingly the responsi-bility of the individual household.

In the cities, where before the reforms a greater number of services were made available to urban households by the factory or neighbourhood organisations, these services have not only continued but frequently, in the interests of alleviat-ing unemployment, they have been expanded by urban neighbourhood service units. It may well be that as urban factories and neighbourhood enterprises are increasingly made responsible for their own profits and losses, the once generous welfare funds of the large state factories may not be so generous or assured.

It is probable that, in both city and countryside, the individual has become more reliant on the household, and in short-term it is likely to remain the most assured source of economic support and welfare. In the longer term it may well be that new public welfare bodies in both urban and rural areas will be established, especially since the ageing of dependants requiring support within the family is likely to stretch the capacity of small family resources to their limits.

Family planning and household size

One of the most momentous and far-reaching policies in its implications for the household and family has been the one-child family programme. To reduce the rate of population growth and develop the economy and levels of livelihood in China, the government decided at the turn of the decade to introduce one of the most radical and stringent of family planning policies, which in effect reduced the number of births permitted to one child per couple. The policy was disting-uished from its predecessors not only by its novel, universal and singular recommendation – one child – but also by the range of incentives and penalties attached to the implementa-tion of the policy and the new degree of state intervention in family affairs which it represented. Of all the new policies introduced by the government during the period of reform, this policy has probably been the most unpopular. This is especially so in the countryside, where the conflict between the demands made on the household as a unit of production and reproduction has been particularly acute. The reproduc-tion of family labour, although essentially a longer-term strategy, is a time-honoured means of augmenting the labour force of the household and securing its future as an economic unit capable of supporting its members, old and young. That peasants in China have customarily perceived a direct correlation between size of the family and its wealth and welfare is frequently reflected in common folklore which links more children with more income and more blessings.

It was evident to many that the households whose incomes rose rapidly in the first few years following the economic reforms were those which were recognisably larger than their neighbours. Moreover, in the countryside, and now for household-based enterprises in the cities, children, and especially sons, are the main source of economic support for elderly parents. The present generation of parents could foresee a future in which one child and its spouse were responsible for the economic support and welfare of seven persons: two sets of grandparents, parents and child.

It was this conflict between the demands of family planning policies and the new economic policies maximising the value of family labour which was one of the factors that led to some relaxation of the single-child rule in the countryside. However, despite some modifications, there are still likely to be stringent family planning controls for the foreseeable future, so that the average number of children permitted per couple is likely to remain at one in the cities, rising to two in the countryside.

Although the composition of the peasant household may continue to take different forms depending on the number of generations and nuclear units residing within any one household, the average size of the peasant household may decline in the next few years, and not only because of family planning policies. The average size of the peasant household in the past fifty years was usually between four and six persons and consisted of two generations, or at the most the nuclear unit plus one or two grandparents. Where there was more than one son, marriage might occasion the establishment of a larger joint household, but more usually among all but the gentry household division took place shortly after marriage. In the past it had been a mark of mobility for peasant households to expand their size and elaborate their family structure once there was sufficient property and wealth to support a larger and more complex household. It might have been expected, therefore, that once the economic reforms had encouraged a peasant household to expand its estate and its labour resources to take advantage of the new income-generating opportunities, there might be a tendency to delay household division for a longer period in order to diversify its economy and accumulate resources. So far, however, there is little evidence that such expansion in household size has taken place. If anything, surveys suggest that there has been a reverse trend with declining household size. A national survey based on the 1982 census suggested that there was a marked rise in the number of smaller one- to two-generation nuclear households and a corresponding drop in the number of larger multi-generational stem and joint households. Instead of delaying division to mobilise family labour resources, it seems that households – at the behest of both the older and younger generations – may now divide sooner rather than later. The partition, however, may not be as complete as it was in the past when the peasant household was fully incorporated into the collective structures and economy. Instead, small individual households have augmented their resources by establishing new forms of co-operation and developing new multi-functional links between kin-related households. A significant trend, therefore, at least in the countryside, is the way in which individual households have joined together with kin-related neighbouring households to invest in common property, share in income-generating ventures which might involve some exchange of labour, and to provide common support for dependants.

The major impetus for kin-based economic associations and co-operation has come from the new economic reforms, which have generated demands frequently beyond the capacity of the small household. The government, recognising this limitation, has encouraged households to establish what it calls 'horizontal ties' between close kin or neighbours to pool resources and jointly operate and manage new enterprises. Those demands that are beyond the resources of the individual household may fall within the capacity of several households through the careful management and distribution of their resources, thus going some way towards making self-sustaining, if not self-sufficient, economic units. Joint ventures may develop on the basis of a single household enterprise which continues to operate after division and household partition. Alternatively, one household may initiate an economic activity which becomes so profitable that kin-related households are encouraged either to contribute their resources to enlarging the venture or to set up a parallel venture which will involve a division of labour and a degree of co-operation. The term 'aggregate' might be appropriate to describe such emerging family forms because despite the fact that families are fragmented into separate households, it is the linkages, associations and relationships between them that will be of major analytical importance. Although, like the household, kin groups also formerly retained some economic and ritual significance within collectives, and to a certain extent within urban neighbourhoods, the reforms and especially the decline in collective productive structures and solidarity have reinvested ties between close kin-related households with a new economic and socio-political importance.

Politics, the household and the family

One of the most significant political developments in the past few years has been the increase in the autonomy, authority and political bargaining power of both the household unit and the larger family group, especially in rural areas. Before the reforms, there had been a clearly defined line of authority in the countryside which combined political and economic controls. This, and the encapsulating nature of the collective structures, meant that the individual household had very little economic or political independence. As a result of the economic and political reforms, there seems to have been some weakening of the Party, state and collective institutions and their authority. This was due to the dispersion of formal economic and political authority and the rise of informal sources of power and status alternative to the Party, leading to plural and uncertain systems of authority and control.

There is some evidence to suggest that peasant households have perceived the balance of power to have been altered in their favour and to have increased their bargaining power *vis-à-vis* the collective and state. In one village, when peasant households were reprimanded for taking independent action against the interests of the village as a whole, they remonstrated that now that the land had been contracted out for use to the peasants they were more independent and could do what they liked. In other cases peasant households have argued against the implementation of the single-child family policy in similar terms, or by inferring that since they now cultivated the land, ate their own grain, and brought up their children on their own, the state had fewer sanctions. Indeed, now that they had taken responsibility for the land, 'there was no need for the state to bother about their child birth'.

This new independence and autonomy has been encouraged by the lesser degree of predictability and control in the local political arena and a greater degree of competition and fragmentation within the village. In the interval between the decline of the old direct agencies of control and the rise of new economic and political bodies, a political vacuum seems to have been created within the village. The household has turned to informal family and kinship associations to gain a measure of influence in the new competition for resources and for protection against undue administrative pressure and the claims of disadvantaged fellow villagers. This competition is a result of the divisions in collective assets and inputs, the acquisition of individual household responsibilities for production, and the distribution of income according to output. One or two studies of allocation and distribution processes suggest that former and present cadres may have been in a position to influence this process and thus favour their immediate kin with better quality lands and a larger share of fertiliser, seeds, capital and other inputs. The individual household may thus turn to kin-related households for support in the competition for such resources, many of which are still scarce in the countryside.

The new village committees provided for by the 1982 Constitution, which are to be a new form of self-management in the public affairs and social services of the village, may provide yet another opportunity for the larger and more affluent families of the village to expand their influence and to further their own interests (see Chapter 3).

One of the main problems facing the newly rich and specialised households has been the exaction of undue taxes and levies by conservative cadres who are working against the reforms or are fearful of a reduction in their authority and privileges. A second problem has been the threats to their property from disadvantaged ,fellow villagers. Although average per capita peasant incomes have risen since 1978, there are still wide variations both in absolute levels of income and in percentage rises. In 1982 the government anticipated that in the next few years, although some 30 to 40 per cent of peasant households would become rich, 15 to 20 per cent of all households were still likely to encounter difficulties in meeting basic needs. In a similar vein, the government forecast that within any one community it is likely that on average richer households would earn two to three times the income of poorer households, and most of the income surveys within local villages or counties do suggest that the range in income figures within regions have widened.

Qualitatively, too, there is evidence of a new degree of polarisation within the village, suggesting that inter-household relations within the rural community may have deteriorated. Media reports note that one of the main problems facing the rich households, and particularly specialised households in villages, has been the threat to, and attacks on, their crops, property and persons. In response, kin-related and neighbouring households have shared facilities and combined to protect their crops as they ripen in the fields.

The decentralisation of collective management has taken place at such a pace that collective assets to facilitate community welfare have frequently been dismantled and distributed among peasant households. For instance, in addition to the collective factories, there are reports that schools and clinics and other such community facilities have been allocated to individual managements or dismantled and divided among peasant households. From such sporadic reports it is difficult to ascertain the scale of such official and unofficial decollectivisation, but it does seem that if the peasant household may not expect to have the same support from the collective as before, then these claims and counter-claims for assistance and welfare by the disadvantaged, disabled and dependent are more likely to be guaranteed, at least in the first instance, by individual or kin-related neighbouring households.

Whether it be in the protection or furthering of their interests, all the available evidence suggests that individuals are more dependent, economically, socially and politically, on their households or family than before, and that there is a new degree of informal interdependence between kin-related households. This trend has largely been brought about by the fragmentation of the village, so that its corporate interests, its politics and its productive capacity are now less important to the individual peasant household. The reduction in the political and economic roles of the collective production unit has meant that the household has become less dependent on village facilities and village government and more on its individually generated ties and alliances within and beyond the village. The fact that the household no longer finds it so advantageous to focus on inter-household relationships within the village, which in turn no longer possess the means to meet its major needs, has turned household attention outwards. In this regard, it is interesting to note the growing tendency for peasants to invest in town and urban centres. Some surveys within villages also suggest that the highest income earners in the villages are usually cadres, ex-cadres, demobilised soldiers, returned students or educated youth – precisely those individuals who are in a position to cultivate alternative relations and alliances beyond the village which give them greater access to raw materials and markets. In sum, now that the new demands on the peasant household stretch its resource capacities to their limits, the collective or village is fragmented and the household is no longer encapsulated by the collective boundaries of the village. So it is the voluntary and informal kin-based cooperation between households within and beyond the village which have been invested with a new economic and socio-political significance. As a result, kin-related households located within cities, towns and distant villages have been incorporated to a greater or lesser extent into aggregate families whose larger family networks may extend outside of the village and across urban, rural or regional divides. In the longer term it is this elaboration of family networks and the incorporation of household or family units into the broader economy, with the simultaneous

weakening of village organisation and the fragmentation of
village cohesion or solidity which may well be designated one
of the most significant of the changes resulting from the recent
reforms.

12

Educational Reforms: Quality, Access and Equity

Keith Lewin

This chapter examines the development of education policy since 1976. The first section summarises key aspects of the existing system; the second explores the most recent Central Committee proposals for reform (CPC, May 1985) in relation to schools, teacher education and universities.

The Chinese education system

China's education system is the largest in the world, and with this comes a complexity that makes generalisation difficult. What is true in one county may not be true in another even in the same province, and is unlikely to be true in other provinces. Nevertheless, some structural features are common. China has adopted a 6–3–3–4 structure for the number of years spent in primary, junior middle, senior middle and higher education. In rural areas it is still common to find five-year, or even three-year, primary schools. Two-year senior middle schools are still the most common, though these are gradually being extended. Higher education programmes vary greatly in length, from one and two years part-time to five years full-time. In most urban areas the age of entry to primary school is about six years; in rural areas seven years or more is not unusual. Kindergarten provision exists for nearly 15 million children, but is concentrated in the towns.

In September 1985 there were about 134 million primary school pupils in 854 000 schools; 39.6 million junior middle pupils in 75 900 schools; and 7.41 million senior middle school pupils in 17 800 schools. Primary schools average about 160 pupils, though many in towns are much larger; secondary schools average about 450 pupils. Senior middle-level provision is diversified: an additional 1.6 million students are in specialised schools (largely for teacher training and technical skills) and 2.3 million in agricultural schools.

Some 1.7 million undergraduates studied in 1016 higher education institutes and universities. In addition there are the students in adult education: more than 1.7 million at higher education level, 5.5 million at secondary level, and 8.4 million at primary level.

Quantitative growth has been dramatic since 1949. Primary school numbers increased six-fold before falling back somewhat due to presently declining cohort size. By 1977 secondary places had expanded to sixty-five times the level of 1949. Virtually all urban, and the majority of rural, children are enrolled in Grade 1, with a claimed net enrolment ratio of 95.9 per cent in 1985. But about one-third of a cohort fails to make the transition to junior middle school. Of those who do, over 30 per cent fail to complete this cycle. Thus by the end of the first year of junior middle school, less than 50 per cent of a cohort are enrolled; this drops to less than 13 per cent for senior middle schools.

Female enrolments are now 45 per cent of the total at primary level, 40 per cent for general middle schools, and 30 per cent for undergraduates.

This quantitative growth has exacerbated the problem of supply of trained teachers. Officially, about 40 per cent of primary and secondary teachers, and 70 per cent of junior secondary teachers are unqualified in terms of the formal requirements.

Curricula at primary level follow central guidelines, but may vary to suit local circumstances. Book publishing is centralised, with standard texts available in major subjects, with some local supplementation.

Timetabling conforms to a recommended pattern, which allocates about 40 per cent of time to Chinese, 25 per cent to mathematics, five per cent to science, 6–8 per cent to physical education, music and fine art, and 4 per cent to political and moral education. At secondary level, mathematics takes the largest allocation of time (19 per cent), along with Chinese (18 per cent) and a foreign language (16 per cent). Among the three basic sciences, physics takes 9 per cent of the time available, chemistry 6 per cent and biology only 4 per cent.

A system of 'key point' schools is in operation at national, provincial and city levels. 'Key schools' are resourced at two to three times the normal level for staff and equipment, and employ the most qualified teachers. These schools are highly selective and admit about 1 per cent of pupils at primary level and 4 per cent at middle school level, on the basis of examination scores. City selection ratios are less stringent, since the majority of key schools are city-based. Key middle schools have quota allocations from junior to senior levels which ensure that, once in the key school system, pupils are likely to stay. It follows that a much greater proportion of key middle school graduates are likely to be admitted to universities or higher education institutes.

Recent reforms

On 27 May 1985 the Central Committee of the Communist Party promulgated a series of educational reforms after wide consultation over a six-month period. The main elements of the reform include:

- a commitment to a universal nine-year cycle of schooling, to be implemented in stages;
- the rapid introduction of technical and vocational schools at middle school level;
- greater autonomy for higher education institutions in planning enrolments in order to respond more closely to the demand for trained and qualified personnel;

- reform of the system of assigning graduates to jobs;
- the development of postgraduate education and research capability, especially in science and technology, and the encouragement of links with industrialised countries;
- a more important role for professionals in planning and management, with less day-to-day involvement of Party organisations.

This policy statement enshrines education's key role in the modernisation of Chinese society and in the drive towards industrialisation. It stresses the importance of developing more effective teaching methods, modernising the content of courses, and increasing the relevance of learning to productive enterprise. In order to support these reforms, public expenditure on education has risen from 6.3 per cent of the national budget in 1977 to more than 10 per cent, and higher education has been expanded rapidly. Unlike many developing countries, educational planning in China is currently taking place under conditions of growth rather than austerity (Lewin, 1987).

Perspectives on change

Schools

At school level, developments since 1976 have reflected a concern with quality, access and equity. It is argued that 'education must serve socialist reconstruction, which in turn must rely on education' and that education should 'constantly pursue new knowledge and cultivate the spirit of seeking truth from facts, thinking independently and daring to make innovations' (CPC, May 1985). Class struggle is no longer to be seen as the 'key link', and the emphasis has shifted to education as a provider of skilled personnel. In practice this has placed the emphasis on achievement in academic subjects, with special concentration on scientific and technological subjects, and a consolidation of school provision.

The qualitative shift towards technical and vocational education at middle school level is striking (Cheng, 1986).

The CPC policy statement is being interpreted to mean that more than half of total enrolment at senior middle school levels should take place in technical and vocational schools. By the middle of 1986 several large cities, such as Beijing and Hangzhou, claimed to have achieved this target (Eraut, Lewin and Little, 1987). However, in large part the reality of this achievement simply amounts to converting and renaming existing schools, which retain much the same staff. Given the magnitude of the task and the rapidity with which it has been undertaken, this was inevitable. Attempts are being made to improve the status of the new schools, even though the 'worn out concept of belittling vocational and technical education is deeply rooted' (CPC, May 1985). The principle of 'training before employment' is being stressed to this end, and units must preferentially employ graduates from these schools. There are some signs that the attractiveness of vocational schools is changing. In 1986 in Hangzhou major employers in the service sector were recruiting directly from trade schools. The most successful students were being offered several times the typical graduate entrance salary to work in joint venture companies. Entry standards to the best technical and vocational schools seem to have reached levels comparable to those in good academic schools.

The formal commitment to universal access to schooling is based on a belief that nine years of compulsory schooling is 'the hallmark of modern civilisation'. It is regarded as economically necessary and affordable, is seen as vital for the social and cultural progress of the nation, and 'is placed at the top of our agenda' (CPC, May 1985). Three observations are pertinent here. First, although the commitment has a very high priority, its implementation is staggered. In the case of the most backward regions the time limit is indeterminate, and this might suggest that for them the priority is not as high as is suggested. Second, there is evidence that in some areas enrolment rates at primary levels have dropped. The reasons advanced for this are ambiguous. It has been suggested that in some cases the 'responsibility system' has resulted in greater withdrawal rates of pupils who have little to gain from staying in school. Where there is little opportunity for employment needing educational qualifications and transition rates into the higher levels are low, drop-out into remunerative employment is to be anticipated (interview, State Education Commission, 1986). Third, as the overall size of the cohort at this level is shrinking, it makes the resourcing of universal provision manageable. In 1983 there were 144 million 7–12 year olds; by 1990 this will be down to 111 million, and it is projected to fall to 91 million by 1995 as a result of the reduced birth rate (World Bank, 1984). China is therefore unlike many developing countries with population growth rates over 3 per cent, where no conceivable rate of school resource allocation can keep pace with increasing numbers of students. However, demographic decline does create its own problems for the school system, not least the problem of redeploying surplus primary school teachers.

Equity has a close bearing on the debate about 'key schools' and the desirability of maintaining them (see, for example *Chinese Education*, 1984). Reintroduced after the Cultural Revolution, as late as 1983 their importance was stressed in order to 'serve as true examples for other schools to follow' (China Handbook, 1983). Their position is now a little less secure. They undoubtedly have an elitist character in the sense of being highly selective and unrepresentative of the social structure of the population. The great majority are urban; many are closely attached to institutions of higher learning; and they enrol disproportionately the children of cadres, professionals and officers in the armed forces. Chances in competitive exams are, as in every other country, weighted in favour of children from educated and wealthy backgrounds, so that access, though competitive, is hardly open to all equally. There has been some criticism of 'key schools' as their role in the maintenance of inequality has again become conspicuous. Nationally, 'key schools' at primary level seem likely to be discontinued. Some city authorities, for example Hangzhou, have carried this policy into junior middle schools, but there do not seem to be any examples of abolition at the upper middle school level. The current status of these schools reflects the balance of ideological debate on the relative importance of nurturing the next generation of intellectuals and experts at the expense of marginal improvements in school quality for the majority.

Teachers

There are four current issues relating to teachers. First, very many are untrained. This is not a major problem at primary level as shrinking pupil numbers have stabilised demand. Problems in distribution remain since rural primary schools are not attractive working environments. Paradoxically, entry standards into teacher training in some rural areas are higher than for cities, reflecting a high level of demand: teaching is a major pathway for rural youth intent on eventually obtaining city jobs. In the cities, on the other hand, there is a wider range of career opportunities, and the status of teaching in relation to other professions is a strong disincentive to follow it as a career. At the junior middle school level teacher supply is particularly strained. The expansion of numbers demanded by universal provision requires many extra teachers. Current projections suggest that the existing 2.9 million secondary-level teachers will have to be increased to between 3.7 and 4.4 million over the next fifteen years, with the largest increases at the junior middle school level (World Bank, 1984). As a result, large-scale in-service programmes are under way to upgrade qualifications, and a considerable increase in the output of initial training is planned. At senior middle level there is a scarcity of trained technical and vocational teachers. Apart from the palliative of redesignating existing teachers, widespread use is being made of part-time teachers with specific skills brought in from their workplaces, and of retired skilled technicians and so forth. These teachers can command high rates of pay – often more than a full-time teacher, even though they lack pedagogical training.

Second, there is a problem of poor teacher utilisation. By international standards teaching loads are typically light. In middle schools a teacher is likely to be allocated about ten to twelve periods out of a thirty-period week (Lewin, 1987). These periods may be with parallel groups and only involve the preparation of three or four lessons. Class sizes are large, typically averaging between 45 and 50, and this creates high marking loads. However, the large class sizes are a direct result of the underuse of teacher time. Yet Chinese teachers do have responsibilities that colleagues elsewhere may not have, such as requirements to undertake home visits to parents for every child each year. Nevertheless, the inefficient utilisation of scarce personnel seems difficult to justify.

Third, the quality of teacher training is a major worry. Knowledge of the subject is stressed to a much greater extent than pedagogy. At some key 'normal' (that is, teacher training) universities, admittedly a special case, less than 5 per cent of time is allocated to pedagogy. Teaching practice usually occupies no more than six weeks of a four-year programme and is unlikely to be closely supervised (Lewin, 1985). Though greater time is given to teaching practice and pedagogical skills in less prestigious centres, it is generally reckoned to be insufficient to guarantee the acquisition of practical teaching skills. There are good reasons for emphasising subject content as a prerequisite for the development of teaching skills, but the latter are central to improving the quality of schools.

Fourth, the status and motivation of teachers is a long-standing problem. Teachers have received only modest pay awards during the 1980s. These have done little more than compensate for falling real incomes, as those of other workers have accelerated over the same period. Teachers' salaries have remained virtually static in real terms since the 1950s (Lo, 1984). Recent exhortations to value teaching as a noble occupation have real currency in Chinese society: teachers are lauded as 'people's soul engineers, people's heroes and gardeners of the minds of the young' (Liu, 1979). But this does not seem to convince the current generation of school-leavers and university graduates. In a study in Dalian middle schools, only 2.8 per cent of children selected teaching as a career (Han, Xiao and Wei, 1984). Teacher motivation is also dampened by the non-financial elements: the lack of mobility, hierarchical authority – largely determined by seniority – and the limited incentives for good teaching. Some changes are occurring, however. Schools visited in 1986 (see Eraut, Lewin and Little, 1987) were subject to community-level bonus systems where teachers might receive the equivalent of an extra month's salary at the discretion of the villagers' committee. Within schools, bonus payments were also being allocated to young staff by committees of senior teachers. In some schools teachers are employed on something approaching a contract which requires inefficient teachers to retrain or be redeployed. This system is embryonic, and one enquiry elicited the alarming prospect that poor teachers would be relegated to poorer schools in less desirable locations.

Universities

University education is growing more rapidly than any other level. Enrolments fell to 83 000 during the Cultural Revolution (figure for 1971), reached 501 000 in 1975, and exceeded 1.7 million in 1985 (Huang, 1984). Since new academic degree regulations were approved in 1981, 35 000 masters degrees and 330 doctorates have been awarded. This growth has compounded problems of teacher supply at the lower level since the best graduates can readily be absorbed into expanding university departments. Again, rapid growth has created structural problems, such as the number of senior academics available to fill positions of responsibility. In 1984 there were 4432 professors out of a total university staff of nearly 114 000. Of these, 85 per cent were over 61, very few having been appointed in the recent past.

Entrance to university is through national competitive examination. The selection ratio of qualified applicants to available places was very low after the Cultural Revolution, but is now high as demand has grown rapidly. The examination is a conventional closed-book, written examination which emphasises knowledge largely dependent on recall (Lofstedt, 1982). The highest-scoring candidates have the opportunity to attend the key comprehensive universities. There have been some complaints about the selection system. It does have 'backwash' effects on the school system, focusing teaching and learning heavily towards the requirements of university entrance. In 1986 it was officially suggested that a proportion of students should be allowed to enter university without having the appropriate entry scores. This might be used to ensure a better balance between different groups, and to compensate for educational disadvantage. It would also allow the admission of students whose talents are not adequately assessed through the entrance examination. It could also, of course, provide preferential access for those with connections.

Expansion has been uneven, with wide variations in total enrolment in different subjects. There is concern that the existing pattern needs careful balancing to achieve the best mix of undergraduate enrolments to meet projected personnel demands. Surprisingly it is the humanities and social science subjects which are thought most in need of boosting (Huang, 1984). Planning is complicated by the new system for determining enrolment numbers, which has introduced an element of response to market demand alongside central planning. It is not yet clear what the limits will be if institutions develop large programmes on their own initiative. The increased autonomy now enjoyed by higher education institutions has created other difficulties. In a particularly notable example, Jiao Tong University in Shanghai has become highly entrepreneurial in the pursuit of industrial consultancies and joint ventures with a commercial character. Opponents of this development stress that the teaching of students may well become a vicitim of the pressures to expand revenue-generating activity.

A final issue concerns the placement of graduates in employment. A 'free' labour market does not exist in China. Instead graduates are usually allocated jobs in state organisations. Counties forward their requirements to provincial authorities who then match them against university output in different subjects. Agreement is then reached on how many graduates will be sent to which units. Students are asked to state their preferences and the university then allocates individuals on advice from administrators and Party secretaries within subject departments. Employing units may compete to get the best graduates; this competition can become acrimonious if one organisation is seen to be poaching graduates notionally allocated to other sectors under national plans. This has happened with teacher training graduates, especially in science and technology, where demand outstrips supply, and potential teachers have been poached from the Ministry of Education. The graduates do not have much influence in this process. One exception to this is graduates of short-cycle vocational universities. These universities are part of the adult education system, where the state does not assign jobs. The graduates from these universities are competitively allocated, and this is used as an incentive to motivate students (Huang, 1986). Changes in the job allocation system and the development of a labour market strike at the concepts of state planning, control and allocation, and are therefore highly significant. The logic of movements in this direction seems compelling, given recent pronouncements on the more efficient use of high-level human resources, and the closer link between performance and reward.

Concluding remarks

Chinese education is in rapid transition. This chapter has only scratched the surface of the many current developments. There are important ways in which existing policy echoes the past, before the dislocations of the Cultural Revolution, and therefore contains within it some of the contradictions that contributed to those years of turmoil. However, at the time of writing, the signs are of a new purposefulness in educational policy that is pragmatically determined; of an unprecedented openness· to the experience of the outside world; and of impressive quantitative expansion.

Whether improvements in quality can match these trends remains to be seen. High-quality teaching and learning undoubtedly exist in many institutions, but the distribution is uneven. ·To balance equity, access and quality whilst pursuing rapid modernisation is the greatest challenge facing Chinese educators, and it is on this that history will judge them.

13
Literature in the Post-Mao Years
Anne Wedell-Wedellsborg

New Directions

The Chinese literary scene some ten years after the death of
Mao Zedong exhibited a variety and vitality unprecedented in
the history of the People's Republic. Economic reforms,
greater intellectual freedom, a massive Western influence, and
the general spiritual climate had combined to pave the way for
the change from the increasingly uniform, basically normative
and politically directed literary output of the earlier decades.
Readers could now choose from a wide range of literary works,
from pure art to pure entertainment, from didactic stories to
pointed social criticism. As a result, Chinese literature had
become a much more sensitive and subtle indicator of social
and intellectual change than was possible when its main
function was to reflect party policy.

Apart from brief spells of liberalisation – notably 1956–7
and to some extent 1961–2 the two decades since 1949 had
seen an increasing ideological and institutional subordination
of literature to politics, a process culminating during the
Cultural Revolution and its aftermath, the decade 1966–76.
Not only did literature become explicitly and directly linked to
the implementation of official policies, serving mainly as
propaganda in the repeated social campaigns, but it was also

caught up in factional disputes among party leaders and bureaucrats. This extreme politicisation, backed up by strict central control of publishing and the media, ultimately led to a situation in which nearly everything that would normally constitute literary material had become a 'forbidden area': love or other 'trivial' themes from the private sphere, feelings which ignored class, the psychological probing of character, the portrayal of people with a wavering attitude to commun- ism, darker aspects of socialist society that could not be immediately attributed to class enemies, and so on. Objective truth, or a personal vision of life, were as out of bounds for writers as formal experiments or endings leaving the reader in doubt as to the message.

With the death of Mao and the subsequent arrest of his close allies, the balance tipped, and the period 1976–86 witnessed intrusions into these forbidden areas, as well as an exploration of new themes and modes of expression. What is especially remarkable about the post-Mao liberalisation is not just the scope, but also that for the first time the Party has not tried to impose clearly defined literary policies, basically allowing writers the initiative in pointing the direction. Campaigns and clamp-downs have occurred, but with the intent of marking the limits of expression, rather than prescribing specific themes or styles. There are several reasons for this relative tolerance. One is no doubt a common wish for a more lenient and harmonious atmosphere following the excesses of the Cultural Revolution. Other factors include the importance attached to the co-operation of intellectuals in the modernisation programme, the usefulness of critical literature for the reformists at certain stages of the power struggle with old leftists, and the impact of the influx of Western culture.

Thus by 1986, while literature seemed to have attained a fairly high degree of independence from the CCP, the process had not been without setbacks, and there had never been any signs that the Party would be willing to relinquish its influence entirely. Literary policy pertaining to ideology is a sensitive area, and the dropping of a tolerant attitude may be a necessary sacrifice in factional disputes, or if political or economic reforms at at stake. Minor oscillations between greater or lesser freedom for writers have occurred throughout the period, and at least three times major campaigns have been initiated. One such was launched in 1981 against the army writer Bai Hua, for his film script 'Unrequited Love', in which it is suggested that the love of Chinese intellectuals for their country is not reciprocated by the state. Again in 1983, several writers came under attack for contributing to 'spiritual pollution' by having allegedly advocated 'bourgeois human- ism' in their works, for being 'non-rational' and influenced by Western schools of modernism, Freudianism and existential- ism, and for implying that 'alienation' may exist in China as well as in capitalist societies. Finally, the beginning of 1987 saw fierce attacks on some outspoken writers who were also Party members, most notably Liu Binyan, till then a proponent and practitioner of social criticism in the form of literary journalism.

Controls

Since the possibility of political intervention remains one of the conditions under which literary works are produced in China, it is instructive to look at the methods used by the party to control literature, and try to assess their effectiveness in contemporary China (Link, 1983). These range from direct intervention in publication and distribution to more subtle manipulation through fear. The primary means of imposing limits is not outright suppression, but the kind of self- censorship induced by more or less implicit threats of public humiliation and eventual punishment, which might be any- thing from loss of job and privileges to severe restrictions of personal freedom. Although drastic measures such as labour camps or banishment to remote areas have not been in use against writers since the Cultural Revolution, the experiences are not forgotten, and the fifteen-year sentence handed down to Democracy Movement activist Wei Jingsheng serves as a warning. There have been demands for the formulation of laws to protect artists and writers against political persecu- tion. In mid-1986, following the appointment of the writer Wang Meng as Minister of Culture, work was initiated to promote legislation, but this was blocked by the clamp-down of early 1987. Given the primacy of Party rule, even if such laws were adopted, it is unlikely that they would have much effect since they could be overruled by the 'four basic principles'.

The most common way of announcing a restriction of literary policy is through speeches by top leaders at literary gatherings, accompanied by editorials in major newspapers. Often the opaqueness and verbosity of official rhetoric can seem difficult to understand, but there are certain key expressions which have acquired a special meaning. For example, reminding writers to 'consider the social effects of their works', to 'stick to the basic principles' and to 'concentrate on the positive aspect' provide clear signals of a narrowing of the scope of literary freedom, while alternatively 'emancipation of the mind', 'originality', 'search' and 'literature as a means of self-expression' belong to periods of relaxation. The speeches and editorials may be followed by critical articles pointing to 'errors' in certain works, and the naming of one or more well-known writers said to incarnate the tendencies to be curbed. The next step is to pressure other famous writers publicly to support the campaign and denounce their colleagues, who in the end will have to submit a 'self-criticism' 'confessing their errors'. Central directives are sent down for group discussions at all levels. In some cases there might be a ban on the publication of works by writers criticised or on certain themes. But generally unspecific formulations will be sufficient to ensure a degree of control. 'Better safe than sorry' has, understandably, been the reaction of most editors and writers. That these procedures do not seem to have quite the same all-embracing, long-term effect as in the past is due to the following considerations.

First, a tacit consensus now exists among many writers and intellectuals that individual interpretations of reality should be allowed, and that Party interference is harmful to literature. This view is even supported by high-ranking people in the Party. In contrast to the period before the Cultural Revolution, when most prominent writers were themselves entrenched in the cultural bureaucracy and in factional fighting, the conflict is now more than ever one between writers demanding creative freedom and political leaders and bureaucrats wishing to control it. During the campaign against 'spiritual pollution' in 1983 it was remarkable how reluctant many writers were to respond to the demand that they express public support for the campaign. Those who did turn against their unfortunate colleagues, like the famous veteran woman writer Ding Ling, later suffered isolation and contempt. In the election to the Secretariat of the Writers' Union in January 1984, she almost lost her seat.

Second, the economic reforms have also influenced the system of publication. Since 1980 publishing companies have no longer been dependent on centrally approved plans for publication, and their success has largely been determined by profit (Hendrischke, 1986). This trend towards a decentralised system of publication, in association with a market-oriented economy, has created for literary magazines enough economic independence and responsibility to make it difficult for their contents to be controlled centrally. This has also meant that public opinion and reading preference have become influential. There is fierce competition between publishing houses, and the profusion of publications makes strict pre-publication censorship and surveillance impractible. In 1985 there were about 700 literary magazines in China, more than 30 of them with a nationwide readership. Much decision-making is thus left to editors who exercise editorial brinkmanship to attract readers, while avoiding what happened in 1982 to the Guangdong-based magazine *Huacheng*. An entire issue was recalled, resulting in heavy economic losses, because of one story that was deemed to have gone beyond the limits: Yu Luojin's fictionalised account of her romantic involvement with a high-ranking official, who was not only much older than her, but also married.

In January 1987, following the dismissal of Party General-Secretary Hu Yaobang and the head of the Propaganda Department, Zhu Houze, it was announced that a Media and Publications Office, directly under the State Council, had been established, with the aim of strengthening the management of the press and the publishing industry. The effect of this still remains to be seen, but clearly firmer control over published material is intended.

Third, for the first time since 1949 literary criticism has emerged as a serious academic endeavour, demoting the traditional political type of review. Furthermore, it is commonly acknowledged that political condemnation of a work is often the best way to arouse a favourable public interest towards it.

Together with a more reticent and cautious attitude on the part of the Party, these three factors are the main reasons why campaigns and clamp-downs have been relatively short-lived and defensive. Though these campaigns have led to temporary halts and setbacks, they have not pushed things back to square one. In the zigzag course of Chinese literature between 1976 and 1986, there has been a gradual development towards more artistic refinement, a diversity of themes and genres, and relative independence from the Party. Even taking into account the 1987 campaign against 'bourgeois liberalisation' and the return to prominence of some orthodox ideologues, it is hard to imagine that this basic development will be totally negated.

It would be wrong to believe that the majority of Chinese writers reject Party authority or the socialist system. On the contrary, most of them basically support the reformers in the present leadership, though not with unquestioning loyalty. This is especially true of writers of the middle generation, those now in their late forties to early sixties. But they do claim the right to write truthfully from their own point of view and in their own way. Many of them consider it their duty to comment on society and the state of the nation, awareness of social issues being one of the hallmarks of the bulk of Chinese literature. But what is more remarkable is the increasing number of writers, particularly among the younger generation, who are either disillusioned with the Communist Party or apolitical, and who express their personal visions through artistic probing and, in a Chinese context, highly experimental modes of writing.

Much has been written in China about the existence of a generation gap among writers, with the Cultural Revolution as the watershed. The oldest generation of writers, who had already established their reputation before the founding of the People's Republic, have not played any significant role in the creative outburst of recent years. But while some of them, like Ai Qing and Ding Ling, have even attacked the new literature, others, most notably Ba Jin, have been active behind the scenes and become widely respected for their support of literary freedom. Writers who started their careers before the Cultural Revolution – some of whom were branded as 'rightists' in 1957 – still tend to be more given to moral judgements and the creation of literary characters that are clearly positive or negative, than their younger colleagues. Those who were at school or just about to begin their education in 1966 formed the artistic *avant-garde* in the literary breakthrough of the late 1970s and early 1980s. They are no less serious and concerned about the fate of China than the older writers, but their work is more ideologically unrestrained and artistically innovative. It is among the very youngest, who have no significant memories of that time, that the most anarchistic and socially independent writing can be found. Such generational differences, while seen by some as a problem, have acted as a dynamic force contributing to the liveliness and significance of the literary scene.

Writers and works

With one or two exceptions, the fiction discussed in this chapter has not been selected for its literary quality, but rather for its representativeness or popularity. At the risk of oversimplifying, it will be discussed in terms of what are seen as the three most significant trends on the literary scene of the post-Mao era. However, these trends are not mutually exclusive. Several writers have contributed to all three, and there are works that with equal justification could be categorised within at least two of them. Yet presenting literature in the context of these three tendencies and the different function each of them has, should tell us something about the realities of contemporary China. The three tendencies are roughly described as: problem literature, documentary literature, and a more 'searching' or ambiguous type of literature.

Problem literature

Problem literature is by far the biggest and broadest category, and also the oldest, continuing a tradition established long before the People's Republic. It focuses on social problems, and sometimes looks at them from a new perspective. It poses questions, yet somehow the answer, which may be a controversial one, is already inherent in the way the questions are presented. The problem stories are entwined with political and moral judgement, and often point to black and white choices. They can be crude, and often express dedication to the leadership or the system. But in recent years an increasing number of artistically more satisfying, and even quite sophisticated, stories have appeared. This literature, apart from its inherent literary merits, acts as a catalyst for public debate. This is so not only because of the stricter control in China of the newspaper and mass media, but also because of the persistence of the traditional concept of literature as conveying the 'way' – that is, the correct basis for social behaviour. The stories discussed below have been the subjects of heated debates, extending beyond their actual contents.

The official chronology of post-Mao literature begins with the publication in November 1977 of a typical problem story, *Class Teacher* by Liu Xinwu (in Barmé and Lee). It deals with urban delinquency and the harmful effects of leftist ideology on school children, and was hailed as the first literary breakthrough into a 'forbidden area'. It is in fact a schematic and poorly written text with a heavily explicit message that happened to correspond exactly with official educational policy at the time. But it dared to tackle existing problems caused by the overpoliticisation of society, which was enough to make it extremely popular. It set off a wave of short stories revealing tragedies caused by the Cultural Revolution. This literature became known as 'scar literature' or literature of 'the wounded', terms derived from the title of a story by a Shanghai student, Lu Xinhua. With its strongly sentimental, artistically unconvincing style of writing, blaming all ills on the 'Gang of Four', this story about the ruined life of a girl who had to cut off relations with her mother, who was wrongly branded as a counter-revolutionary, is the archetypal example of the first wave of post-Mao literature (Barmé and Lee, 1979). But the events and experiences described were real enough to most readers, who for the first time in many years could identify with a literary work.

After becoming famous overnight with *Class Teacher*, Liu Xinwu wrote a number of similar stories dealing with the problems of youth, usually as told by a middle-aged narrator who represents a kind of 'confidence after all' in the system. Since then, and especially after 1980, he has published short stories and novels in which the characters are more psychologically convincing, and in which he probes deeper into human feelings and stresses the importance of compassion and commitment, as well as the difficulties encountered by ordering people in their unheroic daily life. *The Overpass* (1981) was criticised by some for dealing only with trivial matters and for lacking a proper plot, but most readers recognised and sympathised with his description of how unemployment, low wages and cramped housing influences people's search for happiness. In *Black Walls* (1982) (see *Renditions*, 1985) a young man paints the walls of his room black without offering any explanation to his neighbours. This extraordinary and innocent act is used by the author as a catalyst for bringing out some of the more unpleasant characteristics of Chinese mentality: dread of things unexpected and interference with other people's affairs.

Liu Xinwu also wrote one of the first stories after the Cultural Revolution to touch on the subject of love. But it was a story by the woman writer Zhang Jie that really provoked a debate. *Love Should Not Be Forgotten* (in Link, 1984a) set off the first profound discussions of love and marriage since 1949, focusing on the rights of the individual and the repression of feelings resulting from the impact of both traditional and socialist morality. This rather unbelievable story about an elderly woman and her life-long passion for a man to whom she has hardly spoken, had a message that was extremely radical in the context of Chinese society: it is better not to marry at all than to marry someone you don't love.

Zhang Jie has written very different kinds of stories. Her first long novel, *Leaden Wings* (1981) attempts to create a panorama of society in the process of reform. While trying to combine social description with individual portraits she deals with a number of issues, among them generational conflict and conservatism within the Party. But perhaps her most interesting story so far is *The Ark* (1982), which is the first genuinely feminist literature published in the People's Republic. It tells the story of three single women, two divorced and one separated, who live together. They have consciously broken the rules for proper female behaviour: they don't care about their looks, their skin has become like 'air-dried sausage', they smoke and swear, never wash up and live in permanent disorder. They have meaningful jobs, but constantly have to fight against male chauvinism, gossip, and humiliations because of their sex. The necessity, on the one hand, of being tough and insensitive in the world of male dominance, and on the other hand the wish to give way to the woman inside, results in an inner split, effectively reflected in the broken structure of the narrative.

The emergence in China of a women's literature, or at least of works written by an increasing number of women authors, seeing things from a female angle, is an important phenomenon. Apart from Zhang Jie, several of China's most popular and controversial writers are women. Ru Zhijuan and her daughter Wang Anyi, Zong Pu, Yu Luojin (now living in Germany), Zhang Kangkang, Chen Rong, Dai Houying and Zhang Xinxin are the best known. Chen Rong, in her novel *At Middle Age* (1980) (in Link, 1984a) provides a typical example of the fictional presentation of a problem recognised by a significant social group. Through her novel the author speaks on behalf of middle-aged intellectuals who, while living in materially very modest circumstances, make an important contribution to society. The protagonist is an eye specialist, who despite exhaustion never wavers in her total dedication to her work at the expense of her husband and children. At the end the twin pressures of a demanding job and self-reproach for neglecting her family result in a complete physical breakdown. The popularity and impact of this story was such that the name of the protagonist, Lu Wenting, began to be used as a general designation for conscientious female intellectuals of her generation.

Though they are all troubled middle-aged intellectuals, the characters in the long novel *Man, Ah, Man* (1981) by Dai Houying (translated by Frances Wood as *Stones in the Wall*, 1985) are much more moving and convincing than the tired and incredibly noble heroine of *At Middle Age*. Dai Houying's book, which had great difficulty in finding a publisher and was strongly criticised after publication, is among the very first to give voice to the mental wounds and inner confusion of those who had not only been through the Cultural Revolution, but also had been affected by the 'anti-rightist' movement of 1957. The plot concerns the unfulfilled love between Party branch secretary Sun Yue and the thoughtful and shy researcher He Jingfu, who is writing a book on humanism. But the main theme is the broader one of how to cope with deep feelings of guilt or resentment or both. The characters, even the more negative ones, are all caught in a process of self-discovery, each in their own way struggling to find self-respect or meaning in what happened, and might happen again. In a wider sense still the book is about the role of the individual in relation to history. Dai Houying's stand is a strong, in a Chinese context not so obvious, affirmation of the worth of the individual and one forceful and explicit message runs through the book: that humanism and Marxism are compatible.

The story is narrated in turn by the main characters, a technique which, together with the use of symbols and dream sequences, has been considered modernist by Dai Houying herself and many readers. From a Western point of view, the too obvious message, humanism as an ideology of salvation, and the carefully crafted symbolism, would disqualify it as modernist. But that should not detract from its value as the honest and sympathetic testimony of one who lived through those difficult years.

Another writer known for his modernist style, but whose work nevertheless belongs mostly to problem literature, is Wang Meng. Silenced in 1957, he has emerged as one of the influential figures of the post-Mao literary scene. In 1986 he reluctantly accepted the post of Minister of Culture. He is a prolific and versatile writer, whose most conspicuous literary achievements have been his short satirical sketches and his early experiments with a kind of stream-of-consciousness.

Wang Meng was the first officially published writer to try seriously to break out of the confines of the traditional narrative structure of realism. In a number of stories, written between 1979 and 1982, he developed his style, often characterised by a rather verbose mixture of instant impressions and fragments from the past. The title of the story *Butterfly* (1980) (*Chinese Literature*, 1981, No. 1) is taken from the old Daoist philosopher, Zhuangzi, who dreamt he was a butterfly, and when he woke up was in doubt as to whether he was now a butterfly dreaming he was Zhuangzi. The protagonist, whose reflections form the basis of the story, is seen in his various and conflicting roles, as a high-ranking Party official, as a peasant (during the Cultural Revolution) and as a husband and father. Like many other stories from the early 1980s, *Butterfly* represents a search for meaning and coherence in the midst of uncertainty and change, and Wang Meng skilfully lets the sense of disorder be reflected in the narrative structure. Yet in spite of his delving into the psychology of his characters, most of them remain 'types', and his innovative technique has been employed as a vehicle for rather uncontroversial subject matter. As a result most of his stories convey a firm belief in established truth.

In 1986 he published an important work, the long novel *Mutations*, hailed by some Chinese critics as the most significant novel written in the People's Republic. It deals mainly with the period before 1949 and is partly based on material from Wang Meng's own family. *Mutations* shows the mental and emotional distortion resulting from social and cultural constraints, and can be seen as an example of the recent tendency to focus on 'the ugly Chinese', i.e. people under the influence of the most negative aspects of Chinese habits and culture.

There is a current problem in literature known in China as 'exposure literature'. In 1979 the almost masochistic dwelling on individual tragedies in the 'scar literature' was gradually overshadowed by a much more controversial type, exposing the dark side of socialist society. Though often equipped with a 'bright ending', the themes in the most sensational of these stories read like a catalogue of social evils: corruption, embezzlement, abuse of cadre privileges, rural poverty and prison camps. By far the most outstanding was a long piece of reportage, based on real people and actual events, entitled *Between Men and Demons* (1979) (in Link, 1984b), which links 'problem literature' with the second tendency, that of documentary literature.

Documentary literature

Even though reportage existed as a genre before the Cultural Revolution, there are few similarities between the glowingly heroic prose of the 1960s and the often painfully truthful documentary writing of this last decade. Documentary literature today is a wide genre, ranging from engaged reportage close to problem literature, to detached, disinterested sketches of reality. Behind all its manifestations lie an urge to lay bare the truth, to put on record not only the present but also the past, while it still lives in people's memories. They serve an obvious psychological function, reacting against the 'typical characters' or downright lies of the Cultural Revolution.

Between Men and Demons, written by Liu Binyan, tells the unbelievable but true story of ruthlessness, greed and crime in the midst of the Communist Party. It reports the case of a woman, Wang Shouxin, who during the Cultural Revolution was able to amass a fortune and build a huge illegal network, based on bribery and corruption. This network was entwined with the county Party organisation, creating a mutually reinforcing system of economic and political power, totally impenetrable and destructive of people outside it. 'The Communist Party controls everything, except the Communist Party itself', runs one of the most often quoted sentences from this work. And even though Wang Shouxin and her close collaborators were finally found out and punished in 1978, many of those involved were still around and did their best to prevent the publication of this piece.

None of Liu's later works have had quite the scope and dramatic verve of *Between Men and Demons*, but they have all been uncompromising exposés, depicting people as powerless victims of arbitrary political decisions and movements, or of cadres exploiting the system. Liu Binyan, who worked on the *People's Daily* and was a Party member until he was expelled in January 1987, had often declared that precisely because of his trust in the socialist system, he must speak up against injustice. One of his latest works, *The Second Kind of Loyalty*, underlines the necessity of that kind of loyalty, rather than blind obedience. Liu firmly believes that literature should 'intervene in life' and has been as critical of younger writers who turned towards their inner self as of those writers who conformed. He is probably the most widely respected and admired writer in China, but no doubt also intensely hated, not only by those Party bureaucrats directly affected by his investigations, but also by those leaders who feel that his activities are further undermining the already shaken confidence in the Party. On the other hand, no one could write as he did without protection from high places. With the departure of Hu Yaobang he lost that protection.

Where Liu Binyan's writings represent one end of the spectrum in the documentary genre, *Beijing Man* (1985) by Zhang Xinxin and Sang Ye represents the other. This collection of 146 portraits of 'ordinary' Chinese men and women has been an instant success. Termed 'transcribed oral literature' by Zhang Xinxin, these portraits are skilfully crafted self-descriptions, based on interviews. The people portrayed are of all ages, jobs and attitudes, caught in different situations and made to tell their story. For example, a beggar, a vagabond, a cyclist, a husband on honeymoon, a blind masseuse, the son of a famous singer, a book-seller, a crematorium worker, a divorced woman, a boy selling popcorn, speak straight to the reader in all their diversity and individuality.

Other instances of documentary literature include reportage from the Beijing buses, and family histories by Liu Xinwu, a hundred people's account of the Cultural Revolution collected by the Tianjin writer, Feng Jicai, and *A Day in the Life of China*. The latter is also edited by Zhang Xinxin, and is a new version of a book edited by Mao Dun in 1936, in which people from all walks of life tell what they did on one particular day. The day chosen to be recorded for posterity was 21 April 1986, and thousands of people have written to the editor, describing in detail their doings and thoughts on that day.

'Search' literature

Following the success of *Beijing Man*, Zhang Xinxin became something of a literary and mass media star. But in the early 1980s she was known to a smaller circle as the author of a different and not so broadly acceptable kind of literature. Besides *The Crazy Kaffir-Lily* (1983), a satirically absurd story based on a real event, showing the madness generated by rampant profit-making, her most important work at that time belongs to the third important trend in post-Mao literature: an existentially searching mode of writing.

This category is, like the others, very broad, and much more difficult to define. At its best this literature is original both in form and meaning, is many-layered, pays careful attention to language, and would have a value outside a Chinese context as more than a source for sociological information. The authors see their art as self-expression, representing an existential search. Within this broad category of artistically concerned literature, two main currents are discernible: a modernist trend, featuring the alienation and loneliness of the individual, in some ways similar to Western literature of this century, and a more Chinese oriented one that has emerged since 1984 and is known as 'root-seeking'.

One of the most significant modernists is Zhao Zhenkai, better known as the poet Bei Dao. As the editor of the short-lived, but for its time artistically outstanding, unofficial journal *Today* (*Jintian*, December 1978 to September 1980) he exerted an important influence on the literary *avant-garde*. His stories, originally published in *Today*, later appeared in official literary magazines. In a sense the main theme in all of them is the breakdown of communication. They show the loneliness of the individual who knows that there is a truth, a life more honest and fulfilling than what is possible in the present. Thus his main characters are outsiders, cut off from their surroundings because of this insight. *No. 13 Happiness Road* (1985) (see Barmé and Minford, 1986) differs in style from the rest of his stories. It is about a journalist who wants to find out who lives behind the dilapidated wall of No. 13 Happiness Road. The story can be interpreted in several ways, but the reader is to understand that place as a metaphor for the unknown, the undefined. But 'that which no one knows about is a state secret', so the journalist is told by the security chief, and he ends up in the madhouse inside the wall. From the narrative emanates a kind of black humour, engendered through a number of heavily satirical scenes, in which the protagonist seeks out various people and representatives of the bureaucracy in order to ask his seemingly innocent question. Zhao's longest work, the short novel *Waves* (1981), originally dates back to 1974. Both in terms of its subjectivist technique and its philosophical depth, it is an extraordinary achievement given its time and place. It is composed from the chronologically arranged reflections and diary fragments of the five main characters. At the centre stands the young woman, Xiao Ling, whose fate and attitude constitute the underlying themes of the novel: the longing for fulfilment in a world where ordinary human values are crippled, a willingness to give herself, and a capacity for love at the core of an outwardly nihilistic mentality.

Inherent in much of the modernist type of literature is deep criticism of traditional Chinese values – the Confucian virtues of compliance and adjustment, which these writers see as one reason for China's problems. The root-seekers, on the other hand, consciously try to rediscover some uniquely Chinese elements, especially the non-Confucian aspects, such as Buddhism and Daoism, but also tribal cultures, myths and folklore. One of the first and still the most famous example of a literature in which meaning and comfort is found deep in the Chinese tradition is *The Chess King* (1984) (*Chinese Literature*, Summer 1985) by A Cheng. It is about a young man who, in a world of disasters, hunger and absurdities, has managed to preserve his dignity by devoting himself to the ancient game of chess. Outwardly a very simple story, it is in fact a closely-knit and linguistically and philosophically many-layered text.

Whereas modernist writing is very urban, 'root-seeking' literature is firmly linked to the land, and often takes the remote areas of north-western or south-western China for its setting. Much of this writing is based on the experiences of the writers as 'sent-down' youth in the period before 1976. Among its major exponents are Han Shaogong, Mo Yan, Jia

Pingao and He Liwei. The latter is remarkable for his short stories and tales in which hints of the sinister are overlaid with a veneer of idyllic beauty.

Conclusions

Looking back on Chinese literature in the period 1976–86, the common impression gleaned from the three main types of literature discussed above is the overall concern for the individual. In terms of literary technique there is a move away from the omniscient narrator of the realist tradition towards a subjectivist, limited point of view. It is further remarkable that many stories downgrade plot, focusing instead on character, themes or atmosphere.

Future developments depend upon whether Chinese writers' primary responsibility continues to lie with their readers, rather than with their leaders. So far, there is enough to keep Chinese readers going while they, and the world, wait for that great and uniquely Chinese masterpiece, of an artistic scope and philosophical depth as yet unattained, which will tell the story of the Cultural Revolution.

14

China and the Superpowers

Gerald Segal

China has the dubious record of having been in combat with, and the subject of, nuclear threats from both superpowers. This unique status reflects both China's special status in the balance of power, and the wildly changing objectives of Chinese foreign policy. Not surprisingly, China has seen its relations with both superpowers as its main foreign policy priority. There have been four main periods in China's strategy towards the superpowers, but in order to understand the latest period since 1980, a brief review of the preceding three phases is necessary.

1949–1979: shifting alliances

In October 1949, when Mao Zedong declared the establishment of the People's Republic of China, he also announced that the Chinese people had 'stood up'. After decades of humiliation at the hands of rapacious Western great powers, China was concerned to avoid being subservient to any other power. Unfortunately, revolutionary China was ravaged by civil war and badly in need of foreign aid. Furthermore, China had pressing priorities left over from the civil war. Most notably, the communists in Beijing sought unification with 'compatriots' on Taiwan, the last stronghold of the defeated Chiang Kai-shek.

In the war against the Japanese in the 1940s, Mao's forces had co-operated with the United States. But in the late 1940s the United States supported Chiang in his attempt to keep the communists from power, and Mao received limited support from Moscow. By 1949, Mao owed the Soviet Union little gratitude, but did sign a Friendship treaty with Moscow in February 1950 which clearly aligned China with the Soviet camp in the Cold War.

Whatever minimal hope there was that the United States could establish co-operative relations with Mao after 1949 was dashed by American paranoia about 'who lost China', and the outbreak of a new war in Korea in 1950.

When North Korea attacked the South, American troops were drawn in to repel the communist invaders. Beijing entered the war with Soviet support when American troops rolled up to the Chinese frontier. Sino-American reconciliation was dashed on the battlefields of Korea. China relied heavily on Soviet military aid, and from 1953 the Soviet Union supplied large-scale assistance to the Chinese economy. This brought thousands of Soviet advisers to China and helped establish a long-lasting pattern of Soviet methods of management and politics.

Following the end of the Korean war in 1953, while Washington viewed China as the extremist wing of the communist bloc, Beijing saw the United States as an imperialist power, and one preventing the full unification of China. Despite such obvious Sino-American hostility, this phase of close Sino-Soviet co-operation began to fade when the Soviet model was seen to be inapplicable to China's revolutionary needs.

By the mid-1950s, China began experimenting with its own development models. The Soviet Union under Khrushchev made matters worse by trying to improve relations with the United States, and taking a more cautious line on support of revolutionary causes in the developing world. By the time the Soviet Union signed the Partial Test Ban Treaty with the United States and Britain in 1963, the Sino-Soviet rift was already entrenched.

A second phase of China's relations with the superpowers – simultaneous opposition to both – lasted until 1970, taking in the Cultural Revolution. China denounced the Soviet Union for having sold out the revolutionary cause and decried 'contention and collusion' between the superpowers. China supported North Vietnam in the war against the United States, but refused to join with the Soviet Union in 'united action' against the United States. In 1966, China severed Party-to-Party ties with Moscow.

While Sino-Soviet diplomatic relations were maintained throughout this period, China heaped denunciations on 'Soviet social imperialism'. Following the Soviet invasion of Czechoslovakia and the declaration of the Brezhnev doctrine of 'limited sovereignty' for socialist states in 1968, China began to fear that it would be the next Soviet target. China apparently initiated an incident along the Sino-Soviet frontier to demonstrate that China was a tougher nut to crack. But the Soviet Union swiftly retaliated, and in 1969 threatened a surgical strike on China's nuclear capability. Beijing capitulated and opened negotiations in October 1969 about the Sino-Soviet frontier.

This lesson of Chinese vulnerability, and a new American administration under Richard Nixon, led to a third phase of China's relations with the superpowers. Sino-American *détente*, marked by the Nixon visit to China and the Shanghai communiqué in 1972, began almost a decade of a Chinese 'tilt' to the United States in order to deter a perceived Soviet threat. Sino-American diplomatic relations were eventually normalised in January 1979.

The decade of Sino-American co-operation, with talk of 'strategic partnership' and China as 'NATO's 16th member', all rang alarm bells in Moscow. Soviet troop strength along the Chinese frontier was expanded, with 80 per cent of the increase in Soviet defence spending in the decade directed to the east Asian frontier. Border incidents continued, and Moscow improved relations with China's southern neighbours, particularly Vietnam, to build a 'containment' ring. The most important lesson that China learned was that foreign policy adventures born out of excessive hostility towards Moscow were ruining China's foreign policy stature and undercutting its domestic priority of economic reform. China needed a modernised foreign policy.

Modernising China's foreign policy: the domestic roots

China's domestic politics staggered through a two-year interim phase after the death of Mao when Hua Guofeng tinkered with Maoism. The far-reaching domestic reforms that began in 1978 did not reach the foreign policy realm until 1980. While China's 'Four Modernisations' were refined, a fifth modernisation – foreign policy modernisation – began to take shape. The roots of this foreign policy modernisation, and its impact on relations with the superpowers, lie deep in China's domestic politics.

Politics

The nature and problems of China's Four Modernisations are complex. In terms of foreign policy, what was most important was the absence of certainty on the part of the leadership about almost anything except the need for modernisation. That the precise development strategy remained to be worked out by 'seeking truth from facts' left few guidelines for foreign policy.

Unlike, for example, in the Cultural Revolution, when specific radical states and movements were supported because of the governing ideology at home in China, in the 1980s China could seek friends in all directions. The only governing principle was the need for a peaceful environment. Even if the world was not at peace, China was determined to believe that peace could be preserved, and world war was no longer inevitable.

The result for foreign policy was a greater pragmatism than at any time since the 1940s. The danger in such an approach was similar to that faced by a politician at home who rules without reference to ideology: he might be seen as fickle – a fair-weather friend, a carpet-bagger. China's international legitimacy and the likelihood of its being listened to in international forums depended in part on a perception of

China having distinct objectives and a strategy for their achievement.

Economics

The fundamental judgement that China would pursue development pragmatically in a peaceful international environment, left open the question of what development strategy would be tried. The post-Mao modernisation recognised the need for new technology and know-how to speed modernisation. The decision was taken to open the Chinese trading door, although China was inconsistent in deciding how open the door should be, in which direction it should open, and what precisely should come through the portal.

The People's Liberation Army (PLA)

Despite ranking fourth of the Four Modernisations, the improvements in China's armed forces have been prodigious. The main change has been the enhanced professionalism in an armed forces that had spent the last decade of the Maoist period helping to hold the reins of power and keeping order. The obvious modernisation after Mao was to establish stable, moderate government and allow the People's Liberation Army to return to the barracks. Having reasserted civil rule by the early 1980s, the Party then allowed the PLA to get on with enhancing its self-esteem by modernisation. It was obviously too costly to agree to wholesale re-equipment of the PLA when the priority was economic growth. The PLA was satisfied so long as they were promised jam tomorrow and, above all, were allowed to get on with the more essential, less expensive tasks of defence modernisation.

The PLA doctrine of 'people's war' was transformed to 'people's war under modern conditions'. Training, regularisation and discipline were emphasised. In the meantime, some new military technology was acquired: new weapons, ranging from anti-tank technology to submarine-launched ballistic missiles.

Such defence modernisation obviously required a peaceful international environment. China's drubbing in the 1979 war

with Vietnam suggested just how much needed to be done in
the PLA. In the 1980s China has arguably enjoyed its longest
period of peaceful frontiers, with the exception of the conflict
with Vietnam. China has undertaken a series of *de facto* arms
control arrangements with a number of its neighbours, most
notably the Soviet Union, in order to prolong the period of
peace. Between 1982 and 1987, some 90 000 troops have been
removed from each side of the frontier, although no formal
accord on troop reductions was negotiated.

The risks of such a policy of quiet defence modernisation
are myriad. Some neighbours, such as Vietnam, can take the
opportunity to impose their will on China's border regions.
Worse still, China may also get a reputation for being a
'paper tiger'. Appeasement is not necessarily the best way to
guarantee a period of peace for modernisation.

The roots of reform: foreign relations

Since the double shock of the Soviet invasion of Czechoslova-
kia and the 1969 Sino-Soviet border clashes, Chinese foreign
policy had become obsessed by the 'Soviet threat'. Beijing's
belief that Soviet 'social imperialism' was on the rampage led
to Sino-American 'strategic co-operation' and helped put
China in uncomfortable positions on Third World issues, for
example in supporting the Pinochet regime in Chile.

In the late 1970s, when Chinese leaders reassessed the
international scene in the light of Beijing's desire for a
peaceful environment for development, they were almost
surprised to find the Soviet threat had faded. By the early
1980s China had decided that because the Soviet Union was a
lesser danger than previously thought, it was no longer
inevitable that world war would break out soon. China could
take a more relaxed view because it saw that the Soviet Union
was tied down by a failing economy, problems in Eastern
Europe, a protracted war in Afghanistan, leadership instability, and was also unsettled by a resurgent United States under
President Reagan.

Foreign policy under modern conditions in the 1980s meant
that China needed to move to a less hostile anti-Soviet

position. The risks were obvious. Soviet power might only be 'catching its breath' before another imperial push, and by leaning away from the United States, China might jeopardise its economic benefits from new trading relations.

The changing United States

Coupled with the decline in the Soviet threat was the more unsettled relationship with the United States. In the 1970s China had crept towards normalisation of relations with the United States. But the 1979 agreement on full diplomatic relations signed with President Carter was soon shaken by the more conservative President Reagan. As a long-standing supporter of Taiwan and an opponent of communism in all its manifestations, President Reagan was less inclined to curry favour with China. When it became clear that he would not abandon his principles, some decline in Sino-American relations was inevitable.

Vastly increased American defence spending in the first Reagan administration, and the roughhouse rhetoric towards the Soviet Union, meant that the superpower 'correlation of forces' was shifting in the United States' favour. A modernised Chinese foreign policy had to take into account this shift in the balance of power.

Beijing began to drift to a more balanced position between the superpowers, while trying not to appear too soft on the Soviet Union or too hostile to the United States. China knew only too well that a settlement of the Taiwan or Hong Kong problems, and continuing trading relations with the West, depended on not projecting a hostile anti-American image.

Reassessing superpower allies

For much of the 1970s China had subscribed to a peculiar theory of international relations – the theory of the three worlds. It posited that the two superpowers (the First World) were opposed by developed states who were supposed to be their allies (the Second World), in coalition with the developing (Third) world. China, as the leader of the Third World, would try to drive a wedge between the superpowers and their allies, both in Europe and the Pacific.

In the 1980s China came to appreciate that this theory was bankrupt. As far as the Second World was concerned, despite real differences with their superpower allies, the essential ties of alliance remained unbroken. In Eastern Europe, the Solidarity challenge was put down because of Soviet pressure and the fears of the Polish Communist Party that power was slipping away. China had deplored Soviet pressure, but recognised the inevitability of firm Soviet control in its bloc.

In Western Europe, China initially saw the splits in NATO over intermediate nuclear force (INF) deployment as confirmation of its theory of three worlds. But by 1983 it became clear that NATO deployments were going ahead and the alliance was holding. China also came to recognise that the Western alliance was a highly diverse arrangement. China began to pay increasing attention to its Pacific component, improving trading relations with Japan and even boosting trade, formal and informal, with South Korea and Hong Kong.

The theory of the three worlds had not taken into account the diversity of the Second World, and had no place in a modernised Chinese foreign policy.

The complexity of the Third World

The theory of the three worlds also suggested a uniform set of interests among developing states. In the 1950s and 1960s Beijing often out-did Moscow in support for international revolution. But in the 1970s China's Third World policy became muddled when Beijing attempted to pursue radical anti-Sovietism. This approach foundered and, by the 1980s, China took another look at the developing world in the light of its new domestic priorities and the shift to equidistance between the superpowers.

The scene China saw was messy. Conflict raged in the Third World and the superpowers had become increasingly wary of direct involvement, recognising that the friendship of developing states could be rented for a few days, but rarely bought. China, like the superpowers, began to appreciate that the correlation of forces rarely changed for long because of Third World conflict.

The implications of this lesson for China were two-fold. First, there was less reason for China to take an active part in Third World conflict because it mattered less who was winning. This suited China's desire for a peaceful inter-national environment. Second, China could delay any active consideration of close South–South co-operation because the South was so deeply split. China could feel happier about looking after its own short-term, narrower interests, for example with arms sales to both Iran and Iraq in the Gulf war. The main danger of such cynicism was that *de facto*, as opposed to rhetorical, neglect of Third World issues might harm China's longer-term desire to lead the developing world.

Japan and the Pacific century

Students of international relations find it difficult to agree on which, if any, features of global politics have changed since 1945. However, it has become increasingly accepted that the Pacific region has begun to take over from Europe as the focus of economic growth. By the early 1980s the region was becoming less known for its violent wars, and recognised more for the challenge of the newly industrialising countries (NICs) and the Japanese success story.

Of course, China had been at the centre of the violent stage of recent Pacific history. Beijing had taken on the Americans in Korea, played war games over offshore islands with Taibei and Washington, supported Vietnam against the United States, and then tried to teach Hanoi a lesson in a brief, bloody war in 1979.

But China was acutely aware of the changes that had emerged when Vietnam asserted its regional authority and Japan stimulated an economic boom in non-communist East Asia. At first, China's reaction to the Vietnamese challenge was uncertain: it could try to continue punishing Vietnam, risking war with the Soviet Union, jeopardising Western investment in China, and draining the Chinese exchequer; or Beijing could swallow its pride, curb its didactic foreign policy against Vietnam, and emphasise economic growth and regional peace. By taking the latter course, China could mark itself as a participant in the booming part of the Pacific, the non-communist NICs and the proto-NICs of the Association of South East Asian Nations (ASEAN). By trying to dominate communist South East Asia (and North Korea), China risked missing the boat to economic prosperity. By opting for a Chinese version of Japan's Yoshida doctrine (basing national succession on economic power), Beijing took a key step in the fifth modernisation.

Beijing's modern strategy

The layers of China's modern foreign policy overlap. The new trends have not resulted in a new, coherent, guiding theory like the theory of three worlds was supposed to be. But there are a number of major strategies that have become clearer since 1980.

The most striking element is China's more active foreign policy. To be sure, since China took its United Nations seat in 1971 Beijing has broadened its diplomatic contacts. But since 1980 these diplomatic contacts have been extended to include an even wider range of states, including 'pro-Soviet' regimes previously shunned as 'lackeys of social imperialism'.

China's economic contacts have also expanded. The proportion of China's GNP dependent on trade has more than doubled, and certain industries are as reliant on foreign help as they ever were under the Soviet model. China has sought finance and aid from international sources, and made special efforts to join international agencies such as the World Bank and the Asian Development Bank. Chinese students have fanned out across the world seeking expertise and contacts.

Even in the military sphere, China shows signs of developing a more active policy. The creation of a blue-water navy in conjunction with China's burgeoning merchant marine is by now accepted as an important Chinese priority. Beijing's nuclear weapons programme has made great leaps. China has deployed full-range inter-continental ballistic missiles (ICBMs), MIRVed warheads (warheads containing a number of separately targetted bombs) and satellite technology, while developing submarine-launched ballistic and cruise missiles (SLBMs and SLCMs). Even China's airforce is extending its range, acquiring the in-flight refuelling technology that is critical for longer-range deployment.

These types of activities in foreign and defence policy are the result of a combination of motivations for change from China's domestic policy and the evolving international environment. It is one thing to have an active policy, however, but quite another to decide how that activity should be directed.

Balancing the superpowers

Perhaps the most salient component of the foreign policy modernisation is China's more balanced position between the superpowers. This is not the place to recount details of how China manages this delicate game, but all the signs are that Beijing is a talented, if cheeky, player.

At the heart of the game is Sino-Soviet *détente*. Although the march to normalisation often looks more like a meander, by 1987 most observers would accept that Sino-Soviet relations are better than at any time since 1963. Every component of the original split has seen some *détente*. Inter-state contacts are at increasingly higher levels, military tension is vastly reduced, trade is booming, Soviet technicians are back in China, and the two communist powers see almost eye to eye on a wide range of international issues.

Full normalisation of Sino-Soviet relations awaits the resolution or decay of the 'three obstacles'. The frontier dispute is already well on the way to tacit solution, with *de facto* arms control evident in the thinning out of Soviet divisions and the withdrawals and reductions in the PLA. The Afghan issue has all but slid off the agenda as China has watched Pakistan try to sort out a deal with the Soviet Union. Only the USSR's support for Vietnam's occupation of

Kampuchea seems an intractable issue. These three obstacles remain a hindrance to Sino-Soviet normalisation. But the evidence is that the passage of time will eventually make a compromise possible. Sino-American normalisation took nearly nine years from the Nixon visit. Sino-Soviet normalisation has only been underway since late 1982.

Without Sino-Soviet normalisation, or at least a sense that movement is being maintained towards that objective, Chinese foreign policy will slip out of balance. Another, more risky way to keep the balance would be to worsen Sino-American relations. However, China has shown a desire to maintain equidistance by simultaneous *détente*. The visit by President Reagan to China in April 1984 and the small-scale arms deals with the United States suggest that China is serious about keeping Sino-American relations normalised.

Yet China is not prepared to return to the days of strategic co-operation with the United States. While China does apparently allow United States monitoring stations on Chinese soil, and permits navy vessels to rendezvous at sea, China has also tweaked the American nose, for example by cancelling the United States' navy visit to Shanghai in 1984. Although the visit did eventually take place in late 1986, what is important is the Chinese determination to signal a more balanced position between the superpowers at regular intervals. China was taken for granted by the Soviet Union in the 1950s and by the United States in the 1970s. In the 1980s the delicate balancing game should allow China greater pride, and the best of both worlds. Beijing is undoubtedly aware of the old Russian proverb: 'It is uncomfortable to sit on two stools with one backside'. But with booming Sino-Soviet trade and continued Western fascination with the Chinese market, China seems to have found a convenient and comfortable balance.

The Second World

The modernised Chinese foreign policy recognises the states of the Second World as individual cases. From Beijing's perspective, Japan is the main Second World state to be cultivated, yet there remains an important ambivalence in Chinese policy (see Chapter 15).

Further down the list of Second World priorities are the very different cases of the states in Eastern and Western Europe. Western Europeans fall into different categories, but all are basically seen as sources of skills and funds to aid Chinese development. The political/strategic dimension of supporting Western European union in the defence field remains a feature of Chinese policy, but not one with a high profile. Certainly the talk of China as 'NATO's 16th member' is long gone. West Germany leads the way as an economic partner of China, with Britain's performance well below expectations, despite the Hong Kong settlement (see Chapter 15).

By contrast, Eastern Europe is in many ways a more interesting part of China's Second World view. These states are less important in trading terms, although as Sino-Soviet economic relations have taken off, so have Sino-East European relations. East Germany, like West Germany, has led the way in offering China the goods it needs. The East Germans are also particularly adept at tinkering with Soviet plant, adding those more efficient components that appeal to Chinese modernisers looking for a cheaper route to development.

The most stimulating and perhaps longest-term role played by the East Europeans is in the ideological sphere. As China's domestic modernisers struggle with how to mix planned and free markets, China has looked to other centrally planned economies with experience of reforms. The East Europeans, especially the Hungarians, are experts on what can be done to overcome the basic blockages in a centrally planned economy.

Thus the restoration of Party-to-Party ties with the East Europeans, which began in late 1986, suggests that relations are bound to grow closer still.

The developing world

The image of China as a supporter of revolutionary causes in the developing world has always been an oversimplification. But when China began its foreign policy modernisation, the combination of domestic priorities, pragmatism and equidistance between the superpowers ensured that China's revolutionary image was clearly laid to rest.

China's relations with the developing world are now highly complex. On the level of aid and support to revolutionary non-state actors, China has virtually wound up its past programmes. The exceptions include Kampuchean and Afghan rebels and the Palestine Liberation Organisation (PLO). But the shift from assistance to states rather than movements that was underway in the 1970s was virtually completed in the 1980s.

At the inter-state level, China has also cut back on aid and strong support for revolutionary regimes opposed to great power attempts to keep Third World conflict controlled. China's pacifying role on the Korean peninsula is a vivid case in point. Chinese contacts have now begun to emphasise more mutually beneficial trade, and have even moved into the lucrative arms sales business. China has leapt to the dubious position of the world's fifth largest arms exporter, taking special advantage of the Iran-Iraq carnage to earn foreign currency from both combatants.

China has also shifted its rhetorical position on many Third World conflicts. Where it once denounced both superpowers equally, or the Soviet Union exclusively, it has often taken an anti-American line indistinguishable from the Soviet view. China's attitude towards Central America, and its improving relations with Cuba and Nicaragua, suggest the change has been great. In Africa, China holds the United States primarily responsible for South African intransigence. The establishment of diplomatic relations with the Soviet- and Cuban-supported Angolan regime indicates China's new official position, a decade after having supported the defeated revolutionary movement.

Only in Asia, and specifically in South East Asia and Afghanistan, has China been on the opposite side from the Soviet Union. Asia, especially East Asia, is of course the primary Third World area of Chinese concern (see Chapter 15).

Future priorities

Speculating on the future of China's foreign policy is even more complicated than considering the fate of the domestic Four Modernisations. The main priority for Beijing is how to hold a steady course in changeable domestic and foreign environments. There appear to be five main areas to watch closely for signs of change.

Domestic political stability

Despite the much remarked upon corruption and 'bourgeois pollution', China shows no signs of slamming the lid on all reforms. Development will undoubtedly bring further dislocation and unrest, but the present leadership and the successor generation show few signs of cutting off the reform process. The debates, such as they are, are between wings of a reformist movement. Thus the priority of domestic development in a peaceful international environment is likely to remain high.

As a result, the door to China is likely to remain open to foreign trade, investment and social contacts. The door will swing, and no doubt creak on its hinge. Furthermore, China will have more than one open door. The risk of spiritual pollution from Eastern Europe is much less than from the West, and thus the door to the East will be held open by some conservative reformers.

To some extent ideology will remain a guiding force to the type of modernisation, with the conservatives arguing for a slower pace and more planned growth. The unlikely compromise would be limits on co-operation with the West, while contacts with the East are pursued.

Economic priorities

Political stability ultimately depends on meeting economic objectives. Foreigners will play a role in meeting such objectives, but it is an exaggeration to say they will play a leading role. While China's door to trade will remain open, it is far more dubious to argue that it will open further. The

1985 experience with trade deficits, the steep fall in oil prices and the lessons of Third World indebtedness, argue for a cautious Chinese approach.

More specifically, it is difficult to know which tactics will be adopted in the economic strategy. Special Economic Zones have already been scaled down or placed on hold. The joint venture experience is clearly more painful than first expected.

One trend that Western investors would rather not dwell on at length is the possibility that East Europeans will pick up a larger share of Chinese trade. To a certain extent the process is already underway. The advantages for China of trading with a centrally planned economy are evident in terms of foreign currency dealing, indebtedness, and relative certainty of planning. The East Europeans also offer cheaper, follow-on technology which is often better suited to China's conditions.

Few foreign traders with China seem immune from the impact of the pragmatic Chinese approach. Even the Japanese were shocked at the sudden cut-back in Chinese purchases of consumer items. The China market is still available, but it is going to be tougher to develop than many had hoped. The Japanese are perhaps more flexible, and therefore better able to cope with the inevitable hairpin turns in Chinese strategy, but they will get as dizzy as any trader.

Military modernisation

It is unfashionable to argue that the PLA might be a threat to its neighbours. With the armed forces being cut by one-quarter and foreigners setting up co-production deals for arms, or selling prototypes, it seems unlikely that China's military instruments will be anything but defensive. Yet China has a number of unresolved territorial claims, not to mention aspirations towards being a great power, that should not be neglected just because the current and short-term emphasis is clearly on a peaceful international environment. The scenarios for conflict may begin with unresolved Chinese claims on offshore islands, and Taiwan.

Further afield, China seeks regional influence, and with an expanding blue-water navy Beijing may well take a more forceful role in supporting favoured regimes in the developing world. Needless to say, the implications of such a shift in Chinese strategy would be incalculable. But it bears remembering that China has used its armed forces in major operations beyond its frontiers more often than any other contemporary great power, and has certainly been prepared to suffer far higher casualties than either superpower.

The developing world

The pragmatism in China's foreign policy has helped ensure a low profile in the developing world. The main focus remains on Asian developing states, and the non-communist ones at that. This trend looks set to continue so long as the priority is also on a peaceful international environment and a concern with domestic development. Even if such development should prove spectacular over the longer term, it is still unlikely that there will be a 'Chinese model' suitable for other developing states.

The experience of the newly industrialising countries and oil producers suggest that nothing will ever be so simple as South–South co-operation or a New International Economic Order in North–South relations.

Thus the tougher aspects of China's policy in the developing world, restricted aid and increased commercial arrangements, including in the arms market, look like continuing. China has had a remarkably easy ride so far from the developing world. Most states seem satisfied with China's denials of double-faced or miserly policies, and have remained surprisingly quiet about China's entry into the recipient market for aid, thereby depriving others of much-needed assistance. The China mystique still holds sway in much of the developing world.

China's aspirations to lead the developing world may yet be met. It is a long shot, but a world with three genuine superpowers and a rich Pacific region dominated by China would be very different from our contemporary balance of power. Unfortunately, such genuinely triangular politics rests on the shaky assumption of prolonged, successful Chinese growth.

Balancing between the superpowers

It is difficult to imagine China abandoning its policy of
balancing the superpowers: it is one of the most successful
components of China's modernised foreign policy. It seems
far more likely that Sino-Soviet relations will gradually be
normalised, and the process will be marked by an exchange of
visits by top Party leaders. The process may have to await the
withdrawal of Vietnamese troops from Kampuchea (in 1990
as promised?), although more pressure on Vietnam to reform
its foreign as well as domestic policy might be enough to bring
Mikhail Gorbachev to the Great Wall. One pointer to the
future was the signing, in mid-1987, of an agreement on the
demarcation of the Sino-Soviet border along the Amur river,
a product of Mr Gorbachev's suggestion in his July 1986
Vladivostok speech that he might accept the Chinese view on
this issue.

Sino-American relations are suffering the problems of
success. Normalisation has gone as far as it is likely to go
without a major Soviet blunder that drives Washington and
Beijing closer together in strategic co-operation. Just maintaining normal Sino-American relations is not glamorous, but
it is important to the Chinese policy of superpower balance.
Of course, China still does not have properly balanced
relations. But given that the delicate game of keeping
momentum in Sino-Soviet relations while appeasing the
United States is maintained, a more evenly balanced position
is not long off.

15

China and the Regional Powers

Paul Wingrove

Background

Despite China's key role in global politics, the roots of China's international behaviour are fixed in an Asian context in which a regional geography and history have written the rules. Setting this context are almost a dozen countries which border China to the north, west and south: the USSR, Mongolia, Korea, Afghanistan, India, Pakistan, Bhutan, Nepal, Burma, Laos and Vietnam. The borders range from the 50 miles with Afghanistan to the 4300 miles with the Soviet Union. Invasion has come across these borders, or political turbulence has threatened them, so that traditionally China has looked inwards in defending itself – it is a continental rather than a maritime power, despite the long eastern seaboard. China remains sensitive to the potential threats posed by these 'rim' states, and to the importance of managing relations with them: they lie at the far edges of China's territory, bordering areas that are sparsely populated, mainly by China's 'national minorities'. Individual states might pose dangers to China's security, but, more important-ly, in the modern period they have often become the willing or unwilling clients of the superpowers and have brought those powers to the borders of China, threatening China and the Asian power balance simultaneously.

China: Asian power or world power?

China is normally accepted as a world power, but this is a title which calls on some important *caveats*. In so far as China plays on the world stage, it plays at best as an aspirant to superpower status. John Gittings (Chomsky, Steele and Gittings, 1984), among others, considers China to be only 'half a superpower'. In a purely material sense this is inevitable, since China is unique in assuming a global status as a relatively poor Third World state. Strategically, China entered a world already dominated by the bi-polarity of Soviet-American competition, and its foreign policy options are moulded by that configuration. Of necessity, therefore, China's diplomacy is essentially reactive, relying to a large extent on balancing between the superpowers. China has not only managed to operate a reasonably successful foreign policy within these limitations but has, paradoxically, taken them up and transmuted them into a form of strategic virtue. Deng Xiaoping has claimed on more than one occasion that 'China is not a superpower and never will be', arguing that China is qualitatively different from the USA and the USSR in being neither expansionist nor aggressive. Rather China is, according to Deng, materially and morally a part of the Third World. This is a notion which dates back to the mid-1950s when China agreed the Five Principles of Peaceful Coexistence with India, and also sought, at the Bandung Conference of 1955, to align itself with Asia and the Third World. But as Harris and Worden (1986) point out, from the Third World point of view there is a degree of schizophrenia in China's position – materially Third World but playing politics in the superpower league – which engenders some scepticism of China's claims and motives. Thus while Deng's assertion may be queried, and ever more so as China's modernisation and open door policies work their effects, in some senses China does differ from the other superpowers: we have already mentioned the largely dependent and reactive nature of Chinese foreign policy calculations, but there is also an important regional dimension to them. Since 1949 the fundamental concern has been the security of China within the Asian arena, and that narrower focus separates it from the superpowers.

The regional dimension does imply, however, grappling with the foreign policies of the USSR (an Asian power by virtue of its geographical extent) and the USA (an Asian power by virtue of post-war political and military extension into the region). As regards the Asian roles of both these powers, China has been consistent in the line that superpower intervention on the Asian mainland should be opposed by all possible means. This is perhaps the first principle of Chinese foreign policy, of which the second might be that no single Asian state should be allowed to grow to Asian dominance. A third principle would combine the two: no Asian state allied with a superpower should become too powerful, in the sense of rivalling China. These are rough-and-ready rules which can be interpolated from Chinese diplomatic behaviour.

Several consequences follow from this. First, China has paid a great deal of attention to the balance of power among Asian nations and has acted diplomatically or militarily to influence it. This has not always produced results, partly due to inconsistency in China's strategy and tactics. Normal state-to-state diplomacy has been paralleled by Chinese support of Asian insurrectionary communist parties which has created great suspicion of China's motives. Second, in so far as the Asian balance of power has been the concern of the superpowers, to the point of military intervention, China has felt required to meet that challenge militarily. Finally, and most effectively, China has sought a pivotal diplomatic role between the superpowers, setting itself between them in alliance, enmity or 'independence' in order to strike a balance which would guarantee China's security in Asia.

Deterring the superpowers

In support of the contention that China seeks an Asia free of domination by either of the superpowers and the threats they pose, we should note China's sending 'volunteers' into Korea against US forces in 1950. Then in 1954, at the Geneva conference on Korea and Indochina, China appeared determined to prevent the Vietnamese war with France offering an occasion for US intervention, to the extent that a settlement was agreed which, years later, the Vietnamese denounced as a sell-out imposed on Vietnam by the Chinese in pursuit of their own interests (Socialist Republic of Vietnam, 1979). On a number of occasions throughout the 1950s China even resisted proposals from its supposed ally, the USSR, for military and other facilities in China. In the 1960s China aided Vietnam in the war with the USA, but carefully avoided full involvement and an expansion of the war. And in the 1960s and 1970s, with the USSR at first seeming threatening, then filling the vacuum left by the US withdrawal from South East Asia, China turned to the West, drawing on the counterbalancing weight of America and, in a subsidiary role, Japan.

This exclusion of the superpowers from Asia, or the limitation of their influence where exclusion is not possible, is clearly a major theme in Chinese foreign policy, and will no doubt continue to be so, given the attention Mr Gorbachev is paying to Soviet Far Eastern territories, and to Soviet Asian policy. The USA, too, will continue to have an interest in the region, particularly in Japan and the Pacific.

Regional powers

Looking at China's attitudes to the individual states of the region, China has often taken advantage of the complications of Asia's politics to play one side against another where there were gains to be had. This is the case, for example, with India and Pakistan, where China came to align itself, perhaps oddly, with the conservative rulers of Muslim Pakistan, giving support by way of trade and arms, and standing by their partner – at least morally – in the wars with India in 1965 and 1971. This unusual alignment was not inevitable: up to 1954–5 India and China seemed to be able to live with each other. But the differences between Pakistan and India, and India's gradual tilt to the USSR, offered both cause and occasion for Sino-Pakistan alignment. Soviet support for India in the brief Sino-Indian conflict of 1962, and even more so the signing of the Indo-Soviet Treaty of 1971, presented China with the threat – however remote – of encirclement, to which the only available response was continued reliance on the Pakistan relationship. It remains an important one for China, particularly so in the aftermath of the 1979 Soviet invasion of Afghanistan. Pakistan is a major recipient of China's not very extensive aid, and there are persistent (but probably unfounded) rumours that China has provided technical advice on the development of a Pakistani nuclear weapon.

Sino-Indian rivalry is further fuelled by their border dispute, and by an unspoken and almost unacknowledged competition for leadership in Asia and the Third World. India's USSR links, revived by Rajiv Gandhi's visit to the USSR in 1985 and Gorbachev's return visit in November 1986, also set limits to the development of Sino-Indian friendship.

Vietnam: another instance

A similar anxiety about encirclement, again by an Asian state with a Soviet patron, characterised the first few years after Deng's return to office in 1977. In contrast to the case of India, where Soviet influence was rather variable and hardearned, in Indochina a vacuum developed after the withdrawal of American forces from Vietnam in 1975, into which the USSR slipped with an ease perhaps surprising even to itself. Moreover, Russia's influence here was based on Vietnam's post-war debility and consequent need for economic aid and diplomatic support, and was therefore much more secure.

China not only distrusted this latest manifestation of the 'hegemonism' of the USSR, but also the potential for regional hegemonism on the part of Vietnam. Laos was effectively under Vietnamese control after 1975, and Pol Pot's Kampuchea had been in almost continuous conflict with Vietnam from that date, a conflict partly inspired by Kampuchean fears of Vietnamese expansionism – fears which China shared.

Although initially both China and Vietnam seemed to have wanted to limit the impact of this regional war, China's need for an Indochinese client to draw the line against Vietnam and Russia meant taking the part of Pol Pot, offering both material and moral support. With the divisions hardened,

Vietnam finally launched an invasion of Kampuchea in December 1978. This had been preceded by a chain of events which created the most bitter relations between China and Vietnam. In the spring of 1978 thousands of *hua qiao* (Vietnam's Chinese minority) fled the country amid real or anticipated persecution. In June Vietnam became a member of the Soviet and East European economic organisation, COMECON, and in November Vietnam and the USSR signed a Treaty of Peace and Friendship. The Soviet position in Vietnam, with its valuable port facilities, seemed not only threatening but also firmly anchored, with effective encirclement of China finally established. This rapid move of Vietnam deeper into the Soviet orbit was partly protective, in anticipation of its December invasion of Kampuchea, but was also Moscow's reward for loyalty and support of its Vietnamese client in the crucial post-war period.

In mirror image, China had been moving closer to the USA and Japan to balance this new Asian upset. August 1978 saw the signing of the Sino-Japanese Treaty of Peace and Friendship with its 'anti-hegemony' clause, directed at the USSR, and in October 1978 Deng Xiaoping visited Tokyo.

Furthermore, since the May 1978 visit of America's National Security Adviser Brzezinski to Beijing, progress towards complete 'normalisation' of diplomatic relations between China and the USA had been rapid, culminating in the declaration of 'normalisation' and Deng's visit to Washington, both in January 1979, marking the high-tide of the Sino-American relationship.

So while Soviet support for Vietnam had underpinned the invasion of Kampuchea, China's reaching out to Japan and America underpinned the response – China's 'punishment raid' on Vietnam in February 1979. But by this date Vietnam had already routed the Pol Pot regime, and China's attack could be little more than what it was claimed to be: a 'punishment' and a warning – a punishment for Vietnam, and a warning to the USSR. In any case, there is plenty of evidence that China did not want to get bogged down in an unpopular war, with its deleterious effects on the Four Modernisations, not to mention the opportunities for finger-pointing that it would give to the USSR (Keng Piao, 1981). The war lasted three weeks and China came out of it badly, prompting Deng to press for reform of the Chinese army.

Since that time diplomatic struggle has replaced military combat. China, with just a hint of embarrassment, continues to support the claims of the ousted Khmer Rouge now waging guerilla warfare against a Vietnamese-controlled Kampuchean administration. To ease their embarrassment China joined the Association of South East Asian Nations (ASEAN) in promoting a coalition of the unpopular Pol Pot forces with two other resistance groups, those of the more moderate Prince Sihanouk and his former Prime Minister Son Sann. After the creation of this broader-based resistance, China began supplying arms to all three groups in 1982.

Following the rule that any Asian 'hegemonism' is to be opposed, China still resists Vietnamese control of Kampuchea, receiving support from the UN and from the noncommunist states of the region united in ASEAN. Nonetheless these Asian countries have their own reasons for opposing Vietnamese ambitions in Kampuchea, which only coincide at points with China's. Thailand, bordering Kampuchea, is clearly vulnerable to overspill from the conflict and is therefore a strong supporter of China's position. Others, such as Indonesia, are a little more sceptical. They see China, perhaps justifiably, as trying to prevent a local 'hegemony' and weaken Soviet influence, yet if successful in both these things it could only produce a stronger China, and in some Asian eyes that is as much to be feared as any ambitions of the Vietnamese.

The position seems to be at stalemate: China is determined to see an Indochina settlement which denies Kampuchea to Vietnam and weakens the Soviet-Vietnamese link. The formal diplomatic positions of Vietnam and China are so far apart as to make a settlement unlikely, despite the variety of peace proposals that have come from all parties.

Vietnam, of course, has something of an advantage in being in effective control of much of Kampuchea and able, as in 1984–5, to inflict heavy casualties on the Kampuchean resistance while the diplomacy grinds on. Although promising to remove its troops by 1990, by that year the country may be effectively 'Vietnamised'.

It seems that movement will come only if the USSR acts to promote a settlement, and here the signs are ambiguous. One factor which may tell is that, despite the military facilities it obtains, the Vietnamese burden is a heavy one for the USSR, amounting to about $1 billion per annum in aid since 1980, with the Vietnamese apparently falling down in returning the commercial favours and, in Soviet eyes, wasting too much on the Kampuchean occupation. When a high-level delegation visited Moscow in June 1985 it was told, publicly and humiliatingly, that Vietnam had to do better in making deliveries of goods to the Soviet Union (*Current Digest of the Soviet Press*, 1985). Soviet criticism of the Vietnamese leadership probably played a part in the personnel changes of 1986. On the other hand, the new Party Secretary-General, Nguyen Van Linh, still met criticism of Vietnam's economic performance when he visited Moscow in May 1987 – softer in tone, but effectively ending free economic aid, 'shifting mainly from the relations of assistance and commerce to the relations of co-operation in production' (*Soviet News*, 1987).

For the Chinese, this offers some hope that the USSR may find the game not worth the candle, and pressure its client to agree to a settlement. The Kampuchean problem, after all, stands in the way of the full blooming of Sino-Soviet relations, which is important to the USSR. Vietnam, too, is in deep economic trouble and may find the occupation of Kampuchea too burdensome, as well as leading to perpetual dependence on the USSR. If the disadvantages weigh even more heavily, then 1990 might be an opportunity for escape for all parties.

China stands up

In addition to these broad geopolitical themes, we should bear in mind an important sub-plot and subliminal influence in China's foreign policy-making: China's sense of pride in having recovered from its position as the 'sick man of Asia'.

Segal (see Chapter 14) reminds us of Mao's famous pronouncement on the founding of the People's Republic in 1949 ('The
Chinese people have stood up') – a mite un-Marxist in
sentiment, but very revealing.

One of the most important ways in which China feels able
to 'stand up' is in being able to lay claim to territory once
Chinese but seized by, or brought under the control of, outside
powers during periods of political and military weakness. This
legacy of the pre-1949 years is a brittle basket of disputed
borders and territory under foreign control claimed by China,
with China's claims a compound of national honour and
security concerns.

Some of these irritants, 'left over from history' in the
Chinese phrase, have been anaesthetised – a number of
borders had been agreed by the early 1960s – but disagreement on the Sino-Indian border flared into war in 1962, with
discord on the boundary remaining after the cessation of
hostilities. Then again there were threatening military man-
oeuvres and mutual charges of territorial transgression in
1986, notably following the law which made the Indian
'administered territory' of Arunachal Pradesh a full state of
the union in December 1986. In the Chinese view this
unnecessarily exacerbated a border dispute which was at that
point still in negotiation.

On the vulnerable Sino-Soviet border China still holds that
there are large tracts of territory illegally taken from China by
Tsarist Russia under a series of 'unequal treaties'. In 1969
China and Russia clashed militarily on Chenbao (Damanski)
Island, ostensibly over the demarcation of the border on the
Ussuri River, but the acrimony over the technical issue of
where to draw the line was only the symptom, not the cause,
of this clash between the two communist giants. Although the
larger territorial claims remain in dispute between the two
states, in his zeal to accelerate the present phase of the Sino-
Soviet *détente* which dates from 1982, Mikhail Gorbachev has
said he is willing to be flexible on the principle of river border
demarcation, to the point of accepting the Chinese position
(*CDSP*, 1986), a point taken up and hammered into an
agreement in 1987.

Hong Kong

In the era of Deng, the major triumph in the recovery of traditional Chinese territory has been the settlement agreed in September 1984 between Great Britain and China over Hong Kong (*Beijing Review*, 1984). Actually a group of territories taken from China at various times in the nineteenth century, in 1997 all the present British holdings will return to China with the title Hong Kong, China. The colony is promised a high degree of autonomy under the 1984 agreement, a position which is to be bolstered by its being made a Special Administrative Region (SAR) of the People's Republic, with Hong Kong's capitalist system and life-style to remain unchanged for fifty years. The rights of SARs are not spelled out in the State Constitution of 1982, which permitted their establishment: instead they are described in general and optimistically robust terms in the 1984 agreement, and will be incorporated in legal form in a Basic Law for the colony, to be drawn up by the Beijing Government, the first draft of this Constitution for the SAR being available in 1988 or 1989. While the rights set out in the agreement give Hong Kong, *de jure*, a high degree of autonomy (being granted executive, legislative and judicial power, including power of final adjudication; control of all economic matters; control of public order; and basic civil rights of the press, free speech, association, demonstration, strike, etc.), the doubts concern the degree to which the written word is binding on a government in Beijing which in the past has shown little regard for legal nicety. There are already hints that China might exercise firmer control over the colony than the breezy terms of the agreement imply: in April 1987 Deng Xiaoping spoke against London's tentative proposals for direct elections to the colony's Legislative Council, expressing the opinion that universal suffrage would not be appropriate for Hong Kong.

To a degree, the fact that Hong Kong is a stalking horse for the juicier prize of Taiwan may be a protection, since Deng Xiaoping has to demonstrate that his formula of 'one country, two systems' (that is, a single political authority governing two economic systems – socialist and capitalist) can be made to work for Hong Kong – and for Taiwan, as he anticipates (Deng Xiaoping, 1983). Part of that demonstration must rest on the willingness of Beijing to stick to the letter of the agreement and Basic Law when, on any occasion, politics might argue for ignoring them. At present, despite Deng's statement on elections, that seems at least a possibility: after all, China needs the wealth generated by the Hong Kong economy (see Yu Teh-pei, 1986) and cannot afford to jeopardise it. Furthermore, China still seems to believe – despite the evidence – that Taiwan will return to the mainland. In October 1986 Deng Xiaoping was asked by American journalist Mike Wallace why he stubbornly held to this belief: Deng argued the case on the grounds of the 'family feeling' which links the mainland and Taiwan. This is a factor which should never be underestimated: there is indeed a high degree of 'family feeling' among the many Chinese communities throughout Asia which manages to hurdle the barriers of politics. Nevertheless there are few observers (least of all in Taiwan) who believe that there is anything at all to be gained from reunification. That in itself is a danger, since once Beijing comes to believe that reunification is not on the cards, there will be less of an incentive to be on their best behaviour in regard to Hong Kong.

One immediate consequence of the Hong Kong settlement was that it promoted negotiations on the neighbouring Portuguese-held colony of Macao, resulting in an agreement, signed in April 1987, which followed the Hong Kong model. Macao returns to China in December 1999.

Deng's new course

These minor triumphs apart, is there anything new about the course of foreign policy under Deng? Broadly, no: the continuities are the more notable feature. In this area the Deng administration does not feel it has to disavow its past and claim that mistakes must be rectified. In the 'Resolution on Party History' (1981), Mao Zedong's foreign policy is pronounced basically correct, so that no major change of course is called for.

But while there is continuity in the broad picture foreign

policy of China under Deng Xiaoping, he has added a new dimension, based on the 'open door' and the Four Modernisations. The door is open to all comers, transforming China's foreign policy to the point where good diplomatic relations can be cultivated with all states whatever their political colour, in Asia and beyond. Economic growth calls especially for a peaceful regional environment, and thus China's approach to Asia downplays preparation against military threats, as well as support for the once-favoured insurrectionary communist parties of Asia. The economic imperatives of the open door have begun the process of establishing a broader Asian economic base for China, although at present it is one dominated by Hong Kong and, especially, Japan.

With Japan having somewhat reluctantly moved closer to China in signing the Peace and Friendship Treaty of 1978, Sino-Japanese relations after that date evolved from the dramatically strategic to the routinely economic as China's modernisation gathered speed. Even before the 1978 treaty, a Sino-Japanese trade agreement had been reached in February of that year, covering the period 1978–85. Henceforth, China became heavily dependent on Japanese capital, technology and equipment, to the point where Japan became the largest external input into the Four Modernisations.

Between 1979 and 1983 China ordered ninety-seven whole plants from Japan, including the recently completed Baoshan steel plant. By 1984 Japan was China's largest source of external finance, and Japan is also committed to providing capital for the 7th Five Year Plan (1986–90). There is a new type of relationship here, and it brings new problems, in the context of historical memories which refuse to go away. A specific instance occurred in 1984–5, when serious trade deficits with Japan developed as importers of consumer goods soared. More worrying, however, must be the feeling in China that a long-term economic dependence on Japan might be setting in. Some of this worry has already surfaced in student demonstrations in China in 1985: ostensibly aimed at the resurgence of 'militarism' in Japan suggested by Prime Minister Nakasone's honouring the war dead at the Yasukuni Shrine, in part they were fired by the increasing obvious signs of the Japanese commercial presence in China.

Of China's sensitivity to Japan's policies there can be no doubt. The anti-Japanese student demonstrations have their official counterparts: in the protests over the Yasukuni incident; criticism of Japan's sanitising textbooks on the history of the 1930s; anger at the Japanese court decision in 1987 which ruled that a student dormitory belonged to the Republic of China, not the People's Republic; rumblings over trade deficits and the 1986 decision to let Japanese defence spending edge over the psychological barrier of 1 per cent of GNP. On the other hand, this is also part of China's diplomatic style: the thespian employment of guilt for diplomatic advantage.

Sino-Japanese relations are worse in the mid-1980s than they were in the late 1970s, the heyday of 'anti-(Soviet) hegemonism', with the parties suffering the paradox that the harder they proclaim their desire to work together, the more they seem to irritate each other. While there are no indications that the two sides are in a permanently antagonistic relationship, it is nonetheless one between former enemies, between dynamic established power and dynamic aspirant power, between the flashy affluence of Japan and the charming shabbiness of China. This is bound to mix a degree of competitive irritability with the economic and cultural fraternity.

The other leg of China's Asian economic base is Hong Kong. In any one year Hong Kong and Japan might handle over 70 per cent of China's Asian imports and exports (International Monetary Fund, 1986; Yu Teh-Pei, 1986). However, here are signs that the base is broadening a little. Economic relations with ASEAN members and other Asian states are budding if not blossoming, stunted by their past distrust of China and a historically Western orientation. So too are links, direct and indirect, with some of the politically sensitive nations: South Korea, Singapore, Mongolia and Taiwan, but it is still fairly small-scale. The figures for 1985 (distorted somewhat by Japan's burst of exports to China in that year) suggests that the seven or eight Asian nations below Japan and Hong Kong share 20 per cent of China's exports, and only 6 or 7 per cent of China's imports.

China's Asian emergence can nonetheless be a two-edged

sword for some of the less well-developed states of the region. On the one hand China can spin the beneficial web of regional coexistence and co-operation; on the other it becomes a competitor with Asian states for funds and markets. While Asia welcomes China's new stability, moderate politics and moderate economics, there is still a half-posed question concerning the long-term impact on the region.

Pointers

China's Asian policy is only partly described by the above. There are other sensitive areas.

Both the USSR and China have sought a working relationship with North Korea (see Bridges, 1986, for the best short summary of recent developments), but have often had to bite their tongues as this highly independent nation went its own way. China assisted the North in the 1950–3 war with the South, but that has been no guarantee of continuing influence. As Kim Il-song pursued his diplomacy of *juche*, or self-reliance, he oscillated between the USSR and China, and was helped in this by the Sino-Soviet dispute. For both these communist superpowers the incentive for friendship with North Korea was largely the diplomatic advantage of excluding the other, although there are strategic advantages, especially for the Soviet Union. The USSR, however, virtually ceased playing the game as it realised that Kim Il-song was not a predictable ally, and under Brezhnev the policy seems to have been to avoid overarming this Korean unguided missile. This position was reversed in 1984 when Kim visited Moscow and obtained the MiG-23s he had sought for some time, and under Gorbachev the process of revival has gone further, marked in August 1985 by the visit of a large diplomatic party (to celebrate the fortieth anniversary of Korea's liberation from Japanese control), and a naval visit to Wonsan. Nonetheless, in this new phase China has not been excluded, and the ritual exchanges of leaders and various sorts of experts have continued to take place. However, China's aims at present are somewhat different from previously, so that China now stresses the need to reduce North-South tension as a contribution to regional peace and the economic development of China and both the Koreas. Hence China has shown itself more willing to talk and trade with the South (respectively, tangentially and indirectly) and to advise the North that its priorities lie not in remaining an armed camp, but in getting into the market place, preferably following the Chinese model. To the extent that this means less than wholehearted support for the North, there is a risk that China might lose out in competition with the USSR, but this prospect is reduced by Kim's continuing wilful independence, and also by the fact that the Russians still have anxieties about the possibility of conflict erupting from the unresolved issue of reunification, and from the politics that might follow the death of Kim Il-song. Both China and the USSR cautiously seek advantage and influence, but for different reasons, and a genuine change of direction waits upon a change of ruling personnel in the North.

China's most significant Asian neighbour, the USSR, has set about its own economic development, including a renewed drive to develop the eastern regions, and has begun to pick up the pieces of a disastrous Asian policy – mending its fences with Japan as well as China, talking about solutions to the problems of Korea, Afghanistan and Vietnam, and paying court to India and South East Asia. This new dynamism – set out in Mr Gorbachev's speech of July 1986 (*CDSP*, 1986) – will affect China's strategic views in ways that are yet to emerge. While China is in the middle of a cordial, mainly economic *rapprochement* with the USSR, Deng has turned a poker face to Gorbachev's new Asian policy, hinting that the talk of peace and friendship might be cloaking something more tough-minded, and that in the end only actions will speak louder than words.

China's new diplomacy, however, assumes that the military conflicts of the past three or four decades are over (although there are military men who take a less optimistic view). The emphasis in Asia will therefore continue to be on economic growth and co-operation, stability and demilitarisation, and restriction of superpower influence and competition. This is evident from China's attitudes throughout the region.

Trade deals are signed, say, with Malaya or Singapore, while regional communist parties are disavowed or ignored – although in the case of Indonesia, China's past support for insurgent communist parties continues to leave that country looking at China with some disfavour and distrust.

Far to the north, even the frozen relationship with the Mongolian People's Republic thawed with small-scale academic and economic exchanges in 1986–7, and the re-opening of the Ulan Bator-Beijing air route.

Nonetheless, China will not be insensitive to potential threats to basic national interests. With China standing as part of the dynamic convention of American, Russian and Japanese power around the 'Pacific Rim' (see Stuart, 1987), it would be risky to predict anything other than competition and conflict, despite the growing need for co-operation.

Chronology

Sept 1976: Death Mao Zedong; Hua Guofeng succeeds him
Oct 1976: Arrest of Gang of Four
July 1977: 3rd Plenum 10th Central Committee rehabilitates Deng Xiaoping
Aug 1978: Sino-Japanese Treaty of Peace and Friendship
Dec 1978: 3rd Plenum 11th Central Committee: promotes new economic and political line.
end 1978/beginning 1979:
Democracy Movement
Jan 1979: Normalisation of Sino-American relations: Deng in USA
Feb 1979: China's 'punishment' raid on Vietnam
Mar 1979: Deng enumerates 'Four Principles'
July 1979: Special Enterprise Zones launched
Feb 1980: 5th Plenum 11th Central Committee: Hu Yaobang and Zhao Ziyang elected to Standing Committee of Politburo. Party secretariat re-established, Hu Yaobang General-Secretary
Aug 1980: 3rd Plenum 5th National People's Congress (NPC), Hua Guofeng stands down as Premier
1980–81: Trial and sentencing of Gang of Four
June 1981: 6th Plenum 11th Central Committee, Hua steps down as Party Chairman. Central Committee passes 'Resolution on Party History'
Sept 1982: 12th Party Congress. New Party Constitution adopted
Dec 1982: 5th session 5th NPC. New State Constitution adopted
July 1983: Deng's selected works published
Oct 1983: 2nd Plenum 12th Central Committee (CC) launches Party rectification
April 1984: President Reagan visits China
Sept 1984: Sino-British Agreement on Hong Kong
Oct 1984: 3rd Plenum 12th CC launches urban economic reform
Dec 1984: Visit of senior Russian, Arkhipov, to China, indicates degree of *rapprochement*
May 1985: Decision on reform of education system
May–June 1985: Decision on reducing PLA by 1 million to total of 3 million
Sept 1985: Special Party Conference accepts draft of 7th Five Year Plan. Retires veterans from CC and Politburo, brings in younger personnel
Nov 1986–Jan 1987: Student demonstrations
Jan 1987: Resignation of Hu Yaobang as Party General-Secretary
October–November 1987: Thirteenth Party Congress. Resignation of Deng Xiaoping and others from Standing Committee of Politburo. Zhao Ziyang elected General-Secretary of Party by First Plenum of New Central Committee

March–April 1988: 7th National People's Congress. Li Peng confirmed as Premier

November 1987: Li Peng takes up post as Acting Premier

Guide to Further Reading

References are given in full in the bibliography.

General

A traveller's eye view of China may be thought a trifle downmarket for academics, but Kahn-Ackermann, *China – Within the Outer Gate*, is a superbly thoughtful analysis of Chinese society and behaviour, and a good read. See also Bonavia's lively account: *The Chinese* (1982).

We now have an excellent history of China since 1949 in Dietrich, *People's China* (1986), while the longer perspective can be found in Fairbank, *The Great Chinese Revolution, 1900–1985* (1987).

Politics

A good, short introduction to recent changes in politics, international relations and economics is Goodman, Lockett and Segal, *The China Challenge* (1986). Rosen and Burns (eds) *Policy Conflicts in Contemporary China* (1985) have provided an extremely useful collection of documents (plus commentary), covering many aspects of change and conflict in China. In politics (events and institutions), although a little dated, both Gardner, *Chinese Politics and the Succession to Mao* (1982) and Saich, *China – Politics and Government* (1981) can be relied on. More recent, and with quite different perspectives are Womack and Townsend, *Politics in China* (3rd edition 1986) with a political science approach, and valuable appendices; and Blecher, *China: Politics, Economics and Society* (1986), which takes China on its own terms: it is very good on agriculture. Perhaps the best of the bunch for good all round coverage is Domes, *The Government and Politics of the PRC – A Time of Transition* (1985).

Economics

In economics, the list is more or less endless, and the following all have something to offer: Maxwell and McFarlane (eds), *China's Changed Road to Development* (1984); White and Gray, *China's New Development Strategy* (1982); Feuchtwang and Hussain: *Directions in Development* (1987); Riskin, *China's Political Economy: the Quest for Development since 1949* (1987); and, showing that *glasnost* is probably more extensive in China even if not made such a fuss of, Liu Suinian and Wu Qungan (eds); *China's Socialist Economy, An Outline History, 1949–84* (1986) provide a valuable and fairly full Chinese account, with documentary appendices that would on their own make the book worth buying.

Society

China's social order has been well catalogued by Elisabeth Croll's industriousness: see Croll on _Chinese Women Since Mao_ (1983), on _The Politics of Marriage in Contemporary China_ (1981) and _The Family rice Bowl_ (1983); plus Croll _et al._ on China's _One-child Family Policy_ (1985). See also the recent classic study by Unger and Chan: _Chen Village_ (1984); and, on urban life Whyte and Parish, _Urban Life in Contemporary China_ (1984).

Literature

The best book-length study of literature is, so far, Duke, _Blooming and Contending_ (1985), while the literature itself is presented in English in Link's three works (1983, 1984), and also in the books by Barmé and Lee and Barmé and Minford (1979 and 1986). _Chinese Literature_, a quarterly available on subscription from Beijing, presents Chinese writing in translation.

Foreign affairs

In foreign affairs, little yet challenges Yahuda, _The End of Isolationism: Chinese Foreign Policy after Mao_ (1983), although Yahuda ought to be required to update this book. If anything does challenge Yahuda it is Harding (ed.); _China's Foreign Relations in the 1980s_ (1984), a genuinely helpful series of essays with depth, breadth and unity. Kapur, _As China Sees the World_ (1987) has pulled off the trick of getting Chinese academics to write about international affairs. While more than a little restrained, these essays are an interesting read. Harris and Worden, _China and the Third World_ (1986) politely take a hatchet to some illusions about China–Third World relations.

For keeping up to date, _China Now_ (London) provides a 4–5 page summary of recent events in each quarterly issue, while _China Quarterly_ (London) does the same thing in great detail. Official Chinese policy and statements are to be found in _Beijing Review_ (Beijing, weekly).

Bibliography

All-China Federation of Trade Unions (1986) 'Report', SWB, FE No. 8393.

An Zhiguo (1986) 'Improving factory leadership', *Beijing Review*, No. 44.

Bao Xinjian (1986) 'An inquiry into the general goal of the reform of China's political structure', Guangming Ribao, 14 July.

Barmé, G. and Lee, J. (1979) *The Wounded*, Hong Kong, Joint Publishing Company.

Barmé, G. and Minford, J. (eds) (1986) 'Seeds of fire: Chinese voices of conscience', *Far Eastern Economic Review*, Hong Kong.

Barnett, A. D. (1981) *China's Economy in Global Perspective*, Washington, Brookings Institute.

Blecher, M. (1986) *China: Politics, Economics and Society*, London, Frances Pinter.

Bonavia, D. (1982) *The Chinese*, Harmondsworth, Penguin.

Bridges, B. (1986) *Korea and the West*, London, Royal Institute of International Affairs/Routledge and Kegan Paul.

CPC (Communist Party of China) (1985) *Uphold Reform and Strive for the Realisation of Socialist Modernisation*, Beijing, Foreign Languages Press.

CPC (Communist Party of China) (1985) *Reform of China's Educational Structure*, Beijing, Foreign Languages Press.

Cheng Hsiang (1986a) 'A tentative analysis of discussion about reforming the political structure', Wenhui Bao, 21/22 July, in SWB: FE No. 8320.

Cheng Hsiang (1986b) 'News from Beidaihe', Wenhui Bao, 8 August in SWB: FE No. 8335.

Cheng, J. Y. S. (1986) 'The present stage of state building in China and the 1979 electoral law', *Internationales Asienforum*, Vol. 17, Nos 1 and 2.

Cheng, J. Y. S. (ed.) (1986) *China in the 1980s*, Hong Kong, Chinese University of Hong Kong Press.

Cheng, P. (1986) *Chronology of the PRC, 1970–79*, Metuchen, NJ and London, Scarecrow Press.

China Handbook (Editorial Committee) (1983) *Education and Science*, Beijing, Foreign Languages Press.

Chinese Education (1984) 'China's Keypoint School Controversy, 1978–83', *Chinese Education*, Summer.

Chomsky, N., Steele, J. and Gittings, J. (1984) *Superpowers in Collision*, Harmondsworth, Penguin.

Conroy, R. (1985) 'Technological change and industrial development', in G. Young (ed.), *China: Dilemmas of Modernisation*, London, Croom Helm.

Conroy, R. (1986) 'China's technology import policy', *Australian Journal of Chinese Affairs*, No. 15.

Conroy, R. (1988a) 'Domestic sources of new technology for the Chinese industrial enterprise', in M. Lockett and J. Childs (eds) (1988) *Economic Reform and the Chinese Enterprise* Jai Press.

245

246 *Bibliography*

Conroy, R. (1988b) 'China's science and technology policy', in J. Y. S. Cheng (ed.), *China in the 1980s*, Hong Kong, Chinese University of Hong Kong Press.
Croll, E. (1983) *The Family Rice Bowl*, London, United Nations/Zed Press.
Croll, E., Davin, D. and Kane, P. (1985) *China's One-Child Family Policy*, London, Macmillan.
Croll, Elisabeth (1983a) *Chinese Women Since Mao*, London, Zed Press.
Croll, Elisabeth (1981) *The Politics of Marriage in Contemporary China*, Cambridge, Cambridge University Press.
Cui Yueli (1984) 'Some thoughts on health service reform', Guangming Ribao, 25 October.
Current Digest of the Soviet Press (CDSP) (1985) Vol. XXXVII, No. 26.
Current Digest of the Soviet Press (CDSP) (1986) Vol. XXXVIII, No. 30.
Dai Houying (1985) *Stones in the Wall*, trans. F. Wood, London, Michael Joseph.
Deng Xiaoping (1983) *Selected Works, 1975–82*, Beijing, Foreign Languages Press.
Dietrich, C. (1986) *People's China: A Brief History*, Oxford, Oxford University Press.
Domes, J. (1985) *The Government and Politics of the PRC: A Time of Transition*, Boulder, Col., Westview Press.
Duke, M. (1985) *Blooming and Contending: Chinese Literature in the Post-Mao Era*, Indiana University Press.
Eraut, M. Lewin, K. and Little, A. (1987) 'Teaching and Learning in Chinese Schools: Training, Research and Practice', *Education Field Research Transcript No. 2*, Institute of Development Studies/University of Sussex.
Fairbank, J. K. (1987) *The Great Chinese Revolution, 1900–1985*, London, Chatto and Windus.
Falkenheim, V. (1978) 'Political Participation in China', *Problems of Communism*, Vol. 27, No. 3.
Feuchtwang, S. and Hussain, A. (eds) (1988) *Directions in Development: The Chinese Economy in the 1980s*, London, Zed Press.
Field, R. M. (1983) 'Slow growth of productivity in Chinese industry, 1952–81', *China Quarterly*, No. 96.
Gardner, J. (1982) *Chinese Politics and the Succession to Mao*, London, Macmillan.
Garside, R. (1981) *Coming Alive – China after Mao*, London, Deutsch.
Gong Fou-long and Chao Limin (1982) 'The role of barefoot doctors in health services in Shanghai County', *American Journal of Public Health*, Supplement, September.
Goodman, D., Lockett, M. and Segal, G. (1986) *The China Challenge*, London, Routledge and Kegan Paul/Royal Institute for International Affairs.
Goodman, D. G. S. (1979) 'Changes in leadership personnel after 1976', in Domes, J. (ed.), *Chinese Politics after Mao*.
Goodman, D. G. S. (1986) 'The National CCP conference of September 1985 and China's leadership changes', *China Quarterly*, No. 105.

Gray, J. (1973) 'The Two Roads: Alternative Strategies of Social Change and Economic Growth in China' in S. Schram (ed.), *Authority, Participation and Cultural Change in China*, Cambridge, Cambridge University Press.

Guo Zhongshi (1987) 'New Drive to Control Endemic Diseases', *Beijing China Daily* 28 February.

Han, J, Xiao, Y. and Wei, H. (1984) 'The Formation and Development of Youth Ideals', *Chinese Education*, Winter.

Harding, H. (1984) 'The study of Chinese politics: toward a third generation of scholarship' *World Politics*, Vol. 36, No. 2.

Harding, H. (ed.) (1984) *China's Foreign Relations in the 1980s*, New Haven, Yale University Press.

Harris, L. C. and Worden, R. L. (eds) (1986) *China and the Third World: Champion or Challenger?*, London, Croom Helm.

Hendrischke, H. (1986) 'Das Publikationswesen nach 1977', in H. Martin (ed.), *Cologne Workshop on Contemporary Chinese Literature*, Cologne, 1986.

Hillier, S. M. (1986) Unpublished field notes from visits to factory clinics in Chongqing and Yueyang.

Hillier, S. M. and Jewell, J. A. (1983) *Health Care and Traditional Medicine in China 1800–1982*, London, Routledge and Kegan Paul.

Hinton, C. (1986) 'All Under Heaven' (videotape), New Day Films.

Howard, P. (1986) 'Communication, co-operation and conflict in China's countryside, 1978–85', PhD dissertation, Simon Fraser University, Dept of Communication.

Hsiao, W. (1984) 'Transformation of health care in China', New England *Journal of Medicine*, April.

Hu Qiaomu (1978) 'Observe economic laws, speed up the four modernisations', *Beijing Review*, Nos 45–7.

Hu Qiaomu (1982) 'Some Questions Concerning Revision of the Party Constitution', *Beijing Review*, No. 39.

Hu Yaobang (1982) 'Create a new situation in all fields of socialist modernisation', *Beijing Review*, No. 37.

Huang Shiqi (1984) 'On some vital issues in the development and reform of higher education in the PRC', conference paper, World Congress of Comparative Education, Paris.

Huang Shiqi (1986) *Human Resources Development in the People's Republic of China*, Beijing, Second Beijing International Conference on Science and Technology Press.

International Monetary Fund (1986) *Direction of Trade Statistics Yearbook*.

Ishikawa, Shigeru (1983) 'China's Economic Growth since 1949 – An Assessment', *China Quarterly*, No. 94, June.

Jamison, D. T. *et al.* (1984) *China: The Health Sector*, Washington, World Bank.

Jiang Yiwei (1980) 'The theory of an enterprise-based economy', *Social Sciences in China*, Vol. 1, No. 1.

Johnson, G. (1986) 'The fate of the communal economy: some contrary evidence from the Pearl River Delta', conference paper, Association for Asian Studies, annual conference.

Kahn-Ackermann, M. (1982) *China – Within the Outer Gate*, L
Marco Polo Press.

Kapur, H. (ed.) (1987) *As China Sees the World*, London, Frances Pi

Kelliher, D. (1986) 'State–peasant relations in post-reform C
conference paper, Association for Asian Studies, annual conferenc

Keng Piao (Geng Biao) (1981) 'Report of the situation of the Indoc
Peninsula', *Issues and Studies*, Vol. XVII, No. 1.

Kornai, J. (1980) 'The dilemmas of a socialist economy: the Hun
experience', *Cambridge Journal of Economics*, No. 4.

Lewin, K. (1985) 'Curriculum Development and Science Educat
China', *Education Field Research Transcript No. 1*, Institute of De
ment Studies/University of Sussex.

Lewin, K. (1987) 'Science Education in China: Transition and Cha
the 1980s', *Comparative Education Review*, No. 2.

Lee Lai-to (1986) 'Trade Unions in China', Singapore: Sin
University Press.

Li Kejing (1986) 'China's political restructuring and the developm
political science', *Social Sciences in China*, Vol. vii, No. 3.

Li Ping and Li Junyao (1981) 'National survey of cancer morta
China', in Marks, P. (ed.), *Cancer Research in the PRC*, New York,
and Stratton.

Liao Gailong (1981) 'Historical experience and our path of develop
Zhongguo Yanjiu, XV, No. 9, trans. in *Issues and Studies*, XVII, N
12.

Liaowang (1985) 'Proposals for the reform of China's insurance sy
Beijing, 2 December.

Lin Zili (1983) 'On the contract system of responsibility lin
production', *Social Sciences in China*, Vol. IX, No. 1.

Lin, Cyril Zhiren (1981) 'The reinstatement of economics in China
China Quarterly, March.

Link, P. (ed.) (1984b) *People or Monsters?*, Indiana University Press.

Link, P. (ed.) (1983) *Stubborn Weeds: Popular and Controversial L
after the Cultural revolution*, Indiana University Press.

Link, P. (ed.) (1984a) *Roses and Thorns: The Second Blooming of the F
Flowers in Chinese Fiction* Berkeley, Ca., University of California Pr

Liu Suinian and Wu Qungan (eds) (1986) 'China's socialist econo
outline history, 1949–1984', *Beijing Reveiw*.

Liu, S. (1979) 'Be an engineer of the soul', *Chinese Education*, winter.

Lo, B. L. C. (1984) 'Teacher education in the 1980s', in R. Hayhoe,
Contemporary Education, London, Croom Helm.

Lofstedt, J-I. (1982) 'Science requirements in the People's Repu
China', Stockholms Universitet, Institute of International Educat

Ma Hong (1983) *New Strategy for China's Economy*, Beijing, New
Press.

Mao Zedong (1965) 'Instructions on Public Health Work' *Current
ground*, No. 892, 21 October.

Maxwell, N. and McFarlane, B. (eds) (1984) *China's Changed F
Development*, Oxford, Pergamon.

Nathan, A. J. (1986) *Chinese Democracy*, New York, Alfred Knopf.

National People's Congress, Standing Committee (1982) 'The Electoral Law for the NPC and Local Congresses of the PRC', SWB: FE 7212.

National People's Congress, Standing Committee (1986a) 'Electoral Law for the NPC and Local People's Congresses', SWB: FE 8437.

National People's Congress, Standing Committee (1987) 'Decision on intensifying legal education in order to maintain stability and unity', SWB: FE No. 8476.

Nie Lisheng (1987) 'More private health care encouraged', *China Daily*, 8 February.

Nolan, P. and White, G. (1979) 'Socialist development and rural inequality: the Chinese countryside in the 1970s', *Journal of Peasant Studies*, Vol. 7, No. 1.

Nolan, P. and White, G. (1984) 'Urban Bias, Rural Bias or State Bias? Urban-Rural Relations in Post-Revolutionary China', *Journal of Development Studies*, Vol. 20, No. 3.

Oi, J. (1986) 'From cadres to middlemen: the commercialization of rural government', conference paper, Association for Asian Studies, annual conference.

Onate D. (1978) 'Hua Guofeng and the arrest of the Gang of Four', *China Quarterly*, No. 75.

Parker, R. L. and Hinman, A. R. (1982) 'Health services in Shanghai County', *American Journal of Public Health*, September.

Peng Zhen (1982) 'Report on the Draft of the Revised Constitution of the People's Republic of China', *Beijing Review*, No. 50.

Poznanski, K. (1985) 'The environment for technological change in centrally planned economies', Washington, World Bank Staff Working Papers.

Prescott, N., Jamison, D. and Birdsall, N. (1984) 'Determinants and consequences of health resource availability in China', Washington, World Bank.

Putterman, L. (1983) 'A modified collective agriculture in rural growth-with-equity', *World Development*, Vol. 11, No. 2.

Pye, L. W. (1971) 'Mass Participation in Communist China: Its Limitations and the Continuity of Culture', in J. Lindbeck (ed.) *China – Management of a Revolutionary Society*, Seattle and London, University of Washington Press.

Pye, L. (1981) *The dynamics of Chinese Politics*, Cambridge, Mass. Oelgeschlager, Gunn and Hain.

Riskin, C. (1987) *China's Political Economy: The Quest for development since 1949*, Oxford, Oxford University Press.

Rogers, E. M. (1980) 'Barefoot doctors', in *Rural Health in the PRC*, report of visit by the rural health system delegation June 1978, Washington, World Bank.

Rosen, S. and Burns, P. (eds) (1985) *Policy Conflicts in Contemporary China*, Armonk, NY, Sharpe.

Saich, T. (1981) *China – Politics and Government*, London, Macmillan.

Saich, T. (1983) 'The Fourth Constitution of the People's Republic of

China', *Review of Socialist Law*, Vol. IX, No. 2.

Saich, T. (1986a) 'Modernisation and participation in the PRC', in Ch‹ J. Y. S. (ed.), *China in the 1980s*.

Saich, T. (1986b) 'The reform in the year of the tiger', *China Informa‹ Vol. I, No. 1.

Schram, S. R. (1984) *Ideology and Policy in China since the Third Plenum, 1‹ 84*, London, Contemporary China Institute.

Shanghai, (City) (1986) 'Shanghai Spokesman on Student demonstrati‹ Notice of Public Order', SWB: FE 8449.

Shue, V. (1984) 'The fate of the commune', *Modern China*, Vol. 10, N‹

Sklair, L. (1985) 'Shenzhen: a Chinese "Development Zone" in gl‹ perspective', *Development and Change*, No. 16.

Socialist Republic of Vietnam, Ministry of Foreign Affairs (1979) '‹ truth about Vietnam-China Relations over the last thirty years' Ha‹ Government Printing House.

Soviet News (1987) Mikhail Gorbachev, speech on occasion of Visi‹ Nguyen Van Linh, *Soviet News*, No. 6375.

Su Shaozhi (1986) 'Intellectuals and political reform in the PRC‹ interview with Prof. Su Shaozhi', *China Information*, Vol. I, No. 2.

SWB: FE, Daily bulletin of translated materials, *Summary of W‹ Broadcasts: Far East*, Caversham, British Broadcasting Corporation.

Tan Li (1984) 'Medicine offers cash incentives for the healthy', *China D‹ 21 July.

Ting Wang (1980) *Chairman Hua*, London, Hurst.

Townsend, J. (1967) *Political Participation in Communist China*, Berkeley, University of California Press.

Unger, J. and Chan, A. (1984) *Chen Village*, Berkeley, Ca., Universit‹ California Press.

Walder, A. G. (1983) 'Organised dependence and cultures of authorit‹ Chinese industry', *Journal of Asian Studies*, Vol. XLIII, No. 1.

Wang Haiyun (1984) 'Combining medical research on prevention ‹ practical work of epidemic prevention', Jiankang Bao, 27 Decembe‹

Wang Hanbin (1986) Interview in Xinhua, 27 December, in SWB: No. 8455.

Wang Huming (1986) 'Heading for an efficient and democratic poli‹ structure, Shijie Jingji Daobao, 21 July, in SWB: FE, No. 8332.

Wang Shuwen (1982) 'Expanding the powers of the standing committ‹ the NPC is a major measure for perfecting the socialist political syst‹ SWB: FE No. 7023.

Wang Zhaoguo (1986) Report in Xinhua, in SWB: FE No. 8315.

Watson, A. (1983) 'Agriculture looks for "shoes that fit": the produc‹ responsibility system and its implications', *World Development*, Vol.‹ No. 8.

Wei, L. and Chao, A (eds) (1982) *China's Economic Reforms*, Philadel‹ University of Pennsylvania Press.

White, G. and Gray, J. (eds) (1982) *China's New Development Stra‹ London, Academic Press.

White, G. and Benewick, R. (1986) *Local Government and Basic ‹*

Democracy in China: Toward Reform?, Brighton, Institute of Development Studies.

White, G. *et al.* (eds) (1983) *Revolutionary Socialist Development in the Third World*, Brighton, Harvester Press.

Whyte, M. and Parish, W. (1984) *Urban Life in Contemporary China*, Chicago, University of Chicago Press.

Womack, B. (1982) 'The 1980 county-level elections in China', *Asian Survey*.

Womack, B. (1984) 'Modernisation and democratic reform in China', *Journal of Asian Studies*, Vol. 43, No. 3.

Womack, B. and Townsend, J. (1986) *Politics in China*, Boston: Little, Brown.

World Bank (1984) *China: Long Term Issues and Option*, Annex A: Issues and Prospects in Education, Washington, World Bank.

World Health Organisation (1984) *Primary Health Care: The Chinese Experience*, Geneva, WHO.

Wu Shouzhan (1984) 'Since its foundation, Janyang hospital has never used government financial support' Jiankang Bao, 11 December.

Xue Muqiao (1981) *China's Socialist Economy*, Beijing, Foreign Languages Press.

Yahuda, M. (1983) *The End of Isolationism: Chinese Foreign Policy after Mao*, London, Macmillan.

Yu Guangyuan (ed.) (1984) *China's Socialist Modernisation*, Beijing, Foreign Languages Press.

Yu Teh-pei (1986) 'An analysis of economic ties linking Hong Kong, PRC and ROC with special reference to trade', *Issues and Studies*, Vol. 22, No. 6.

Yuan Wenqi *et al.* (1980) 'International division of labour and China's economic relations with foreign countries', *Social Sciences in China*, Vol. 1, No. 1.

Zhao Zhiyong (1984) 'Fuzhen hospital has reformed the rural system of epidemic prevention and health care', Jiankang Bao, 11 December.

Zhuang Jia (1985) 'We must actively support individual doctors in opening their own clinics', Hainan Ribao, 7 June.

Zweig, D. (1985) 'Up from the village into the city: reforming urban-rural relations in China', conference paper, 32nd North American meeting, Regional Science Association, Philadelphia.

Zweig, D. (1986) 'Agrarian radicalism and the Chinese countryside, 1968–81' unpublished manuscript.

Index